Lessons from Latin America

LESSONS FROM LATIN AMERICA

INNOVATIONS IN POLITICS, CULTURE, AND DEVELOPMENT

FELIPE AROCENA *and* KIRK BOWMAN

UNIVERSITY OF TORONTO PRESS

Library and Archives Canada Cataloguing in Publication

Bowman, Kirk S., author
    Lessons from Latin America : politics, culture, development / Kirk Bowman and Felipe Arocena.

Includes bibliographical references and index.

Issued in print and electronic formats.

ISBN 978-1-4426-0947-1 (bound).—ISBN 978-1-4426-0549-7 (pbk.).—ISBN 978-1-4426-0550-3 (pdf).—ISBN 978-1-4426-0551-0 (epub).

    1. Latin America—Politics and government—1948–. 2. Latin America—Social policy. 3. Latin America—Social conditions. I. Arocena, Felipe, author II. Title.

F1414.B68 2014   980.03   C2013–908651-X

                                C2013–908652-8

We welcome comments and suggestions regarding any aspect of our publications—please feel free to contact us at news@utphighereducation.com or visit our Internet site at www.utppublishing.com.

North America
5201 Dufferin Street
North York, Ontario, Canada, M3H 5T8

2250 Military Road
Tonawanda, New York, USA, 14150

ORDERS PHONE: 1–800–565–9523
ORDERS FAX: 1–800–221–9985
ORDERS E-MAIL: utpbooks@utpress.utoronto.ca

UK, Ireland, and continental Europe
NBN International
Estover Road, Plymouth, PL6 7PY, UK
ORDERS PHONE: 44 (0) 1752 202301
ORDERS FAX: 44 (0) 1752 202333
ORDERS E-MAIL:
enquiries@nbninternational.com

Every effort has been made to contact copyright holders; in the event of an error or omission, please notify the publisher.

The University of Toronto Press acknowledges the financial support for its publishing activities of the Government of Canada through the Canada Book Fund.

This book is dedicated to our students, in particular those who have studied with us throughout Latin America. We have learned far more from them than they have learned from us.

CONTENTS

ILLUSTRATIONS

FIGURES

TABLES

ACKNOWLEDGMENTS

We are grateful for the support of our colleagues and institutions. Generous support was provided by the Departmento de Sociología de la Universidad de la República, the Comisión Sectorial de Investigaciones Científicas de la Universidad de la República, the Sistema Nacional de Investigadores de Uruguay, the Fulbright Commission, the Ivan Allen College at Georgia Tech, the Center for Business Education and Research at Georgia Tech, the Coca-Cola Foundation, and the Sam Nunn School of International Affairs.

We acknowledge the comments and contributions from our colleagues and peers. Mariana Banús, Rachel Benkeser, Gabriel Di Meglio, Michelle Dion, Jeremy Ferris, Ayanda Francis, Stephen Kay, and Molly Ward all made contributions or provided research support of note. We thank Richard Manning for his excellent translation from Spanish of part of the book.

This project was well served and improved by extensive comments from the anonymous reviewers. Our experience with Anne Brackenbury and the University of Toronto Press could not have been better.

Finally, we wish to acknowledge the laughter and joy provided by Manuela, Micah, Kole, and Tomás.

INTRODUCTION

How would you feel if someone called you an underdeveloped person? How would you react if someone said your son or daughter, or sister or brother, was underdeveloped? You would probably be deeply offended and insulted, and at the very least you would ask what arguments were being used to define you as underdeveloped. What adult human being has the right or the arrogance to label another adult incomplete or not fully developed? This kind of behavior is no longer acceptable, not even when referring to individuals who are physically, psychologically, or intellectually dysfunctional; those we now call "people with different abilities," instead of the old terms "handicapped," "disabled" or "deformed." It is even less acceptable today to argue there are groups of people with particular physical characteristics that make them superior to other groups. From the point of view of intellectual abilities, there is no such thing as superior or inferior races. Scientific racism and Darwinism applied to the social realm have been dead and buried since the Nazis' delusions were discredited and abandoned. So why do we continue to use the term "underdeveloped" when describing the Latin American countries? Why do we still accept that some countries are defined as developed (read: mature, complete, advanced, modern) and others as underdeveloped (read: backward, incomplete, childlike)?

If this reasoning is right, why do we go on accepting that Latin America, this collection of diverse countries and nations spread between two continents and an isthmus, which is part in the northern hemisphere and part in the southern, which has every kind of climate, race, and ecosystem, and where human beings flourished thousands of years ago, is an underdeveloped region? Isn't Latin America the birthplace of some of the world's most elaborate and beautiful mythologies and cosmologies, such as those of the Mayas and the Incas? And much more recently, haven't artists, writers, poets, painters, and musicians emerged from that region who transformed modern culture? Doesn't it contain the largest areas of vegetation humankind has preserved? Doesn't it still have the world's biggest reserves of potable water, which is one of the key natural resources for the future? Isn't it one of the regions that, taken as a whole, has the most sustainable environmental indicators? Isn't it where a good part of the food that human beings eat, such as potatoes and maize, were first cultivated? So what is the basis for this idea we keep perpetuating: that Latin America is an underdeveloped region? Is it because it is not as rich as other parts of the planet? If this were logical, then someone who is poor would be underdeveloped compared to someone who has more money, which is absurd. Is it because Latin America has less technology to dominate other countries with weapons? If this were the reason, we would have to say Sparta was more developed than Athens (the cradle of classical civilization), because it beat the Athenians in the Peloponnesian War, or that Germany with all its barbarism in World War Two was more developed than France.

So why do people still say Latin America is underdeveloped? We believe the explanation can be found in the logic of colonization. This logic was based on a strategy of devaluing the conquered population. Its great triumph was when the people who were colonized felt inferior to the colonizers, acknowledged them as superior, and wanted to be like them. This logic of colonization remained in force long after the conquests, and it was still alive when the Latin American countries achieved political independence and the ruling elites wanted to be like Prospero.[1] The Latin Americans were ashamed because most of them were relatively dark-skinned, and they tried to Europeanize themselves by adopting institutions from the Old World and implanting them in a completely different political, social, cultural, and economic context.

This book is inspired by this line of thought, which can be traced back to a long list of authors, including Frantz Fanon, Richard Morse, Enrique Dussel, Leopoldo Zea, Aníbal Quijano, Edward Said, Aimé Césaire, and Charles Taylor. However, our aim is not to take a Manichean anti-imperialist, anti-colonial stance and just praise the virtues of societies before colonization and condemn the colonizers for their excrescences. That would be to fall into an error very like the colonizers' logic. It would be to exaggerate the advantages and potential of Latin America (as some patriots and nationalists do when they glorify it) and magnify the disasters of the rich world, and to curse it like Caliban (as anti-imperialists did with an outdated demonizing strategy as in the 1960s).

Our approach in this book is inspired by the conviction that Latin America is not a sick man that has to be cured, an underdeveloped child that has to be taught, or a corrupt place that has to be cleansed. Obviously some countries in the region have problems, but there are problems all over the world. Many Latin American countries had serious difficulties in the past, but in recent years they have tackled them in ways that are intelligent, or at least interesting, even if not particularly successful. We are not saying that some "lessons" we cite in this book should be adopted as prescriptions or models for other countries outside the region. We are merely trying to show how the rest of the world would do well to take note of approaches that have emerged in some spheres such as cultural rights, inequality, racism, women's participation in

---

1 Prospero is the Duke of Milan in Shakespeare's play *The Tempest*. He is exiled and, along with his daughter Miranda, lands on a deserted island. It is not totally uninhabited because someone else, Caliban, is living there, but the European duke does not regard this supposedly deformed and incomplete being as a real person. He considers him underdeveloped. But Caliban is still human enough to be able to procreate with the young girl and have children, and to curse her father in the language he has learned. Caliban does not want to be like his colonizer. Thus *The Tempest* is one of the greatest allegories for colonization that we have.

politics, social security, the armed forces budget, and even soccer and music. Thus the "lessons" can also be seen as new contributions from Latin America in these areas.[2]

Almost all the Latin American countries have done well in the last ten years, and some people regard this as a historic time in the region. Democracy rules, the dictatorships are gone, national economies are growing at unprecedented rates, poverty is decreasing every year, inequality is not as bad as it was, there are no more guerrilla movements except in Colombia, indigenous groups and people of African descent are finally getting their rights recognized, and women are progressing along their arduous path toward equality.

This favorable context can be seen very clearly from the United Nations Development Program (UNDP) *Human Development Report 2013: The Rise of the South: Human Progress in a Diverse World*.[3] It states that "Latin American countries have resumed their upward trajectories of human development and growth" (UNDP 2013, 22) and that "Latin America, in contrast to overall global trends, has seen income inequality fall since 2000 but still has the most unequal distribution of all regions" (p. 14). On life satisfaction, an indicator that is being used more and more to measure the subjective perception of quality of life, Latin America is the region with the highest average at 6.5 (on a scale of 1 to 10). This compares favorably both to the world average of 5.3 and to the highest score for an individual country, which is 7.8 in Denmark.

In a recent book, *Nuestra Hora: los Latinoamericanos en el Siglo XXI*, Raúl Rivera (2010) says that Latin America is in a good situation and that we should shake off the "feeling of insignificance and the view that history is passing us by and that we are an irrelevant region." And we are pleasantly surprised when he puts the widely held negative view of Latin America into a comparative context: it is not so poor after all, when we consider that its economy as a whole is the fourth largest on the planet and that 60 per cent of the population is middle class. Nor is it particularly violent in the context of the twentieth century, which saw dictators such as Hitler, Mao, Stalin, and Pol Pot and the millions of deaths they were responsible for, and bearing in mind that the guilt for today's death toll in the drug wars must be shared by those who dominate the drug business, namely the U.S. itself. Rivera (2010) maintains that Latin America ". . . is the richest region in the emerging world and we are in a marvelous position to learn from the industrialized countries' mistakes and to develop our own model."[4]

---

2   There has been widespread international acclaim for the very high level of the arts in Latin America: as seen in music such as the tango, samba, and salsa; composers such as Astor Piazzola, Tom Jobim, and Abel Carlevaro; writers such as Juan Carlos Onetti, João Guimarães Rosa, and Juan Rulfo; painters such as Joaquín Torres García and Frida Kahlo; essayists such as Gilberto Freyre, Ezequiel Martínez Estrada, and Octavio Paz; and many more. The same can be said of football (soccer), since just three South American countries have won nearly as many World Cups as all the European countries combined.

3   With commendable sensitivity, at no time does the Human Development Report employ the term "underdeveloped." Countries are categorized as having very high, high, middle, or low levels of human development.

4   These quotations are also found in an interview with the author that appeared in the Uruguayan newspaper *El País* on June 12, 2011. See also Weitzman (2012).

In recent years there have been numerous innovative public policies throughout the region, all the way from the Rio Grande to Tierra del Fuego. This upsurge has come about partly because Latin America is so heterogeneous, and partly thanks to the third wave of democratization that started in 1974 with Portugal's "Carnation Revolution" and spread rapidly. In many cases Latin America has even been a pioneer, for example in demilitarization in Costa Rica and Panama, in social security reform in Chile, in multicultural policies for indigenous peoples in Bolivia, in quotas to increase women's representation in the Argentine Congress, and in equity programs to transfer resources to the poor in Brazil. Public policy reforms in Latin America have been creative, innovative, and exploratory, and they could contribute to helping other countries that face similar challenges.

We do not have the space to examine all the novel initiatives in just one book, and we have had to leave aside such projects as environmental protection policies in Costa Rica and Ecuador, new energy policies in Brazil, urban planning in cities such as Curitiba, health system reforms in various countries, and state control of the production and sale of marijuana in Uruguay. These are all instructive and fascinating experiences, and it is a pity we cannot include them here. Perhaps we will be able to remedy this in a future publication.

The real origins of this book go back to a trip we made with our students. The two authors worked together directing study programs in Latin America for the Georgia Institute of Technology. On one of our trips we visited the United States embassy in Argentina several times, and we asked the diplomats to talk to the students. One particularly lucid student asked the same question to the cultural, economic, and military attachés and to the head of the diplomatic mission: What positive lessons could the United States and the rest of the world learn from Argentina and Latin America? The replies were very illuminating. The Americans either laughed because they thought the question inappropriate, or answered sarcastically because it seemed ridiculous to even consider this possibility.

This book is organized in ten chapters. The first ("Would You Like to Go to South America?") is an analysis of the stereotyped images of Latin America that have been constructed in the United States. Each of the other nine chapters is a reflection on a subject, public policy, or problem that was originally analyzed, implemented or resolved in one or more of the Latin American countries. These chapters are divided by subject matter into three sections. The first section is "Politics: Elections and Participation." In Chapter 2 ("Gender and Representation"), we examine essential policy dimensions such as women's access to positions of power. Chapter 3 ("Counting the Votes and Aggregating Political Preferences") deals with mechanisms to secure transparency in national elections and foster civil society participation in community problems. Chapter 4 ("Demilitarization and Peace Promotion") is an analysis of the move in some countries to reduce their military budget or do away with the armed forces altogether. In the second section of the book, "Cultural Rights: Racism, Discrimination, and Multiculturalism," we tackle cultural rights and focus on multiculturalism and the challenges of integrating three groups into the societies in which they live, namely indigenous populations, people of African descent, and immigrants. We approach this theme in Chapter 5 ("The Awakening of Indigenous Culture: The Case of Bolivia") by analyzing the extraordinary changes in the situation of indigenous people in Bolivia, where for the first time in history an Aymara Indian was elected president. In Chapter 6 ("Brazil: Where Were the Blacks?"), we survey the very recent public policy package in Brazil designed to reduce racism against the population of African descent. Chapter 7 ("Latino Immigration into the United States") examines the impact the fifty million Latinos living in the U.S. have made, including how they have turned it into a bilingual country. In the third section of the book, "Social Policy, Inequality, and the Beautiful Game," we focus on inequality, an insidious weakness in Latin America, which is the most unequal region in the world and ranks even lower on this indicator than Africa, the poorest continent. However, we find in Chapter 8 ("The Delayed Revolution and the Rise of the South") that considerable progress has been made toward closing this wound. Brazil is the giant of the continent and for decades the most unequal country, but now it has taken firm steps toward tackling this problem by implementing robust social policies to redistribute wealth and has raised itself to the level of Costa Rica, one of the most egalitarian. Chapter 9 ("Retirement with Dignity") examines another widespread innovation: the implementation of social-security policies for workers who retire. In this area Latin America has developed systems derived from the initial Chilean model, which in spite of criticisms can be found to a greater or lesser extent in all the reforms. The tenth and final chapter ("Global Lessons from the Beautiful Game") is an analysis of the activity for which Latin America is best known in the world: football (soccer). The region as a whole, and especially Argentina, Brazil, and little Uruguay, has made a tremendous impact in this sport and soccer holds some important political lessons, so it certainly deserves its own chapter.

In a way our choice of subjects is arbitrary because we could have included other themes, such as music, the environment, or the third wave of democratization. However, we feel our selection covers some of the main dimensions of life in society, such as politics, culture, economics, and sport, and includes countries of very different sizes, ranging from Mexico, Costa Rica, and Panama in Central America, to Chile and Brazil farther south. We have also examined significant population sectors whose rights were disregarded in the past but are today at the center of the trend toward recognition, namely women, indigenous groups, people of African descent, and immigrants.

This book is the product of a long-lasting collaboration between a Uruguayan sociologist and a political scientist from the United States. We have very different experience and different disciplinary perspectives, but we share the same curiosity to observe and the same fascination with the region. Over the last ten years we have discussed the ongoing changes in Latin America in a wide variety of places—cafés in Montreal, a park in Curitiba, restaurants in Buenos Aires, strolling on the *Rambla* in Montevideo, and on the Georgia Tech campus in Atlanta. One or both of us has done extensive fieldwork in Argentina, Bolivia, Brazil, Chile, Colombia, Costa Rica, Cuba, Honduras, Mexico, and Uruguay.

ADDITIONAL READING

Césaire, Aimé. 1972. *Discourse on Colonialism*. New York: Monthly Review Press.

Rivera, Raúl. 2010. *Nuestra Hora: Los Latinoamericanos en el Siglo XXI*. Santiago de Chile: Pearson Educación de Chile.

Weitzman, Hal. 2012. *Latin Lessons: How South America Stopped Listening to the United States and Started Prospering*. Hoboken, NJ: John Wiley & Sons.

CHAPTER ONE

WOULD YOU LIKE TO GO TO SOUTH AMERICA?

INTRODUCTION

Robert Cohn read *The Purple Land* by William Henry Hudson and then read it again and yet again. Cohn was a Jewish American writer in his early thirties. He had published a fairly successful novel in the United States; he had money and had gone to Paris to get to know the inter-war avant-garde. But he was bored with his life, he was tired of Paris, and everything seemed tedious. After reading Hudson, he thought a trip to South America would break the monotony. A trip like that to far-away lands would be a real accomplishment in his drab existence. One day in Paris, Cohn met his friend Jake:

> "Would you like to go to South America, Jake?"
> "No."
> "Why not?"
> "I don't know. I never wanted to go. Too expensive. You can see all the South Americans you want in Paris anyway."
> "They're not the real South Americans."
> "They look awfully real to me."
> "All my life I've wanted to go on a trip like that," Cohn said . . . . "I can't stand to think my life is going so fast and I'm not really living it . . . . I want to go to South America."

Hemingway fans will have guessed that Cohn is one of the characters in *The Sun Also Rises*, the iconic book of the "lost generation" of American writers. *The Purple Land* was written a long time ago, and according to Hemingway it "tells the imaginary and splendid adventures of a perfect English gentleman in an intensely romantic land

and in a well described landscape." It was the perfect image for Cohn: it promised an escape from his disenchantment with his overly rational, materialistic American life that not even Paris could alleviate. Besides, he had run out of ideas and imagination, and the trip could provide material for a new book.

Cohn's images of South America were based on Hudson's book, but they are obviously not historically accurate or modern. They stand in stark contrast to the predominant perception among Americans today, which is less romantic, less appealing, and more racist. American images of Latin America range from the racist idea of an area inhabited by inferior savages, an idea that has its roots in a Protestant perspective—we will call this the *enlightened stereotype*—to another stereotype of primitive savages, but this time romantically idealized by the U.S. counterculture—we will call this the *romantic stereotype*.

United States foreign policy toward Latin America has passed through various stages. First there was Pan Americanism, which began in the early nineteenth century and which was aimed at forming a new West to oppose old Europe, and involved the Monroe Doctrine with its stance of non-intervention—except, of course, when debts had to be collected. Then there was the Big Stick policy of Theodore Roosevelt and the policy of intervening to remedy economic problems. Following that came the Good Neighbor Policy of Franklin Roosevelt, which supposedly forbade direct intervention, although in fact this rule was ignored time and time again. Next came the Alliance for Progress of the 1960s, which was to replicate the Marshall Plan in the Americas, and more recently President George H.W. Bush's Four Plus One proposal to form an international market like the Southern Cone and join with Mexico and Canada to set up NAFTA. Thus U.S. international policy has involved a variety of approaches in the last hundred years; but whatever the rhetoric, Latin Americans have always perceived it as imperialism. From any objective analysis of the relations between the two regions one must surely conclude that the Americans see Latin America in terms of their own economic interests, security, and hegemonic aspirations. Latin Americans think the image the U.S. has of them is tainted by political relations and international strategies. Be that as it may, our approach in this chapter is not to examine political events but to work on another plane: we will analyze U.S. images of Latin America in terms of how they have been used to justify or "legitimize" official political action.

American culture has manufactured a series of images of the lands south of the Rio Grande, and these have been repeated as mythical themes throughout the country's history. In his 1992 book *The United States and Latin America*, the historian Frederick Pike partly succeeds in analyzing them. In his view, the myths and stereotypes that Americans have of Latin America date back to the conquest of the Wild West, the original American frontier. Looking back to when the immigrants from Britain first met their first *other*— the native North Americans—we can find interesting clues to help us understand the images of Latin America that Americans (white Protestant Anglo-Saxon Americans, obviously) created. The conquest of the West from unspoiled nature and from its original populations gives us the first images of civilization in opposition to barbarians. And, as Latin Americans know only too well, the myths that sprang up around those opposing forces have been endlessly repeated ever since. The image that Americans have of themselves is intimately linked to the interaction between "civilized" and "barbarian," and this inevitably brings us to the relations between culture and nature.

The term "culture" was originally associated with cultivated land, earth planted and worked by man, and subsequent metaphors have added new meanings. Thus, when we speak of a cultured man we mean someone who has cultivated his own nature, shaping, working, and refining it. Therefore, one meaning of the word "culture" involves the notion of man transforming nature and interacting with it, be it the transformation a society makes in its surroundings or the transformation an individual makes of his or her own inner nature. Culture and nature have never gotten along in the modern world. Quite the contrary in fact, because in spite of any romantic intentions the over-all picture is of domination, exploitation, and opposition. And now, as we stand on the threshold of postmodern times and ecological apocalypse, a new kind of interaction between nature and culture is beginning to emerge, and this new relation is crucial for the future of the human species.

The first colonists in North America did not consider this new relation between culture and nature. They believed that everything natural, virgin, and wild had to be changed by human effort and used to feed production:

> Since their earliest arrival to the New World, Americans tended to equate wilderness and Indians, seeing the latter as the personification of the former; and from this equation derived the race-war aspects of America's frontier expansion. One basic reason for the nature–Indian connection in American perception was the native's alleged preference to live in harmony with nature . . . . The failure of "savages" fully to exploit the natural resources of the land they claimed justified the actions of civilized men as they seized Indian property. Frontiersmen, therefore, cleared "the wilderness of primitive men in order that civilization might root and flourish." (Pike 1992, 4)

Thus, in the early days, nature and the Indians were seen through the filter of Puritan thought with a leavening of ideas from the Enlightenment. Nobody expressed this connection better or more succinctly than William Golpin, an ex-army Colorado governor, when he pronounced in 1873, "Progress is God" (Pike 1992, 3).

Once the western frontier had been tamed, the Americans started to look south for new lands that they could organize and civilize. In the nineteenth century the images of Latin America they began to construct were no different from those they had of their own western frontier, which was now well on the way to being civilized. The new frontier was south of the Rio Grande, and they used the same thinking to interpret and try to change it. This new frontier was also inhabited by savages, lazy natives, and alcoholics—unpredictable and passionate people who were controlled by their sexual appetites, which revealed the worst sin of all: godlessness. On top of that they were poor.

1.1. THE ENLIGHTENED STEREOTYPE OF THE SAVAGE

In the nineteenth century not many people went south. Before the advent of modern communications, the images people had of the inhabitants of foreign lands came from travelers' tales published in travel books. Most of the early stories about Latin

Americans were about Mexico and the Caribbean, but the same stereotype of the primitive savage was repeated by anyone who happened to go farther south. The Americans' most common stereotype was their image of the Mexicans, who were especially denigrated because a large part of the western United States was first settled by Mexico and was conquered in a bloody war. The Mexicans were seen as having wasted the favorable natural conditions of California, and by the same token the other Latin Americans had done nothing to exploit their luxuriant rich lands. It seemed that with little effort compared to what the Americans had expended in crossing the desert, the North Americans would be able to make the natural environment of South America *productive*. This was their work ethic and they felt there was nothing they could not achieve in the exuberant and fertile lands of Latin America.

The same question occurred again and again: how is it that the Latin Americans are so poor when they live in such a rich environment? And the answers always had to do with lack of character, physical weakness when faced with wild nature, lack of discipline, lack of perseverance, the inability to stick to a rigid plan of action—all of which can be summed up as their childishness. They were seen as children, savages, primitives—human beings who had not yet been shaped by culture. Pike provides ample evidence:

> One might well fill a long book with quotations from nineteenth- and early twentieth-century American travelers and diplomats disgusted by the laziness that seemed an ingrained way of life south of the border. Here follows what I judge to be a representative sampling. From a traveler in Mexico and Central America: "It [dictatorship] is a form of government not entirely unfitted to a people in the bulk utterly indifferent as to who or what rules them so [long as] they are left to loaf in their hammocks in peace." From a diplomat who served in the same region: "the bland climate [predisposes them toward] an indulgent, easy and voluptuous life." From an observer of Mexico in the 1880s we learn that "only the children show energy, spark, and vivacity" [but] unhappily these children "will grow up and become Mexicans!" In Panama, Colombia and Venezuela travelers garnered the [same impressions] . . . . A traveler to Brazil disparaged the swarms of beggars, contrasting "the graft and enterprise of Americans with [the] laziness" of nearly all Brazilians, regardless of class. (Pike 1992, 71)

Some comparisons between historical figures, religious attitudes, sexual customs, and institutions can illustrate the stereotype, constructed by the U.S. in the nineteenth century, of South Americans as primitive savages. Let us compare, for example, George Washington with Simón Bolívar. These two heroes of independence in the two regions had opposite personalities and behavior, and they can be seen as prototypes of the images the Americans had of themselves and of their southern neighbors. Washington symbolizes the triumph of reason over passion, of reality over unrealistic fantasies, of austerity over luxury, of serenity over impulsiveness, of abstinence over weakness of the flesh, of rationality in affairs of state over impulsive arbitrary decisions. Bolívar, on the other hand, even though he liberated vast lands from Spanish dominion, was seen by the Americans as an authoritarian, passionate, womanizing mixed-blood who was incapable of planning policy once freedom had been won. And on top of that he set free the most primitive people of all, the Negro slaves, something Washington did not do. The differences between them can even be seen in how their lives ended: Washington died in comfortable old age, while Bolívar was poor and afflicted with tuberculosis. Who could ever write a novel about Washington like Gabriel García Márquez's 1989 account of the last days of Bolívar, *The General in His Labyrinth* (Pike 1992, 63–66)?

In the American national myth it was mainly cowboys who conquered the West. And it is partly true: many of the pioneers who settled that territory and bravely confronted the indigenous redskins were in fact cowboys, and they have been immortalized by Hollywood. Many of them also became prosperous, hardworking ranchers. Not only were they brave conquerors of the region, but they also devoted themselves to dominating nature and making it productive. Comparisons between these American cowboys and the gauchos of South America made the nineteenth-century stereotype of the primitive Latin American even more negative. In none of the three livestock areas—the Venezuela plains, the Brazilian south, and the Pampas–River Plate region of Argentina and Uruguay—were the locals capable of transforming wild territory into productive ranches. Instead they were always nomads, never interested in production and rarely fighting the Indians.

In American legend, cowboys played a much bigger role than the state in taming the Wild West, and in fact they would have done it by themselves on their own initiative. In Latin America, on the other hand, it was the state that conquered territory occupied by the Indians, and the plainsmen or gauchos were more of a hindrance than a help in the spread of civilization. We have the contrast: Facundo Quiroga versus Daniel Boone, Lampião versus Bat Masterson. The former of each pair slows down modernization; the latter makes it bloom. A key work that sheds light on this issue is the 1870s epic poem by Argentine writer José Hernández, *Martín Fierro*, which implicitly attacks the Buenos Aires government for its efforts to impose civilization and destroy the gauchos, and makes a hero of Fierro, who resists being sent to the frontier as a soldier. *Martín Fierro* is one of the most important works of Argentine literature, and it highlights the differences between the United States and the South American frontier experience. Contrary to the depiction in *Martín Fierro*, Hollywood has always portrayed Hispanic cowboys and Mexican mestizos (mixed-blood) as cowards and alcoholics. Another example of this prejudice concerns Theodore Roosevelt. One day the American author Stephen Crane sent him a new short story he had written, *A Man and Some Others* (1897), in which a cowboy is shot dead by a gang of Mexican "greasers." Roosevelt responded with the comment that he wished someone would write another story in which the cowboy wins the gunfight, because "it is more normal that way" (Pike 1992, 203)!

Approximately one million Africans were transported to the United States as slaves, but ten times that number, some 10 to 12 million, were taken to Latin America. In several Latin American countries large numbers of slaves escaped and set up their own independent communities beyond the reach of the authorities. In Brazil these communities were called *quilombos*, and in Spanish America they were called *palenques*. The best-known *quilombo* in Brazil was in Palmares in the north-east; it consisted of around 20,000 runaway slaves and was suppressed with much bloodshed at the end of the seventeenth century. Some *palenques* and *quilombos* survived in Spanish and Portuguese America until modern times. The Americans were appalled at this phenomenon and saw it as a typical example of Hispanic ineptitude and a failure to organize a civilizing crusade. But the Americans were frightened when the slaves in Haiti revolted and created a large *quilombo* not far from their coasts. There was another big *quilombo* in eastern Florida, which at that time was outside the United States but far too close for comfort, and the Americans were terrified of it for decades. To make matters worse, many escaped slaves made their way to Spanish Florida and joined the Indians, and the authorities were unable to suppress this threat. One result of this free community was interracial procreation, which produced mulattoes and mestizos. The Americans made several incursions into Spanish territory and finally in 1821, as a result of this pressure, they obtained legal rights to that region in eastern Florida. This military effort was the U.S. solution to the problem of *palenques* and *quilombos*, but since the Latinos had been unable to do the same thing, this was further proof of Anglo-Saxon superiority and another triumph of civilization over barbarianism (Pike 1992, 141–44).

A parallel can also be seen in religion. According to one of the best-known historians of Protestant (and thus anti-Catholic) America, Ray Allen Billington, "The average Protestant American of the 1850s had been trained from birth to hate Catholicism; his juvenile literature and school books had breathed a spirit of intolerance . . . . [His] religious and even his secular newspapers had warned him of the dangers of Popery. From early childhood on, Americans were shaped to believe that to be a Catholic was to be a false, cruel and bloody wretch . . ." (qtd. in Pike 1992, 76). Indeed, Protestants saw Rome as "the whore of Babylon." It is not difficult to make the connection between this metaphor and the idea of Latin America as a great brothel or *quilombo*. The Catholic priests in Latin America were perverted and wanted the whole year to be one long party. And the festivals! Saint George, Saint Sebastian, Saint Cono: there was always some saint to celebrate with a party. How is any work ever going to get done when there's a party every week? And to make matters worse, the Catholic religious rites were mixed with pagan customs and involved alcohol, food, and sensual dancing. The Catholics could commit all manner of excesses and then confess and be forgiven. This is why areas where Catholicism is dominant were more licentious and hedonistic than those controlled by the Protestant faith. The prototype of these excesses is carnival; a festival like that would never have developed in a Protestant society. And besides, Protestants could not stomach the Catholic belief that the poor would inherit the earth and be exalted. To be poor and wretched in this world is a sure sign of being damned, of not being chosen by God. The poverty of the Catholic world was a reflection of the sin in which they lived.

This is how the stereotype of the primitive and decadent Latino south came into being. The United States was built by expanding west, and this secular conquest of the country's internal frontier put its stamp on the population's identity. No other myth has so deeply marked the Americans as the expansion and colonization of hitherto unproductive lands. But by the end of the nineteenth century the American frontier had come to an end. Those undertaking the expansion had reached the geographical limit—the sea—and also the limit of exploiting nature. Where could they spread now? Where could they go to devour more virgin land? There was only one possibility: south. At the beginning of the twentieth century, U.S. imperialism in South America thus became government policy and intensified even more in the years to come. The American dream had to go on at all costs; if the country did not move it would die. Thus in the new century, armed with the same stereotype of savages that they had applied to the Indians on their internal frontier, the Americans justified their expansion to the south. And now they had even more reasons: to combat the vices of Catholicism, to correct the decadence of cross-breeding, and to exploit an untouched environment that was blessed with even greater natural riches than their own country.

That story comes later. First we should clarify why these negative stereotypes of Latin America are not true. They are derived, symbolic constructions imposed by a Protestant Anglo-Saxon cultural matrix on the Iberian cultural matrix, which was not understood because it was a different way of adapting to the New World.

1.2. THE ROMANTIC STEREOTYPE OF THE SAVAGE

It would be unjust not to balance the stereotype of a savage described above with an account of another stereotype that some Americans have cherished. This stereotype is also that of a primitive person but is instead in the style of Jean-Jacques Rousseau's noble savage, and it reflects the fact that some people admired and were dazzled by Latin America. This featured in much twentieth-century counterculture and can still be found in the twenty-first century as well. But we should be careful of this representation as it frequently borders on racism. It is the inverse of the racism we examined above, a form of racism couched in different terms, because in this second image the idea that the Latinos are incapable of improving or solving their problems is just as strong as in the first image. However, they are seen from a benevolent and romantic perspective instead of from an enlightened standpoint.[5] The crucial difference between the two views is that this second stereotype does not justify active intervention or an attempt to change human beings who are different; instead, it romanticizes them and tries to preserve them as they are.

The empty lands and native inhabitants that the first British colonists found in North America did not just awaken the urge to take possession and conquer; they also inspired respect for nature in opposition to the civilizing stereotype. Nobody expressed this perspective and the praise for nature better than Walt Whitman (1819–92). But another American artist of the last century—a painter, Frederic Edwin Church (1826–1900)—went into ecstasies, not only over the natural world on his own frontier, but also over wild nature in the South American tropics. On his travels in South America, Church painted typically romanticized landscapes of enormous size to reflect the religious awe that virgin nature inspired in him. He felt this land should

---

5 The previous stereotype can be deemed "enlightened" in the sense of being directly influenced by the French Enlightenment.

not be ruthlessly transformed, but quite the contrary: it should bring about a change in man and in his decadent civilization. In this romantic vein, nature should be felt, apprehended in its regenerative purity rather than dissected by scientific knowledge in pursuit of domination.

In the first years of the twentieth century, some sectors of the American aristocracy reacted against the increasing materialism on which their civilization was based, and in turn developed ideas sympathetic to the elites in South America. They recognized in those elites a culture, manners, and cordiality that were superior to those of the American aristocracy. Pike, borrowing from a Uruguayan writer called Rodó, baptized these people "the North American Arielists."[6] They thought that, as with wine, the Hispanic aristocracy was more noble for being more mature, principally in its maintenance of relations with the Old World and for putting spiritual life ahead of the material world. The Americans have always had a complex that they are culturally inferior to the Old World of Europe, and they transferred this perspective to the aristocracies of the Hispanic countries, who lived in much greater harmony with tradition and knew how to enjoy the most sublime things in life. With a sharp distinction between the Hispanic elites and the barely civilized primitive masses, the U.S. aristocrats also perceived the need to live life aesthetically:

> Again and again, in fact, Americans in the late nineteenth century wrote admiringly of the courtesy of wellborn Latin Americans . . . . The South Americans, [Theodore] Roosevelt observed, "often surpass us, not merely in pomp and ceremony but in what is of real importance, courtesy: in civility and courtesy we can well afford to take lessons from them." (Pike 1992, 196–201)

Rodó's message that the U.S. was overly materialistic had its counterpart in the United States itself, but it was always a minority view and usually fizzled out or was overtaken by Yankee economic interests, which proved Rodó right. The Latin American elites might have been very cultured and courteous, but they did not know how to keep their populations in line or make their countries prosper. When the United States turned south to its new frontier it could not tolerate the social disorder it found there. The revolts and internal squabbles that were so frequent in the Latin countries disrupted economic progress and went against American interests, and they had to be suppressed. Just as previously the Americans had had to handle Indian skirmishes on their internal frontier because they hindered the pioneers' material progress, now they had to put their neighbors' house in order. This mindset gave birth to the Monroe Doctrine to back up the civilizing message of the U.S., which was to create wealth, and Americans had to spread this gospel throughout Latin America. In his 1905 supplement to the Monroe Doctrine, Roosevelt let it be known that if the Hispanics "were able to act 'with reasonable efficiency' and keep order and pay their

---

6 *Ariel* was a book written in 1900 by the Uruguayan José Enrique Rodó (1872–1917) in which he severely criticizes the materialism in U.S. culture. The book was an immediate and enormous success.

debts then they did not 'have to fear United States intervention.' However, 'chronic errors, or impotence that resulted in a loosening of the bonds of civilized society' would force the United States, 'much against its will,' to assume 'the exercise of an international police power'" (Pike 1992, 174). And thus began the great conquest of the new frontier. Spain was expelled from Cuba in 1898, thus leaving the way clear for American industry.

1.3. AMERICAN COUNTERCULTURE AND FASCINATION WITH THE MYTH OF THE PRIMITIVE

The discipline of anthropology developed enormously in the early years of the twentieth century, and along with World War I this started a real revolution in how the West perceived itself. The prevailing evolutionist, Darwinist, and racist theories that postulated different societies having different rates of progress and development were overturned by a new anthropological theory: cultural relativism. This involved the notion that white Western societies cannot be seen as superior to others, because they are more advanced only in terms of technological production. But even in the area of technology the new currents from anthropology called the supremacy of the West into question. Why is building a skyscraper considered a symbol of technological progress when compared, for example, with the architecture of the Pueblo Indians? Why is land exploitation with machines and fertilizers seen as more technically advanced than the cultivation of communal land with traditional techniques such as those practiced by the descendants of the Incas in Peru? Why should the former be considered superior if it leads to land exhaustion, while the latter maintains soil fertility for centuries? Perhaps the only point beyond dispute was that the West had the technological superiority to dominate the rest and, if it came to the crunch, to eliminate them. But ironically, the world that was considered more advanced at that time nearly destroyed itself in World War I.

In Europe in the inter-war years there were very close connections between the various strands of the political avant-garde and the aesthetic and anthropological avant-garde, and they fed into each other. One of the most important results of the cultural movement generically termed avant-garde was that it challenged the foundations that had supported the vision of the Western world since the French Enlightenment in the eighteenth century. It called into question Western people's relation to nature, to science, to politics, to other societies, and to technology itself. It tried to turn the accepted scale of values upside down, and what had previously been seen as merely the background against which the West progressed was now seen as valuable and worth saving for its own sake. The United States was not isolated from this cultural movement, and indeed the Americans had their own avant-garde. This too was interconnected with anthropology, and it challenged the foundations of the country's culture and hence the prejudices underlying the U.S. vision of Latin America (Pike 1992, see Chapter 7).

Something of the role that Émile Durkheim, Georges Bataille, Marcel Mauss, and the Museum of Man in Paris played in the European avant-garde was played in the United States by the anthropologist Franz Boas (1858–1942), although his style was very different. Boas was an immigrant from Germany who arrived in the United States in 1889 and within ten years was the leading professor of anthropology at Columbia University. In 1911 he published *The Mind of Primitive Man*, which gained wide recognition in the 1920s. Boas's main contribution was to disseminate the notion of cultural relativism in American intellectual circles, and this superseded the evolutionist and Darwinist ideas of the best-known anthropologist in the Anglo-Saxon world up to that time, Lewis Henry Morgan (1818–81). Morgan had provided scientific justification for North American racism against the Afro-Americans, the Indians, and obviously the Latin Americans too. It was under Boas's influence that the great American anthropologists Ruth Benedict and Margaret Mead were trained, and also another immigrant, Edward Sapir. There is surely a connection between Boas's cultural relativism and the fact that the two *women* anthropologists mentioned above came to fame. The relativism that emerged in the context of different cultures was later extended to matters of gender and to the relations between the whites and the other ethnic groups that had previously been discriminated against by the WASPs (White Anglo-Saxon Protestants).

In this intellectual environment that criticized Western materialism, in 1926 D. H. Lawrence published *The Plumed Serpent*, which describes Mexico as a mythical future place where civilization and primitivism would shake hands and go on happily together. Lawrence was a friend of Mabel Dodge (1879–1962), one of the most prominent figures in the initial North American counterculture that opposed the expropriation of the land of the Pueblo Indians, whom the counterculture admired for their community with nature. A fair proportion of the avant-garde, in the United States as well as in Europe and Latin America, saw communism as a possible solution that might reverse the downhill slide being experienced by the capitalist, materialist, individualist world. Communism and primitivism merged thanks to scientific anthropological studies of ethnographic societies organized with no state and no private property.

In 1919 Waldo Frank (1889–1967) published a book entitled *Our America*. Frank, who was a devotee of Whitman and of Moscow, describes a United States corroded by the most savage materialism and lacking in spirit: "Here (the U.S.A.) is a land saturated with empty spiritual paths: a land so ravaged by the accumulative urgency of current business and by Puritan philosophy that there is no space left for any spiritual force to be born" (Frank 1972, 227). In later years Frank's interest turned to Spain, and he visited the country and produced a book about it, *Virgin Spain* (1926). Then he traveled in Hispanic America; his accounts of it dazzled many intellectuals in the 1930s, and he became one of the most widely read American writers in Latin America. He was not the typical Yankee who despised the south; quite the opposite—he saw it as a possible source of redemption for the West.

It is hard to gauge how much the American counterculture movement influenced international politics at that time because there were other factors in play—for example, the difficult economic situation after World War I—the trauma of the Great Depression after 1929—but in any case the Monroe Doctrine and the Big Stick were replaced by the Good Neighbor policy. One aspect of the Good Neighbor policy—which was carried forward mainly by Franklin D. Roosevelt—was that direct United States intervention in Latin America stopped. The Monroe Doctrine that justified United States intervention in the financial affairs of the Latin American countries did not have many supporters during the New Deal. It was only at the start of the 1950s and the Cold War that the U.S. would again resort to direct action and bring about the overthrow of the democratically elected Jacobo Arbenz in Guatemala.

During the 1920s and 1930s, some of America's leading intellectuals and artists moved toward supporting and even identifying with oppressed groups. There was a great upsurge in the struggle to help African Americans, but this soon lost impetus and was only revived when the civil rights movement bloomed again in the 1960s. The counterculture also publicly defended Native Americans' rights and helped the Pueblo people to a famous victory. Underlying these new values was the feeling that the structure of U.S. society bred alienation, and many of the adherents of this ideological movement moved toward socialist, anarchist, or communist positions. They greatly admired the Mexican Revolution of 1910 and hoped it would spread to the rest of Latin America. Their devotion to cultures that had not yet been disenchanted by production-based materialism was proportional to the extent to which they rejected the United States. The counterculture avant-garde consisted of a relatively small group of people, but they made a lot of noise and were in tune with the social disillusionment caused by the Great Depression, the Second World War, and the natural world's own reaction to overproduction and overconsumption: the creation of deserts.

However, the avant-garde's fascination with Latin America did not last long. The United States emerged from World War II as the self-proclaimed savior of mankind, and this changed how the country was perceived on the world stage: now it was not so bad after all. The development of the atomic bomb had involved a huge financial effort and coordination between scientists and the military, and it symbolized the manipulation of nature for the good of the human race. Atomic energy opened up new possibilities for exploiting the country's internal resources, and the external frontier no longer seemed so important. And what followed—the postwar era—was without doubt one of the saddest periods in United States culture. Rage had been building up for years against Americans who criticized their own country and constantly attacked the WASP status quo, and this exploded in a vicious and sustained reactionary backlash led by Senator Joseph McCarthy. Now was the time to put the United States in order and get rid of the cultural and political agitators. But it was also vital to establish order abroad, and America took on its role as the world's policeman again with renewed energy. Latin America was very near and was straying far too close toward communism, so it was time to apply the same remedy as McCarthyism was espousing at home: the witch hunt. The pendulum of foreign policy swung a long way to the right, the U.S. picked up its Big Stick again, and the racist stereotype of Latin Americans as savages resurfaced.

However, the counterculture, which was the soul of criticism of the modern world, had not entirely disappeared. It welled up again in the 1960s when there was an anti-establishment explosion that had considerable repercussions in politics. On the U.S. home front there was a "second" liberation of the African Americans. The slaves had been formally freed in the Civil War in the nineteenth century, but in practice their situation had changed very little and they were still the victims of discrimination in everyday life. In the 1950s and 1960s, the black movement revived and fought for human and civil rights, and this brought about a definitive and positive change in the racist stereotype of Americans that had weighed so heavily on their shoulders.

At around the same time the Cuban Revolution focused U.S. attention on the Hispanic countries again. Waldo Frank, the writer who had traveled in Spain and Latin America some time previously, interviewed Fidel Castro in Cuba and again became fascinated with the possibility that a real change in America could come from the south. Frank envisaged a new society based on principles diametrically opposed to those underlying the alienating world of industrial capitalism. In fact, in the incandescent 1960s there was a great wave of enthusiasm for the Third World in general, and this included a new romanticism about Latin America. Susan Sontag (1933–2004) went to Cuba and later traveled to Vietnam, where she ". . . found people she couldn't help regarding 'as children—beautiful, patient, heroic, martyred, stubborn children.' Among these people, she discovered, 'the phenomenon of existential agony, of alienation, just don't [sic] appear'" (Pike 1992, 324).[7] This image Sontag sketches of the Vietnamese could well be extrapolated to describe a vision of Latin America where new blood was also fighting to create a different kind of society. Indeed, the image of children has always been associated with primitive people. Children and "primitives" have not yet been corrupted by repressive, adult, modern, disciplined civilization. Some decades ago the German artist Paul Klee wrote in his diary, "I would like to be a child, a primitive, and know nothing of Europe." And one of the most famous American writers, J. D. Salinger, made a child the only character in *The Catcher in the Rye* (1951) who is not in some way rotten: the only person the teenager Holden can communicate with is his little sister. In fact, the image of a child expresses very well the way in which Americans stereotyped Hispanics. This image can express opposite things depending on the point of view of the person who interprets it. On the one hand, it is frequently used to symbolize the negative primitive stereotype the U.S. manufactured for Latin Americans, and it can send an authoritarian and racist message wherein the child is someone who has to be "cultivated." But, on the other hand, the image is charged with hope and a vision of utopia, although this often involves an overarching idea of paternalism.

1.4. AN INTERMEDIATE SYNTHESIS: LATIN AMERICA IN CARICATURE

In an excellent 1993 book, *Latin America in Caricature*, the American writer John J. Johnson shows—using newspaper cartoons—the images Americans constructed of the Hispanic American South. He reproduces 131 cartoons that appeared at various times in the twentieth century in the American press and thus achieves a solid and convincing synthesis of the prevailing stereotypes. In keeping with the connection we make above between the image of the child and U.S. views of Latin America, one of the figures the cartoonists use most to represent Latin America is in fact a child. There are children that have to be educated by Uncle Sam, dirty children that have to be washed by Uncle Sam, children fighting who are disturbing Uncle Sam when he's trying to rest, children who are ill and have to

---

7   The Sontag quotation is from *Trip to Hanoi* (1968).

take Uncle Sam's medicine, and children who have to grow up so they can be called civilized and walk on their own without Uncle Sam's guidance. Sometimes Uncle Sam is severe and gets tough when the kids are naughty, and sometimes he has the face of an easy-going old man—when the children are well-behaved or have done something right.

There are other figures, too, that are repeated throughout the century, such as Latin America as a passive woman who must be seduced and fertilized by the virile Anglo-Saxon man. Very often the representation of Latin America is monolithic and the figure is a black man, an Indian, or a Latino who is usually scruffy, wearing a Mexican hat, or sleeping a big siesta. The images representing the different countries in Latin America are all alike, and while it is true that cartoonists need to do this to give the pictures force, it is also true that such homogenization reflects an ignorance of the specific characteristics of each of the different countries that make up the continent. Few Americans know that in the River Plate region people of African descent and indigenous populations are minorities, and few can distinguish a Brazilian mulatto (of mixed race, dark-skinned) from a Mexican mestizo.

In the late 1960s and throughout the 1970s, the subjects of militarism, revolution, and social reform came increasingly to the fore and many of the cartoons featured military generals or contrasting extremes of wealth and poverty. The conclusion Johnson draws after analyzing 131 cartoons is particularly telling:

> If it seems . . . that the cartoons included herein victimize the people of Latin America, it is because the cartoonists ordinarily have portrayed the republics as politically and economically impoverished and culturally deprived. Concomitantly, for the most part, they have been willing participants in a "grand design" to strip Latin Americans of any inherent ability to compete on equal terms in this hemisphere by denying the very qualities required to compete in Western societies. (Johnson 1993, 28)

The cartoons are drawn for the American public and in most cases they do no more than reproduce symbols from the collective imagination. In 1940, the Public Opinion Research Office carried out a nationwide survey in which the interviewees had to choose from a list of nineteen words those they thought best described the people of Latin America. The eight terms selected most have negative connotations: dark-skinned was mentioned by 80 per cent of the interviewees, quick-tempered by 49 per cent, emotional by 47 per cent, religious (Catholic) by 45 per cent, backward by 44 per cent, lazy by 41 per cent, ignorant by 34 per cent, and suspicious by 32 per cent. Only three favorable words (friendly, proud, and imaginative) were chosen by more than 20 per cent of the people interviewed, and none by more than 30 per cent, and none of the other favorable words (intelligent, honest, brave, generous, progressive, efficient) was selected by more than 15 per cent of the interviewees (Johnson 1993, 18).

In this chapter we have focused exclusively on analyzing stereotypes constructed in the United States but there is no doubt that these same "caricatures" can be found in the European images of Latin America.

Figure 1.1: Room for All, If They're Careful.
Credit: William Allan Rogers, *New York Herald*, 1904.

CONCLUSIONS

The United States is changing with dizzying speed, and it is no longer possible to talk about U.S. stereotypes of Latinos in the way we have been doing up to now. When we consider today's Americans, we have to take account of the different cultures that have been developing and imposing their customs and visions of the world. The African American population can certainly not be identified with any of the past images described above; i.e., those images were created by a WASP worldview in which African Americans did not participate. And today's women are also developing their own perspectives, which they want to explicitly differentiate from those that predominated in the past. Similarly, the populations that originated in Latin America and have now put down roots in the United States (the Hispanics or Latinos) form part of the group labeled as "the Americans," and their culture, language, music, literature, beliefs, and

Figure 1.2: The Monroe Doctrine Now Seems to Have a Little Brother.
Credit: John T. McCutcheon, *Chicago Tribune.*

lifestyles are spreading more and more. But as we are analyzing American images of Latin America we shall pause briefly and examine the people who without doubt will do most to modify the previous stereotypes, namely the Latinos in the United States (a subject we will examine in greater depth in Chapter 7).

Today in the United States there are some 50 million Hispanics. In the country as a whole they make up around 16 per cent of the total population, in New Mexico 38 per cent, in Texas 25, and in California 23. There are 1,500 Spanish-language newspapers and 250 radio stations. Tijuana, a Mexican border city across from San Diego, had a population of around 60,000 in 1950, but today there are 1.5 million inhabitants (many of whom cross the border every day). According to the 2010 Census, 60 per cent of the people in the metropolitan area of Los Angeles are Asians and Latinos. In New York there are advertisements and signs in Spanish all over the city; in Miami you hear more Spanish spoken than English, and the same applies to the area near the southern border and on the west coast. The Chicano cultures of immigrants from Mexico and the *Nuyoricans* of Puerto Rico in New York are gaining strength, their language and symbols are entering the flow of the mass media, and what is most interesting is that

Figure 1.3: We're Taking a New Look at It.
Credit: The Washington Post, 1964. Reprinted by permission of the Herb Block Foundation.

both movements are fighting hard not to lose their cultural roots. Hispanics have managed to achieve an interesting cultural transformation insofar as they are adapting to their dual identities in a creative way and saving their vernacular traditions by combining them with the experience of living in the United States. The outcome is quite the opposite of cultural assimilation: it is an astonishing revitalization of their own traditions. They are handling their experience of living in two places, of living on the edge, on the border, in the tension between two cultures, by updating their traditions and forging a synthesis between their past and American modernity. One of the best-known members of the Chicano movement, Tomás Ybarra-Frausto, who was associate director of the Rockefeller Foundation, has expressed it as follows:

> . . . while traditions are maintained for the sake of historical survival, it is also the case that the "real" tradition is to break with tradition, to desacralize and

actualize it. The past is thus revitalized, and inherited cultural trappings are recontextualized to suit present needs and functions. (1992, 214)

On January 30, 1994, the following headline appeared on one of the culture pages in the *New York Times*: "Burying The Frito Bandito Once And For All." This was a reference to a film that was being made about the Cisco Kid by the Chicano director Luis Valdez (who directed *La Bamba*). In the article we read: "This film is part of a great effort to counteract ninety years of omissions and distortions in how Latinos have been represented in westerns." It is an eloquent example of how the stereotype of the greaser analyzed above is undergoing a big change in American imagery. Now the Chicanos are also Americans. The mythical western and southern frontiers of the White Anglo-Saxon Protestants are imploding into the United States, the flood has come and the stereotype of Hispanics as savages is fading. This is a long-term process, and it does not depend only on the Hispanic populations in the United States, but also on what the people who live in Latin America are doing in their own cultures and societies. That process is what the rest of this book is about.

The images that Latin Americans are constructing of themselves are changing too. Postcolonial thought has become more prevalent since 1992, and there has been increasing criticism of the stereotypes analyzed in this chapter. The theory of culture and progress in human rights has also changed, partly under the influence of multiculturalism and interculturality (see, for example, Taylor 1993). Frantz Fanon has been an important figure in promoting an understanding of the psychology of colonized people: they end up internalizing the stigmas that colonizers put on them to dominate them more completely. This has happened with Latin Americans, a phenomenon that Richard Morse sums up as follows: "The heart of the matter is that Hispanic America has always been seen, even by its own classic thinkers, not as autochthonous but simply as obsolete" (Morse 1982, 168). In his book, Morse sets out to show how the main traditions of thought in Latin America (which he refers to as *Iberoamérica*) infused these societies with a certain antidote against falling into the disenchantment that has affected the rest of the Western world, where the current scenario is very much like what the Frankfurt School predicted (individualism, consumerism, rationalism, crisis in the relation with nature). In other words, a civilization like the industrialized West, as analyzed by Weber, Nietzsche, Spengler, Adorno, and Horkheimer, should be less likely to emerge in Latin America, which is another kind of West with different philosophical and political foundations. In short, the world Robert Cohn was alienated from is not so common in Latin America.

This book is an attempt to highlight and discuss some aspects of Latin America that seem to us not to be "obsolete;" on the contrary, they can be considered innovations in economics, politics, culture, and society. In the chapters that follow, we analyze subjects such as the following: women's participation in politics in Argentina, Brazil, Chile, and Panama (which have all elected women presidents); social distribution policies to reduce poverty; social security systems; innovations in electoral systems in pursuit of greater transparency; the new indigenous movements, such as the one in Bolivia that led to the election of the first indigenous president; Afro movements and the conquest of civil rights, as seen in Brazil, where for the first time an Afro-Brazilian,

Joaquim Barbosa, has become president of the Supreme Court; and football, with its inexhaustible supply of players, clubs, and national teams that are always at the top of the world rankings. These are all dimensions in which Latin Americans, instead of being ashamed, can inspire the world.

LESSONS LEARNED

- The stereotypes of Latin Americans that were created in the United States were overwhelmingly negative and labeled them as passive, lazy, dirty, irrational, incapable, and backward.
- To a large extent these images provided a cloak of legitimacy for United States superiority and the right to intervene in Latin American countries' affairs as a way of re-establishing order, democracy, or progress, even when the real motives for direct intervention were economic.
- These negative images have been changing in the last twenty years thanks to the 50 million Latinos living in the United States today, who have gradually managed to disseminate more positive images of Latin Americans.

DISCUSSION QUESTIONS

- How and why are negative stereotypes of a group of people created?
- Are there still negative epithets about Latin Americans? If so, what are they, and have they changed from those of earlier times?
- How can people who are negatively stereotyped end up believing they really are as they are portrayed?
- With the rise of Latin American global figures such as Lula, Lionel Messi, Pope Francis, Rigoberta Menchú, and Gabriel García Márquez, will the stereotypes of Latin Americans change for the better?

ADDITIONAL READING

Arocena, Felipe, and Eduardo De León. 1993. *El Espejo de Próspero*. Montevideo: Vintén Editor.

Lander, Edgardo (compiler). 2000. *La Colonialidad del Saber: Eurocentrismo y Ciencias Sociales. Perspectivas Latinoamericanas*. Buenos Aires: CLACSO (Consejo Latinoamericano de Ciencias Sociales).

Moraña, Mabel. 2008. *Coloniality at Large: Latin America and the Postcolonial Debate*. Durham, NC: Duke University Press.

Schoultz, Lars. 1998. *Beneath the United States: A History of U.S. Policy toward Latin America*. Cambridge, MA: Harvard University Press.

PART ONE

POLITICS: ELECTIONS AND PARTICIPATION

CHAPTER TWO

GENDER AND REPRESENTATION

INTRODUCTION

When comparing the distribution of men and women elected to national legislatures, one would find considerable variation both around the world and within every region. The highest percentage of women in parliaments is not in the expected countries of Scandinavia, where women have made significant electoral gains for decades. In fact, Rwanda leads the world in the percentage of women in the legislature at 56 per cent, while Nicaragua (40%), Argentina (39%), and Costa Rica (39%) lead the western hemisphere. In contrast, countries from around the world and with very different cultural characteristics and levels of economic development elect legislatures with fewer than 10 per cent of the seats held by women. The wealthy European Union country of Malta has 9 per cent, the poorer Asian country of Mongolia has only 4 per cent, and Algeria has 8 per cent; meanwhile, in the Americas, women make up a mere 9 per cent of the chamber of deputies in both Brazil and Panama.[8]

In this chapter we use historical and contemporary evidence from Latin America to explore the important issue of gender representation in national parliaments. What could explain such a wide variation in electing women representatives around the globe? Is it cultural or economic? How much do attitudes toward women matter? Or are electoral architecture and electoral rules more important? Why should anyone care if women are elected in significant numbers?

Latin America is a particularly useful laboratory for understanding these issues, as the region is, notwithstanding the data from Brazil and Panama cited above, the

---

8   These data come from http://www.quotaproject.org/.

world pioneer and leader in policies and practices to increase the percentage of elected women. In 2009, 11 of the 26 countries in the world with electoral quotas for women were located in Latin America. This results in some interesting case studies and fascinating electoral rules. Latin America also exhibits wide variation in both attitudes toward women and the percentage of women elected. This chapter presents the history of women's elected political representation in the region and explains the impact of attitudes and electoral architecture on the election of women.

2.1. WHY DOES IT MATTER?

There are three principal arguments for wanting a significant number of women in democratic parliaments. The first is that it responds to an issue of fairness and justice. If women make up more than 50 per cent of the population, shouldn't they also hold a significant percentage of political power? A parliament made up exclusively or largely of men is unrepresentative, and it limits the distinguishing feature of republican governments whereby elected officials act on behalf of the overall population.

Second, women have long lagged far behind men in economic, political, and social power. Women have suffered from discrimination and violence for thousands of years. In many parts of the world, public opinion polls reveal widespread public attitudes that men are superior to women, that women should not work but should stay at home, and that women are inferior in politics. It is important to have large numbers of elected women at the national level to counter these views and provide role models for young people. With such role models, negative attitudes toward women should decline over time.

Finally, women bring important new issues to the national arena and to the area of policy development. In parliaments with large numbers of women, pioneering policies have been developed on such social issues as child care, senior care, child support, women's health, birth control, sex crimes, and other similar issues of particular importance to women.

The argument that supports a significant percentage of women in office as a matter of fairness or justice is philosophical and open to debate. The other two stated reasons include an empirical dimension. Is it true that attitudes toward women change over time after large percentages of women are elected to the national parliament? Is it true that parliaments with large numbers of women tackle women's issues with more frequency than do parliaments with very few women? These are important questions, and the experience in Latin America provides some clues and some answers. We will turn to these issues after describing the evolution of women's involvement in elections in Latin America.

2.2. EVA PERÓN AND THE EMERGENCE OF ELECTORAL QUOTAS FOR WOMEN

Argentina was the first country in the world to use quotas to increase the number of elected women in parliament. This was largely a result of the influence and policies

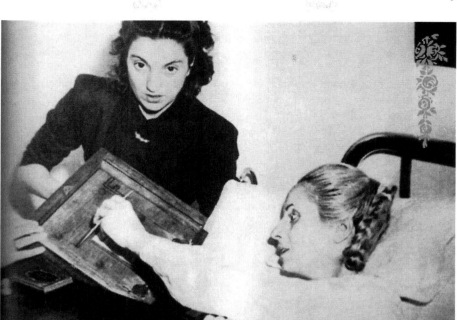

Figure 2.1: Eva Perón Voting from the Hospital in 1951. Courtesy of Kirk Bowman.
Credit: Eva Duarte de Perón (Evita). Otelo Borroni and Roberto Vaca. CEAL, Buenos Aires
page 72, 1970.

of Eva (Evita) Perón (1919–52). Eva was the charismatic and influential wife of Argentine president Juan Perón (1895–1974), who was minister of labor under a military regime from 1943–46 and who governed as an elected president from 1946 until being exiled by a military coup in 1955.[9]

When Juan Perón was first elected in 1946, politics was exclusively a men's club, as women had no voting rights. In June 1947, however, Evita undertook a humanitarian mission to Europe, where she proclaimed that the twentieth century would be remembered as the Century of Victorious Feminism and that victory would begin in Argentina. Evita focused her energy and influence on the cause, and in September 1947, Law 13.010 was passed, giving all Argentine women the right to vote. Evita subsequently animated the efforts to register women and provide identity cards for voting in the next elections, and Evita herself received identification card number 0000001. The card is still proudly displayed in the Eva Perón Museum in Buenos Aires.

---

9 Juan Perón was elected again in 1973 but died in 1974, leaving his third wife and vice-president Isabel Perón as president. The country descended into chaos, and Isabel Perón was overthrown in a coup in 1976. The generals ruled the country and executed the "dirty war" until 1983.

With women's suffrage in place for the 1951 presidential and legislative elections, Evita and the Peronists put in place the world's first voluntary gender quotas for candidate selection, resulting in the election of 23 women to the Argentine Chamber of Deputies and 6 senators to the Argentine Senate. This resulted in women making up 15 per cent of the Chamber of Deputies, the highest percentage of any democracy in the world and a percentage that is similar to the 17 per cent women elected to the U.S. Congress six decades later.

The use of quotas has spread throughout Latin America since 1990. Once Uruguay's recently enacted quotas go into effect for the 2014 elections, every Latin American country with multiparty elections, except Venezuela, will have electoral quotas for women functioning at the party level or at the national level. Nevertheless, even with quotas spread throughout the region, some countries have lots of women elected and others have very few. Table 2.1 presents the percentage of women in lower house seats in Latin America, Canada, and the United States in 1990 and 2011.

Table 2.1 Percentage of Women in the Lower House, 1990–2011

	1990	2011	Type of Quota
Argentina	6	39	Legislated/enforced
Bolivia	9	25	Legislated/enforced
Brazil	5	9	Legislated/enforced
Canada	13	25	Voluntary by some political parties
Chile	8	14	Voluntary by some political parties
Colombia	5	13	Legislated/enforced
Costa Rica	11	39	Legislated/enforced
Cuba	34	43	No multiparty elections, no quotas
Dominican Republic	8	21	Legislated/enforced
Ecuador	5	32	Legislated/enforced
El Salvador	12	19	Voluntary by one party (FMLN)
Guatemala	7	12	Voluntary by some parties
Honduras	10	18	Legislated/enforced
Mexico	12	26	Legislated/enforced
Nicaragua	15	40	Voluntary by parties
Panama	8	9	Legislated/enforced
Paraguay	6	13	Legislated/enforced
Peru	6	22	Legislated/enforced
United States	7	17	None
Uruguay	6	15	Legislated/enforced for 2014
Venezuela	10	17	None

A quick look at these data produces some interesting questions. Nicaragua leads the hemisphere for electing women in countries with multiparty elections, with 40 per cent women. Why would one of Nicaragua's neighbors (Costa Rica) have 39 per cent while the other neighbor (Honduras) only has 18 per cent? And why does Argentina have 39 per cent while one of its neighbors (Chile) only has 14 per cent and another (Brazil) a mere 9 per cent?

Political scientists have studied these questions for the past two decades and developed a very good understanding of the factors that determine the election of women.[10] The percentage of women in legislatures is a result of two components: the first is public attitudes toward women; the second is the electoral system.

2.3. POLITICAL ATTITUDES TOWARD WOMEN

In a world where women were valued as equal to men, there would probably be no need for any organized efforts to elect more women. Unfortunately, this is not the case. Latin America is well known as a region characterized by *machismo* and male chauvinism. But is there truth in this stereotype?

Latinobarómetro is a public-opinion organization based in Chile that each year surveys 19,000 citizens across 18 Latin American countries on a wide range of topics. In 2009, a large number of Spaniards were also surveyed. Two of the questions provide useful information for our understanding of attitudes toward women that could affect elections and the number of elected women:

  1. *It is preferable for a woman to stay in the house and men to do the work.*
  2. *Men are better political leaders than are women.*

For both questions, respondents could answer with Strongly Agree, Agree, Don't Know/No Answer, Disagree, or Strongly Disagree. Figure 2.2 presents the percentage of the population in each country that agree or strongly agree that men should work and that women should stay at home. In other words, they believe in traditional family structures where women raise children and are homemakers.

Spain, which shares many religious and cultural values with Latin America, is by far the country with the lowest percentage of supporters of traditional family roles (13%). Given the strong traditional-family policies of the Francisco Franco dictatorship that lasted from 1936 to 1975, one can conclude (and survey data support), that attitudes can change relatively rapidly.

In Latin America there is tremendous variation in attitudes toward traditional gender roles. Less than one-third of the population believes that women should stay at home in Argentina, Brazil, Costa Rica, Chile, Peru, Uruguay, and Venezuela. In contrast, 59 per cent of the population of Honduras and 52 per cent of Guatemalans do

---

10 This chapter borrows extensively from Alcántara Sáez (2008), Carrio (2005), Htun (2005), Jones (2009), Thames and Williams (2013), and Wicks and Lang-Dion (2007).

Figure 2.2: Proportion of Population that Believes That Men Should Work and Women Should Stay at Home

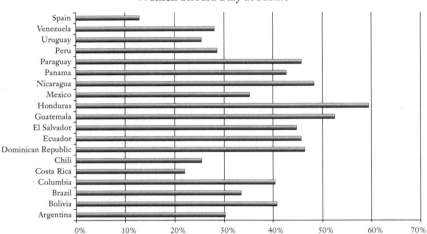

Source: Data from Latinobarómetro. http://www.latinobarometro.org/latino/latinobarometro.jsp.

not support women working outside of the home. More than 40 per cent of those living in Bolivia, Colombia, the Dominican Republic, Ecuador, El Salvador, Nicaragua, Panama, and Paraguay also support men working and women staying at home.

It is easy to explain the theoretical linkage between these attitudes and elections for women. If a large percentage of the population believes that women should stay home and raise children, there would be a predisposition against voting for women to get out of the home and into a political job such as elected representative. In fact, there is a very strong correlation of 0.90 between the percentage of the population who is does not believe that women should stay home and the percentage of the population that believes that men are better politicians than are women, as shown in Figure 2.3.

The attitudes of Latin Americans and Spaniards on the superiority of men as politicians are presented in Figure 2.4. While there is a strong correlation between Figures 2.2 and 2.4, there are some important differences. For one, Costa Rica (16%) has nearly the same attitudes as Spain (14%). Costa Rica has the longest continuous experiment with measures to ensure significant female representation in the legislature. Could it be that having lots of women in politics changes attitudes, resulting in fewer people believing that women were inferior to men in politics? The three countries with the highest percentage of the population who believe that men are superior politicians are Panama (44%), Honduras (49%), and the Dominican Republic (53%). In every Latin American country with multiparty elections, except Costa Rica, at least 25 per cent of the population believes that men are better politicians than are women. This is a significant electoral hurdle for women candidates, as one could assume that between 25 and 53 per cent of the population would vote for a male candidate over a female candidate merely because of gender.

Figure 2.3: Relationship between Traditional Gender Attitudes and Belief That Men Are Better Politicians

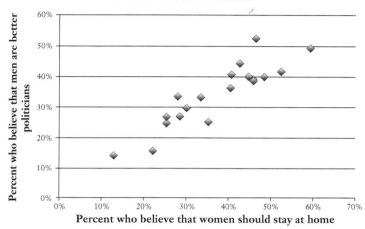

Source: Data from Latinobarómetro. http://www.latinobarometro.org/latino/latinobarometro.jsp.

Figure 2.4: Proportion of Population That Believes That Men Are Better Politicians

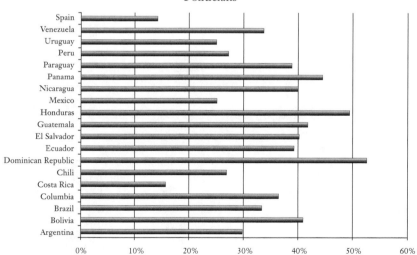

Source: Data from Latinobarómetro. http://www.latinobarometro.org/latino/latinobarometro.jsp.

2.4. TWO DECADES OF EXPERIMENTATION

In 1990, Latin America was characterized by a very small percentage of women elected in national parliaments (eight per cent overall) and a significant percentage of the population with attitudes that inhibited the electoral success of large numbers of women.

Starting in 1990, four decades after Argentina first experimented with gender quotas, Latin Americans began to develop new policies and practices to elect more women legislators. What would have been the options available to Latin American political leaders who wanted to increase the number of elected women legislators? Would the electoral system need to be altered? There are three general strategies.

The first strategy is to change attitudes and empower individual female candidates with resources, training, experience in local politics, and other opportunities. For example, EMILY's List (the acronym stands for "Early Money Is Like Yeast") is an organization in the United States that aims to elect more pro-choice Democratic women to the U.S. Congress and governorships, while pro-life conservatives have Susan B. Anthony's List. A wide range of organizations work to empower and prepare women to succeed in electoral politics around the world. This is the only strategy in effect in Venezuela (with 17% women legislators), as well as in the United States (also 17%).

The second strategy is for political parties to embrace the election of women as a party strength and to introduce voluntary quotas for women in electoral lists. This was what Evita Perón first implemented in 1951, and it has been hugely successful in the Scandinavian countries of Denmark, Norway, and Sweden. In some cases a dynamic develops whereby parties compete with each other for the highest number of women. Party A announces that 30 per cent of its elected representatives will be women, and Party B responds by announcing that 40 per cent of *its* elected representatives will be women. The voluntary party quota strategy is in effect in Chile (with 14% women legislators), El Salvador (19%), Guatemala (12%), and Nicaragua (40%), as well as in Canada (25%).

A third strategy is for the legislature or courts to mandate candidate selection rules for all parties that specify particular electoral positions for women candidates. Mandated rules are in effect in Argentina (with 39% women legislators), Bolivia (25%), Brazil (9%), Colombia (13%), Costa Rica (39%), the Dominican Republic (21%), Ecuador (32%), Honduras (18%), Mexico (26%), Panama (9%), Paraguay (13%), and Peru (22%), as well as more recently in Uruguay.

As these figures show, there is tremendous variation in success within each of the quota strategies. The voluntary party-level quotas produce 12 per cent women legislators in Guatemala and 14 per cent in Chile, while at the same time leading to the top performer in Latin America in Nicaragua (40%). The national mandated quotas also result in tremendous variation, with Argentina and Costa Rica at 39 per cent, and Brazil and Panama at a regional low of 9 per cent. This extreme variation suggests that these cases hold the keys to understanding legislative elections and gender representation.

2.4.1. THE SUCCESSFUL CASES

2.4.1.1. Costa Rica

Costa Rica has the longest continuous experience with gender quotas in the region. Prior to 1994 there were no quotas, and women held a mere 11 per cent of the legislative seats. Following the success of Scandinavian voluntary party quotas in the 1970s that produced impressive gains, Costa Rica recommended but did not require that political parties implement policies to elect more women. This policy depended on the good will of individual parties, and in the end it was not successful in electing more women. The Costa Ricans responded by requiring parties to submit electoral lists where 40 per cent of the candidates were female. However, the parties could nullify the spirit of the law by placing women at the bottom of the nominating lists. So in 1999, Costa Rica went further still and required that parties have women as 40 per cent of the "electable positions" on party lists, where "electable position" is a seat that the party won in the previous election. Going even further, Law 8765 of September 2009 states that the principal of parity requires alternation on the candidate lists (the so-called zipper-system): "All nominations to election will comply with the mechanism of alternating by sex (woman-man or man-woman) in a way that two persons of the same sex cannot be subsequent on the nomination list." These rules will go into effect for the 2014 elections and will likely increase the percentage of women legislators to above the current 39 per cent.

In two decades, Costa Rica has made tremendous strides and has learned that recommendations and good will are not enough; instead, specific and mandatory rules that ensure both the percentage and the placement of women on the party list are necessary. In the 2010 elections, Costa Ricans elected not only 22 women in a 57-seat legislature, but also a female president, Laura Chinchilla. Chinchilla was first elected to the legislature in 2002, in the first elections that required 40 percent women in electable position.

As shown in Figure 2.4 on page 27, Costa Rica is the country in Latin America with the lowest percentage who think that men are better politicians than women. Supporters of quotas argue that having large numbers of elected women will provide role models and erode traditional views of women.

2.4.1.2. Argentina

While Argentina originated gender quotas in 1951, subsequent military coups and decades of turmoil reversed those policies such that by 1990 women constituted a mere 6 per cent of the legislature in the lower house. In 2011, by contrast, women constituted 39 per cent in both the lower house and the senate. Argentina mandates quotas on all parties and, like Costa Rica, uses the concept of "electable positions." There must be one woman on the party list for every two men. In addition, parties without representation or with only one or two seats to renew are obliged to have a woman as one of the top two candidates. Parties that are renewing three or more seats can have its first woman as the third candidate.

It is in the senate that the most interesting interplay of quotas and electoral systems occurs. Argentina has a senate of 72 members, three from each of the provinces and from the Autonomous City of Buenos Aires. Senators serve six-year terms, and every two years one-third of the provinces elect their three senators. The party that receives the highest number of votes in each province elects two senators, while the second place party elects one senator. Following the mandated electoral quota rules, each party must have a woman as one of its top two candidates, since by definition each party renews zero, one, or two seats (two is the maximum number of seats that a party can win in each provincial election for the national senate). Therefore, the interplay of the quota law and the electoral rules results in at least one woman elected to the senate in each provincial election and a senate composed of at least 33.3 per cent women.

2.4.1.3. Nicaragua

Nicaragua elects its 92-member unicameral legislature through party lists and proportional representation for 90 seats, plus one seat for the losing presidential candidate and one seat for the outgoing president or vice-president. Nicaragua has the highest percentage of women in the legislature in the hemisphere, and yet it has no mandatory quota. The jump in the number of women legislators from 21 per cent in 2010 to 40 per cent after the 2011 elections resulted from voluntary quotas in the FSLN (Sandinista) party.

The FSLN has a 30 per cent quota for women in its party statutes and has long elected large numbers of women. The FSLN won 69 per cent of elected legislative seats in the 2011 elections, and an astounding 34 of the 62 (i.e., 55%) elected FSLN candidates were women. The FSLN's embrace of women candidates has not rubbed off on the other major parties, however. Only 3 of 26 (12%) of elected candidates from the Liberal Independent Party (PLI) were women, and both elected members of the Liberal and Constitutionalist Party (PLC) were men.

The future in Nicaragua is therefore uncertain. The continuation of large numbers of women in the Nicaraguan parliament requires either the continued domination of the Sandinista party, with most women candidates, or the rapid increase in the number of women candidates in other political parties. Neither of these scenarios is assured, and the success of women candidates may be sadly ephemeral.

2.4.2. THE DISAPPOINTING CASES

2.4.2.1. Brazil

Brazil has a woman president, Dilma Rousseff, and moderate levels of voters who believe that men are better politicians than women. Brazil also has had a mandated quota provision of 30 per cent women candidates on party lists since 2000. With this combination of moderate attitudes and mandated quotas, one might expect Brazil to do far better than its 9 per cent female elected members of the chamber of deputies. Why are women so underrepresented in Brazil? The answer lies in the powerful effect of electoral rules on outcomes. Brazil has a large lower house, with 513 deputies and proportional representation. Parties put forward party lists, and women must make up 30 per cent of the candidates. A positive outcome for women candidates is undermined by two elements of the process.

The first difficulty is that the 2000 quota provision was watered down when implemented as parties only need to meet the quota if the party submits candidates of the stipulated maximum for candidacy. The stipulated maximum was raised from 100 to 150 per cent of the total fillable seats per voting district as part of the quota law.

Therefore, the law has little real effect, as parties can submit a smaller list or a list with the 30 per cent women on the bottom of the list.

But there is an even greater problem in Brazil: Brazilians vote for open lists. They vote for individuals, and the party receives a proportion of seats based on the total percentage vote received by all party candidates. The final ordering of the party list is determined by the voters. In this system, there is no way to ensure that women constitute any percentage of elected candidates, and no way to place women in the first or second or third, or indeed any, position. Unless Brazil changes its electoral system, attitudes must be dramatically improved, women candidates must be nurtured and supported, and parties must start favoring female candidates. Without such measures, improvement in Brazil will continue to be slow and disappointing.

2.4.2.2. Chile

Chile has some of the most pro-women attitudes in Latin America, and some of the political parties have stringent voluntary quotas for women candidates. Yet Chile has one of the lowest percentages of elected women in parliament. Why? As with Brazil, the electoral system has a powerful effect on the number of women elected.

Chile has binomial voting districts with proportional representation. The country is divided into 60 districts for the chamber of deputies, and each district elects two legislators in proportional representation. This binomial system was instituted as dictator Augusto Pinochet (1915–2006) was leaving power, as a way to limit the electoral power of Pinochet's opponents. Why and how? Pinochet was worried that single-member districts or multi-member proportional representation would result in a large majority for the left and center-left parties, and could lead to potential investigations into, and punishment of, the human rights abuses committed during his dictatorship.

The binomial voting district by proportional representation has a powerful effect on the distribution of seats. A party or party coalition must win 66.7 per cent of the votes in a district to win both seats. A losing party or coalition can win one of the two seats in a district by capturing a mere 33.4 per cent of the vote. This is an electoral system that strongly benefits the electoral power of the minority coalition! It also means that the second candidate on a party list is almost never elected, as almost every binomial district election gives one seat to the majority party (coalition) and one seat to the runner-up party (coalition). Therefore, even if a woman were in the second position on every voting district in the country, there would be very few women elected. The only way to ensure more elected women would be for a national mandate or voluntary party quota of having a woman in the first position in 30, 40, or 50 per cent of the districts.

2.5. WHAT ARE THE EFFECTS OR CONSEQUENCES?

For the purposes of legislation and public policy, does it matter if more women are elected? This is a very difficult question to answer, in part because the gains are too recent. One might assume, however, that women have greater interests in such policies as child care, corruption, senior care, domestic abuse, reproductive rights, and so on, and that having more women legislators would lead to more action in these areas.

The evidence is beginning to emerge that large numbers of women in a democratic legislature results in a shift in legislation (Carrio 2005; Wängnerud 2009). Argentina, for example, has passed important legislation on reproductive rights, marriage rights, and sexual harassment legislation. There is a strong established correlation between the number of women in parliament and the amount of corruption, with more women parliamentarians correlated with lower levels of corruption. Unfortunately, neither the direction of causation nor the causal linkage is known with confidence: we do not know if having more women in parliament reduces corruption, if low levels of corruption result in electing more women, or if both variables are correlated with other variables.

The challenge of understanding the relationship between women in parliament and corruption highlights a similar difficulty of measuring other substantive effects of electing more women. The most extensive review of the research is found in Wängnerud (2009). Wängnerud admits that it might be too early to know the effects of electing women on substantive outcomes and that the extant research might be characterized as immature. However, after viewing all of the major existing empirical studies, she concludes: "The result that emerges from the empirical research is that female politicians contribute to strengthening the position of women's interests. There is need for more research on women in parliaments, especially regarding substantive representation" (65).

We propose that there are two other areas where electing large numbers of women to parliaments has a positive impact. The first is the effect of having large numbers of female parliamentarians on attitudes toward women in society. As we noted, there appears to be a correlation between having large numbers of women in parliament and more favorable public opinion toward women as politicians. Over time, having more women in parliament may eliminate or reduce the cultural impediments to women in politics and perhaps the quotas could disappear. More time and studies would be required to fully understand this relationship.

Second, we can already begin to identify paths to power—i.e., election to higher office—available for women in countries with electoral quotas that favor women. Effective quotas result in large pools of female legislators and a greater probability that women will eventually become presidents. Current presidents Laura Chinchilla of Costa Rica and Cristina Fernández de Kirchner of Argentina both served in legislatures with effective electoral quotas for women.

CONCLUSIONS

From Argentina to Rwanda, the last decades have witnessed a revolution in the participation of women in politics. Latin America has the earliest and most extensive experience with institutional arrangements for electing greater numbers of women.

There are three ways of electing more women to parliaments: changing attitudes toward women, voluntary quotas by political parties, or enforced quotas on all parties. In Latin America, public-opinion polls reveal a strong bias against women in politics, which provides a large hurdle for women to get elected in large numbers without other reforms. Voluntary quotas have largely proven insufficient in the region, with the exception of recent elections in Nicaragua where there was a very large number of women parliamentary candidates from the ruling Sandinista party. These gains by women politicians in Nicaragua may be temporary, relying as they do on the ongoing success of the Sandinista (FSLN) party in winning large numbers of seats and on the continuation of voluntary pro-women policies by the party.

Argentina and Costa Rica have had the longest experience with quotas, and the results not only appear to lead to a greater prominence of substantive issues of interest to women but have also contributed to the election of female presidents who previously passed through the process of being candidates and being elected to the legislature under the quota system. In contrast to the voluntary and potentially ephemeral policies in Nicaragua, the rules in Argentina and Costa Rica guarantee the election of large numbers of women in these two countries. And with Uruguay joining the group of countries with electoral rules that guarantee a significant number of women legislators, the expansion of the proportion of women politicians will continue.

LESSONS LEARNED

- Attitudes toward women in the region make it difficult for women to win large numbers of seats without electoral quotas.
- More and more countries in the region are establishing rules and institutions that guarantee the election of large numbers of women for the legislative branch.
- Voluntary quotas, which work well in Scandinavia, are unlikely to have significant long-term effects.
- Open-list elections, such as those in Brazil, and low-magnitude districts, such as those in Chile, are likely to result in legislatures dominated by men.

DISCUSSION QUESTIONS

- What other factors do you think could be affecting the gender representation in parliament in these countries?
- Do you think that different political ideologies (previous or current) influence the attitudes toward women's political representation/participation?
- What are some arguments against quotas? Do the positives outweigh the negatives?
- Why has women's access to politics increased in Latin America?
- Why is there so much variation in representation among countries in Latin America?
- How does having women in office affect policy?

ADDITIONAL READING

Araújo, Clara, and Ana Isabel García. 2006. "Latin America: The Experience and the Impact of Quotas in Latin America." In *Women, Quotas, and Politics*, ed. D. Dahlerup, 83–111. New York: Routledge.

Baldez, Lisa. 2007. "Primaries vs. Quotas: Gender and Candidate Nominations in Mexico, 2003." *Latin America Politics and Society* 49 (3): 69–96.

Campo, Esther Del. 2005. "Women and Politics in Latin America: Perspectives and Limits of the Institutional Aspects of Women's Political Representation." *Social Forces* 83: 1697–1725.

Franceschet, Susan, and Jennifer Piscopo. 2008. "Gender Quotas and Women's Substantive Representation: Lessons from Argentina." *Politics & Gender* 4: 393–425.

Jones, Mark P. 2004. "Quota Legislation and the Election of Women: Learning from the Costa Rican Experience." *The Journal of Politics* 6: 1203–23.

Schwindt-Bayer, Leslie. 2012. *Political Power and Women's Representation in Latin America*. New York: Oxford University Press.

Zetterberg, Pär. 2009. "Do Gender Quotas Foster Women's Political Engagement? Lessons from Latin America." *Political Research Quarterly* 62: 715–30.

WEBSITES

Statistics on women in national parliaments:
Inter-Parliamentary Union. http://www.ipu.org/wmn-e/classif.htm.
World Bank. http://data.worldbank.org/indicator/SG.GEN.PARL.ZS.
Women's Environment and Development Organization. http://www.wedo.org/wp-content/uploads/5050_parliamentsfactsheet03.pdf.

CHAPTER THREE

COUNTING THE VOTES AND AGGREGATING POLITICAL PREFERENCES

INTRODUCTION

The world watched with disbelief in November 2000 as journalists, elections officials, armies of attorneys, state courts, and finally the Supreme Court investigated and
eventually intervened to decide the winner of the United States presidential election
between George W. Bush and Al Gore. In the critical state of Florida, which in the
end was the state that decided the winner, at one point only 327 votes separated the
candidates, while irregularities affected tens of thousands of votes. Many observers
around the world were stunned to learn that the U.S. electoral system was riddled with
inconsistencies, politics, and errors. These included the following:

- The official in charge of elections in the United States is the secretary of state
  in each individual state. These local officials are members of national parties and
  partisans by definition. Indeed, the official in charge of overseeing a credible and
  fair election in the troublesome state of Florida was Secretary of State Katherine
  Harris, a prominent Republican who also served as the co-chair of George W.
  Bush's Florida election campaign.
- A private company was paid millions of dollars to "scrub" or remove felons and
  other voters from the official voting rolls in Florida. Tens of thousands of individuals were wrongly removed from the rolls.
- Voting in some districts—often wealthy ones—takes far less time and effort than
  voting in other districts—often poor ones.
- Voting procedures and error rates differ from voting precinct to voting precinct
  within the same state. In Florida, the world learned of hanging chads, where voters
  in some voting precincts used punch cards to vote but where one or more of the

corners of the paper fragments (chads) remained connected to the punch cards and were not counted. The voting districts in Florida that used punch cards had a higher rate of uncounted votes than other districts that used other voting machines.

In the end, it was impossible to know for whom the majority of Florida voters wanted for president, George W. Bush or Al Gore. An activist and conservative-leaning Supreme Court—with no explicit constitutional jurisdiction over elections within states—weighed in and by a 5–4 decision handed the presidency to George W. Bush and froze any additional vote counting in Florida.

Many citizens and politicians in the United States were indignant. How could a system of elections provide confidence in the will of the people when the process was politicized and riddled with errors? Politicians and political groups promised answers and fixes.

Presidential elections in 2004, 2008, and 2012 continued with many of the same inherent weaknesses from 2000. Elections are still overseen and administered by partisans at the state level, leading to charges that Republican secretaries of state in Florida and Ohio intentionally provided too few voting machines in Democratic-leaning voting districts, resulting in lines of up to eight hours. Critics also allege that Republicans

Figure 3.1: Votomatic Machine Used in Some Districts of Florida.
Credit: Clariosophic.

are imposing unnecessary voter identification requirements in an effort to reduce voter turnout by minorities and the urban poor, traditionally solid Democratic voters: "I knew something was afoot when my wife reported that a 90-year-old woman had to be turned away from voting early at our local polling place. Her crime: She didn't have a driver's license. Why would she? She wasn't able to drive anymore. As the embarrassed election judge fumbled for a solution as the woman sobbed—this was the first election she missed in her life (and might be her last)—it struck me how regressive this whole idea of voter policing has become" (Wasik 2012, n.p.).

Aggregating votes is never simple, and it is even more difficult in large countries with hundreds of millions of citizens. Counting votes in Brazil, a country larger than the continental United States and with nearly 200 million people, has long been a challenge. The Brazilian electoral system is open-list proportional representation, and the ballots have hundreds of candidates. Prior to 2000, Brazilians were required to write in the name or candidate number of their preferred candidate. With high levels of functional illiteracy, many Brazilian voters would leave their ballots blank due to embarrassment. In the 1994 elections for the lower house of the Brazilian parliament, 42 per cent of the votes were blank (Hidalgo 2013). As Hidalgo notes, "The paper ballot also created delay and facilitated fraud. Vote counters had to interpret the handwriting of the voters and allocate the vote among thousands of candidates, a monumental task that would often take several weeks. In many regions, vote counters bought off by political machines could surreptitiously allocate blank votes to their favored candidates and invalidate votes cast for the opposition. In the northeastern state of Bahia, for example, fraud was used to perpetuate the rule of oligarchic political families, seemingly invulnerable to the increased political competition that accompanied Brazil's transition to democracy" (Hidalgo 2013, n.p.).

Like voters in the United States after the 2000 electoral debacle, Brazilians were embarrassed with the poor-quality elections, the delays in announcing winners, and the potential for fraud embedded in the system. Unlike the United States, however, Brazilian officials made a radical shift. Since 2000, all 140 million voters in Brazil have been using compact, portable voting machines and a satellite-based communication system so that votes from the mega-city São Paulo to the villages of the Amazon can be rapidly tabulated. In 2011, Brazil implemented an Intel-based voting machine that incorporates fingerprint identification of voters. Every voter in the country uses the same voting machine, and all votes are tabulated within hours of the polls closing. Roughly the size of a small toaster oven, the Brazilian voting machine has a 10-hour battery life, which is useful for isolated communities without electricity. When the voter punches in the number of their candidate, headshots appear on a small screen, allowing the voters to verify their candidates. In 2000 Brazil became the first country to hold a completely automated election (see Figure 3.2).

This chapter is about aggregating the preferences and votes in Latin America in a manner that instills confidence, even in close elections. We will first introduce the challenges and requisites of electoral administration and identify a longstanding democratic deficit in electoral oversight—highly partisan electoral officials. We will then present an early effort to resolve this problem—the de-politicization of the electoral tribunal in Costa Rica in 1949—and a recent effort to restore confidence in electoral

Figure 3.2: Universal Voting Machine in Brazil.
Credit: Antonio Cruz, Agencia Brazil. Licensed under the Creative Commons Attribution
license (CC-BY-SA).

processes—in Mexico leading up to the 2000 elections. But the actual voting process and administration are not the only dimensions of voting that matter. Participation in politics and policy at the local level in areas other than voting is also crucial for the establishment and aggregation of preferences, or the will of the people. To highlight the importance of political activity beyond the ballot, we describe the political process in one of the world's smallest autonomous units, the Kuna Indians of the San Blas islands in Panama, and continue to explore the innovative interest aggregation of participatory budgeting in Porto Alegre, Brazil.

3.1. ELECTION ADMINISTRATION REFORM IN COSTA RICA AND MEXICO

In October 1989, Costa Ricans celebrated 100 years of democracy in an international event attended by U.S. President George H.W. Bush and all the presidents of Central America. There are very few countries that can rightly claim a full century of democratic rule, and Costa Rica is in fact not one of them. In his excellent but often ignored 1951 book, Rafael Obregón details every military coup, attempted coup, rebellion, and war involving the Costa Rican armed forces, from the first civil war of 1823 through to the last attempted military coup in 1949. Obregón lists 115 military and political conflicts during this period and suggests that Costa Rican political development up until 1948 had more similarities with other Latin American countries than Costa Ricans like to admit (1951, 3). Lehoucq (1992) and Salazar (1995) describe a political system typically of a republican and civilian nature, but one in which power was gained through fraud, intrigue, single-party power, and outright imposition of presidents by their predecessors. Despite electoral reforms throughout the 1940s, it is difficult to argue that things were getting better instead of worse. Calderón Guardia was imposed by his presidential predecessor León Cortés in 1940 and gained 84.3 per cent of the vote (Salazar 1995, 202). An educated and charismatic "caudillo" or strongman, Calderón had a fierce rupture with his mentor, the previous president León Cortés, soon after, and in 1944, Calderón handed the presidency to Teodoro Picado in highly suspect elections in which Picado defeated León Cortés with 66 per cent of the vote (Salazar 1995, 231). The period 1940–48 is replete with violence, ethnic persecution of Costa Ricans of German, Spanish, and Italian heritage, assassination attempts, electoral fraud, U.S. concern with communist power, strikes, riots, abuse of state and police power, rumors of palace coups, plots to overthrow the government, terrorist activities, and dangerous class tensions (see Bowman 2002). Lehoucq, who may be the most informed scholar on early-twentieth-century Costa Rican political history, also disputes the democratic nature of Costa Rica prior to 1948: "Since 1882, outgoing presidents have imposed their successors on at least six different occasions. During the same period also, opposition movements have launched twenty-six rebellions against central state authorities—three of which succeeded in installing a new incumbent in the presidency. . . . The use of violence and fraud to capture state power only declined in the aftermath of the 1948 civil war," a violent conflict with between 2,000 and 4,000 deaths (1996, 334–35).

Costa Rica faced many of the same problems as other electoral republics—elections that did not meet minimal standards to eliminate fraud and manipulation by officials that would provide confidence in electoral outcomes. Episodes of fraud and vote manipulation led to rebellion by the losers, and the absence of confidence in the voting process reduced support of the system by the population. In Costa Rica's neighbor Nicaragua's history, decades of electoral manipulation eventually led to violent revolution. According to Pastor,

"Carlos Fonseca Amador, one of the founders of the Nicaraguan Sandinista National Liberation Front in 1961, offered this justification for their revolution: 'Peaceful changes between different factions of the ruling class, which have been rather frequent in other Latin American countries, have not taken place in Nicaragua. This traditional experience predisposed the Nicaraguan people against electoral farces and in favor of armed struggle.' The Nicaraguan experience of 'electoral farces' was hardly unique. Elections have often been manipulated by the incumbent regime." (Pastor 1999, 2)

At a minimum, official electoral bodies must impartially and effectively act at three different periods. Before the elections, election commissions must impartially register voters, prepare voter lists, and prepare ballots listing the approved candidates. In some countries such as Iran, large numbers of candidates are eliminated from the ballots for political purposes. In other countries, voters are purged from the voting lists or not allowed to register. On election day, election commissions must provide for equal access of all voters to vote and a process to tally transparently and correctly all votes and to provide results quickly. If some voters wait in line for five minutes and others for ten hours, or if some voters use voting machines with a significantly higher non-count rate than other voters, then the equal access principle of voting is not met. Finally, after the voting occurs, electoral officials must investigate and adjudicate complaints, verify the final count, and certify the final results.

There have been many attempts to create free and fair electoral processes that create confidence in the electorate. In Argentina, the conservative National Autonomist Party (PAN) controlled the country through an oligarchic democracy from 1880 to 1916, winning elections through a combination of electoral fraud and restricted suffrage. After controlling the country for so many years, PAN was losing its edge and starting to be seen as corrupt and illegitimate, and the opposition Radical Party began to gain support. PAN President Roque Sáenz Peña (1851–1914) tried to recover support and momentum for PAN by instituting the secret ballot and obligatory voting for all males over age 18. The reforms enfranchised many native-born middle- and working-class men. Sáenz Peña needed an organization to oversee the elections that would be seen as neutral and fair by the population in order to restore confidence in the elections, so he selected the military, as the only neutral actor, to run the elections. The reforms backfired on PAN, however, as the Radicals of Hipólito Yrigoyen (1852–1933) were swept into power in the elections of 1916. The conservative PAN could never again win a contested election, losing to the Radicals in 1922 and 1928. The old conservative order then turned to the previously apolitical and neutral military to oust Yrigoyen in the first military coup in the country in 1930. The legacy of that coup was profound and devastating. From 1928 until 1999, no elected president handed presidential power to another elected president at the end of his full term in office.[11]

Returning to Costa Rica, that country had constitutionally proscribed its military in 1948–49, so that was not an option for overseeing elections. So how precisely did Costa Rica make the transition from elections that were characterized by fraud and a lack of confidence to elections that were free, fair, and legitimate? The answer lies in institutions. In 1949 Costa Rica established the Supreme Electoral Tribunal as the fourth branch of government, providing power and autonomy to the institution and eliminating partisanship. The Supreme Electoral Tribunal comprises three permanent magistrates and three alternate magistrates. During elections, five magistrates serve. The magistrates are selected by the Supreme Court in staggered six-year terms and are chosen for their judicial experience and not their political pedigree. The Supreme Court justices are chosen by the Legislative Assembly, which is chosen by the voters. The Supreme Electoral Tribunal is therefore twice removed from the political process.[12] The Tribunal is charged with safeguarding Costa Rican democracy and the

---

11   Radical President Raul Alfonsín did pass power to Carlos Ménem in 1989, but instability and hyperinflation forced Alfonsín to relinquish power before the end of his term.

12   In the United States, in contrast, electoral officials are embedded in the political process.

sanctity of elections. Toward that end, it is charged with birth and death registration, maintaining voter registration for all Costa Ricans and achieving the registration of virtually the entire voting-age population of nearly 3 million, issuing voter registration cards, overseeing campaign finance, designing ballots, overseeing the election-day processes, counting the votes, adjudicating any charges of wrongdoing, and certifying the results. As an independent branch of government, the rulings of the Supreme Electoral Tribunal are final and are not subject to appeal to any other branch of government.

Security forces have often meddled in battles for political power in the history of Latin America, frequently serving to support or undermine the incumbent. In Costa Rica, however, there is no formal military. The security forces and police serve under the authority of the Supreme Electoral Tribunal during elections, as a final safeguard to democracy and as a symbolic demonstration of the authority and autonomy of electoral officials. Establishing a de facto new branch of government to oversee democratic elections is thus a Latin American policy innovation.

After the Costa Rican institutional innovations for autonomous and politically neutral electoral commissions in 1949, other countries, including India, have followed suit. One of the most interesting cases is that of Mexico. Since its founding in 1929, the Institutional Revolutionary Party (PRI) ruled the country for seven decades. From 1929 until 1982, the PRI won every election with at least 70 per cent of the vote, leading observers such as Mario Vargas Llosa to describe the PRI as the perfect dictatorship and far less than a democracy.[13] The PRI became a symbol of corruption and fraud, and more progressive elements within the party split away and formed the Party of Democratic Revolution (PRD), led by Cuauhtémoc Cárdenas (b. 1934), son of PRI icon and leader Lázaro Cárdenas (1895–1970).

Mexican elections were administered and organized by the Secretary of Interior, always a PRI official and highly partisan. In the 1988 elections, between Carlos Salinas (b. 1948) of the PRI and Cuauhtémoc Cárdenas of the PRD, the Secretary of Interior announced a delay in tabulating the vote, claiming that the tabulating machines had crashed. After a lengthy delay, Salinas and the PRI were pronounced the winners with 50.89 per cent of the vote. The PRD reported massive fraud, and Salinas ended his term amid scandal and unpopularity. He was, however, able to impose Ernesto Zedillo (b. 1951) as his successor in 1994, in elections that were also seen as highly irregular. State elections in Quintana Roo, Tabasco, and the Yucatán were deemed highly fraudulent (McCann and Domínguez 1998). Zedillo not only started office with limited legitimacy due to perceptions of fraud, but also inherited a highly publicized violent revolt by the Zapatistas in Chiapas and a collapse of the Mexican peso.

In response, Zedillo enacted many significant electoral reforms. No longer would the PRI candidate be hand-selected by the outgoing president (the *dedazo*), but he or she would be selected through a primary system. The mayor of Mexico City would

---

13 Vargas Llosa made this statement on Mexican television in 1990, and it quickly became an adage for the country.

no longer be appointed by the ruling party but would instead be elected. The Federal Electoral Institute would no longer be a highly partisan vehicle but would be autonomous, and its members would be selected by a consensual procedure in the legislature, seeking professional and non-partisan members of the electoral officials. The highly partisan Secretary of Interior would no longer head or serve on the Federal Electoral Institute.

These reforms had immediate effects. The PRD's Cárdenas won the mayorship of Mexico City, opposition candidates won many governorships, and the PRI lost the majority in the lower house of the Mexican Congress for the first time in history. Most importantly, after some seven decades in power, the PRI lost the presidency in 2000 to the opposition PAN candidate Vicente Fox (b. 1942). The reforms were enhanced again in 2007 to remove the power of third-party activists in elections. Third parties and individuals are no longer allowed to purchase radio and television ads to influence elections. In addition, the amount of money available for campaigning has been sharply reduced and restrictions have been placed on the content of political speech. Yale law professor and expert on U.S. elections Heather Gerken portrays the Mexican reforms as follows:

> It is hard not to be impressed with Mexico's electoral reforms during the last two decades. For a scholar who studies the United States, a mature democracy that is often run badly, it is refreshing to see a relatively young democracy run so well. It is also heartening that an "electoral meltdown" can result in serious reform and grassroots engagement. The fiasco that confronted the United States in 2000 prompted Congress to pass the toothless Help America Vote Act, which addressed only the symptoms of the Florida debacle, not its root causes. The 2006 crisis in Mexico,[14] in sharp contrast, resulted in serious and systemic reform. In the United States, election reform is almost entirely an elite enterprise, with little by the way of grassroots involvement. In Mexico, election reform is a source of genuine participatory engagement. The failure to pass serious election reform in Mexico after 2006 would have raised serious questions about the legitimacy of the State. The failure to pass serious election reform in the United States after 2000 barely raised an eyebrow. (2009, 166)

Elections in Mexico are far from perfect. Mexico suffers from high levels of corruption and political violence, including violence against journalists, with approximately 100 journalists having been killed or disappeared since 2000, undermining the democratic process. Institutions have improved, but they also need time to mature and gain confidence. However, the improvement over the PRI-controlled electoral institutions is pronounced and important.

---

14 The PRD candidate accused the PAN government of electoral manipulation as PAN candidate Felipe Calderón defeated PRD Andrés Manuel López Obrador in a razor-thin victory.

3.2. ENHANCED POLITICAL PARTICIPATION IN SAN BLAS AND PORTO ALEGRE

For many democratic theorists, voting is not sufficient political activity for a healthy democracy (Pateman 1970). There have been many experiments in Latin America involving greater citizen input into political decision making. In this section, we will present the enhanced participatory experiences of the Kuna Indians of Panama and the citizens of Porto Alegre, Brazil.

Approximately 40,000 Kuna Indians live in Panama, mostly on the San Blas islands of the coastal Caribbean. The Kuna political system is an unusual hybrid of traditional chiefdom politics and is the product of centuries of adaptation and change in a socially marginalized environment that has existed at the frontier between major colonial and neocolonial systems (Howe 1986, 8). The Kuna have a long experience with autonomy. During colonial times, they established trade relations with Britain and other European nations; the authorized political autonomy of the Kuna territory goes back to at least 1871, when it was ceded by Colombia to the Kuna people. However, when Panama gained independence from Colombia in 1903, the new national government sought to assimilate the Kuna into the mainstream population, issuing two laws, in 1908 and 1912, that authorized the government to civilize and Latinize, respectively, the indigenous populations. Because Panama had no standing army, governmental policy centered on forced cultural assimilation rather than violent coercion.

The Kuna did not respond passively to this governmental attempt at ethnocide. In 1925, the Kuna successfully rebelled against Panama, and through U.S. mediation formed a treaty with the Panamanian state, thereby achieving regional autonomy. In 1938, the region was officially recognized as a Kuna *comarca*, which is a political division of territory governed by indigenous authorities and institutions. However, the law designated an intendant as the maximum authority in the *comarca*, charging him with overseeing the traditional governance. The adoption of an Organic Charter by the reunited Kuna Congress in 1945 can be regarded as the most tangible outcome of this process. This fundamental document contains an institutional design that is essentially still in force and was recognized by a Panamanian law in 1953. This structure was recently further advanced in the "*Ley Fundamental de la Comarca Kuna Yala*" of 1995 (Foss 2012, 4).

The Kuna geographic territory is presented in Figure 3.3. The Kuna political system consists of five fundamental authorities. The Kuna General Congress dates to 1872 when a shaman called on the widespread and sometimes discordant Kuna communities to federate and establish a common assembly. Today the Kuna General Congress is the supreme institutional legislative power. It also holds executive powers by managing numerous social and environmental projects. Each Kuna community, regardless of size, has one vote in the Kuna General Congress. Another traditional institution is the *Saila Dummagen*, a council of three important local leaders who are directly elected by the Kuna people from a list of candidates. This Council of Leaders is subordinate to the Kuna General Congress. A third institution, the General Congress of the Kuna Culture, was founded in 1972 and has the mission of safeguarding Kuna culture and spiritual life by teaching the Kuna language and cultural patrimony such as traditional Kuna medicine at schools.

Figure 3.3: Kuna Yala, Autonomous Indigenous *Comarca* of Kuna.

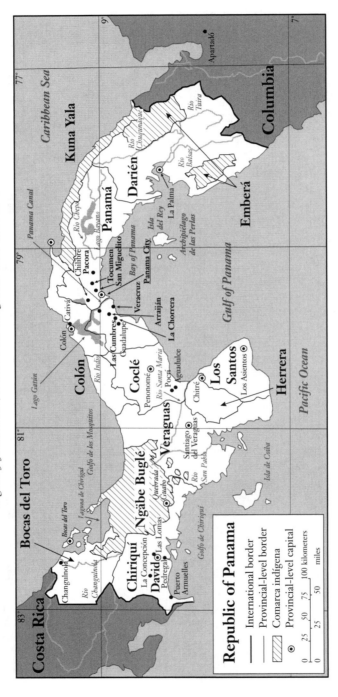

Source: Sabine Cretella, from CIA World Factbook data (1995). Licensed under the Creative Commons Attribution–Share Alike (CC-BY-SA).

Figure 3.4: Kuna Woman Selling Traditional Kuna Molas.
Credit: Markus Leupold-Lowenthal. Licensed under the Creative Commons Attribution-Share
Alike license (CC-BY-SA).

In addition to these three national Kuna institutions, there are two local political actors. The Kuna political system is highly participatory and combines both theocratic and democratic components. Each community has a local decision-making body known as the local Congress House (*Onmaked Nega*), where Kuna can deliberate and discuss local and national issues. There is also a local leader or *Sahila* who is both a religious and political leader. The *Sahila* is elected and in charge of local political, judicial, and social affairs in the community and sings the sacred history, legends, and laws of the Kuna in the Congress House. In turn he is interpreted by a circle of speakers and advisers.

James Howe, who is the leading scholar of Kuna political institutions, lauds this system, which has developed over 400 years despite challenges and changes:

> More than just the strongest of Panama's three primary Indian groups, they are the great success stories of indigenous America, and much of that success they owe to their democratic institutions. True, the local gathering and the Kuna General Congress can at times be parochial, arbitrary, slow, inconsistent, and contentious, but in the long run they have proved more reliable than individual Kuna leaders (when the latter perform well, collective scrutiny and review deserve some credit), and they have certainly done much better than have many tribal politics of a more authoritarian sort.

Much of the success, moreover, of Kuna democratic institutions, in regional and national as well as local arenas, arguably depends on wide-spread and lifelong political participation. For all the didactic efforts of gathering leaders to slant political learning one way or another, it is undoubtedly something much more diffuse and less consciously directed, namely, early and prolonged exposure to politics, taking place in San Blas literally at the parental knee, that most encourages participation and activism. It is practice in local settings, moreover, that makes the Kuna ready and able to speak for themselves in national ones. Thus this case lends credence to the arguments of Pateman (1970) and others that national systems are best served by the democratic attitudes and skills nurtured through participation in smaller constituent units— the neighborhood, the workplace, the local *junta*, or, for the Kuna, the village gathering. (Howe 1986, 261)

While the process of institutional innovation began centuries ago among the Kuna, the democratic innovations in Porto Alegre began less than 25 years ago. A military regime guided Brazil from 1964 to 1985, and then democracy was restored in 1988. The new constitution of 1988 called specifically for political participation of civil society in the elaboration of public policies and required popular participation in the development and implementation of social and health policies. At the same time, a fledgling left-wing Worker's Party (PT) was beginning to win local elections. The party's platform included direct citizen participation in decision making and improving infrastructure and services for the poor. These two trends met in the city of Porto Alegre in 1989, when the city became the first to use participatory budgeting (PB). Participatory budgeting was successful and very popular in Porto Alegre, and this led to the PT being re-elected four times and governing the city until 2004. Since 1989, some 1,200 cities worldwide have implemented some form of participatory budgeting.

Porto Alegre is the capital of the southern Brazilian state of Rio Grande do Sul and has a population of 1.5 million. Like many Brazilian cities, Porto Alegre was formerly characterized by wide disparities in income and living conditions. Sewage, roads, and other services were much better in the middle-class and wealthy parts of the city, and absent in the marginalized *favelas* or poor shantytowns. The newly elected PT administration developed participatory budgeting as a mechanism for using the preferences and input of the population to determine the distribution of the discretionary part of the budget, of more than US$200 million per year.

The process of participatory budgeting in Porto Alegre is fully described in Abers (2007) and elsewhere as "radical democracy," transformed civil society, and elevated democratic consciousness among the participants; we will provide only a brief overview of Abers's description here. Some 15,000 people participate in budget assemblies each year; the participants are, on average, poorer than the general population but believe that their contributions matter in budget making. Research has shown that poorer regions of the city have received greater and greater shares of the budget since the process began, leading to a reduction in inequality and a dramatic improvement in infrastructure and public services in poor neighborhoods. Almost all decisions approved by the PB process are eventually implemented by the government.

The process has been very open, and any adult who wants to participate can do so. The process originally consisted of 16 budget regions, each of which would put forward preferences for spending. Over time, however, the actors determined that infrastructure and other investments should also include thematic priorities, and a second set of thematic assemblies emerged. Themes could include infrastructure foci such as sewage or paving roads, or more cultural themes such as sports. The entire budgetary process includes neighborhood assemblies, regional assemblies, election of delegates, and regional budget forums. This funnels into a citizen-led Municipal Budget Council, which

- analyzes and approves a general budget before the mayor sends it to the city legislature;
- defines the distribution of funds among regions and themes;
- designs and approves an investment plan based on regional and thematic priorities; and
- monitors implementation.

The process has both contentious and competitive dynamics, which provides a critical voice to many who previously only participated by casting a ballot. Abers argues that this competition has strengthened democracy by empowering and enhancing civil society associations. For example, the number of neighborhood associations grew from 380 in 1990 to 540 in 1998 (2007, 86). In addition, the PB process has resulted in social learning through several ways (Abers 2007). First, citizen participants had to listen to the demands of others and argue the competitive worth of their own needs and demands. Prioritizing budgetary needs over months resulted in empathy and a spirit of compromise between neighborhood delegations. Second, open discussions led citizens and neighborhoods to learn that their needs and problems were often shared by others. Participatory budgeting began to focus on regional issues and proposals, and these were often given higher priority than demands by individual neighborhoods. Third, the process of participatory budgeting educated citizens about the importance of the decision-making process itself. Participants soon learned that the decision-making rules were often as important as the programmatic merits. Discussions of the rules taught many important lessons about power and democracy. In Abers's words:

> Simply creating a space for participation was not enough for all this to occur. It is important to mention three critical factors that transformed PB Forums into both spaces for expanding civic organizing and for social learning. First, participants were drawn into the process because they saw it as a means to reach their ultimate goals. This may seem obvious, but so many participatory spaces today fail to address needs that ordinary people see as relevant, focusing instead on complex or abstract technical issues. Second, the PB had credibility because the government respected the decisions made by delegates. This credibility was important because it made participation something worth investing hours of time and much emotional energy. Third, participants received

support. Community organizers hired by the government were crucial because they helped local groups with the operational aspects of mobilizing. They also helped them coordinate debates and encouraged more collaborative and cooperative values in the discussion process. (Abers 2007, 88)

Implementing and sustaining participatory budgeting is complex and difficult, as it depends on a genuine willingness and commitment on the part of elected officials and bureaucrats to listen to citizens—often poor citizens—as well as on the organization and participation of citizens, neighborhoods, and civil society organizations. After the PT was defeated in 2004, there have been claims that the new government only pays lip service to PB, and in many cities that have tried to replicate Porto Alegre and install a similar system, the PB process influences only a minuscule part of the budget. In cities like Porto Alegre, participatory budgeting has greatly enhanced citizen participation in the practice of governing. At its best, it is an innovative and highly desirable model of preference aggregation that expands democratic practice.

CONCLUSIONS

Democratic practice has come under criticism in recent years because of failures in the electoral processes in many countries and for turning into low-intensity democracy, where citizens have little input in determining political outcomes. This chapter has described the failure of democratic processes as undermining confidence in elections and then presented some innovative examples from Latin America. Two models of more engaged political participation were then discussed.

We argue that elections are open to charges of abuse and manipulations when the electoral officials are highly partisan and when the process of voting lacks consistency among all voters, two problems that plague elections in the United States. The reforms in Costa Rica in 1949 and in Mexico between 1996 and 2006 are two cases that illustrate how institutions changed to build confidence in holding elections and aggregating votes. In both cases, the objective of electoral officials was to increase participation through near-universal voter registration and to reduce partisan interference through autonomous and non-partisan electoral administrations. In Costa Rica, the electoral administration is a fourth branch of government, while in Mexico the electoral administration is an independent body within the judicial branch.

Democratic theorists hold that voting is not sufficient for a vibrant democratic political culture, and two cases demonstrate different models of enhanced political participation. In Panama, the Kuna of the San Blas Islands have developed a fascinating model of self-government that combines extensive political participation at the village level and an autonomous congress for the entire Kuna nation. In Porto Alegre, Brazil, political, societal, and historic forces led to the creation of the innovative process of participatory budgeting. When implemented with genuine commitment from political leaders and sufficient levels of civil society, such a process can empower citizens, particularly those in poor neighborhoods.

Democracy is under threat when citizens feel powerless and when they feel that their preferences in elections and policy making are ignored. There are many ways to enhance popular support in democracy, and the lessons from Costa Rica, Mexico, the Kuna, and Porto Alegre are interesting examples of the ways in which democratic practice can improve and citizenship can be strengthened.

LESSONS LEARNED

- Institutions matter, and electoral oversight institutions in Latin America work best when they are autonomous and apolitical.
- Once a region plagued with fraudulent and illegitimate elections, Latin America has made great strides in improving confidence in elections.
- The Kuna of Panama present an alternative form of participatory government, and democracy need not look identical in all cases.
- Porto Alegre demonstrates the possibilities of enhanced participation in the budgeting process. Perhaps policy making from below could take place in other domains.

DISCUSSION QUESTIONS

- What do you think the biggest voting impediments are today?
- Why have other countries not adopted completely automated elections?
- What are the minimal standards for having a fair and democratic election?
- Does increased democracy lead to less election fraud?
- Differences in waiting times at polling locations plague many countries, including the U.S. What are some ways to remedy this? Do some actors want long waiting times?
- In Argentina, Sáenz Peña elected the military to run elections because it was a "neutral actor." Would this work in other countries?
- Do institutions provide the solution for credible elections?
- Is it possible to have both highly partisan election officials and fair elections?
- Is voting sufficient political activity for a healthy democracy?
- Why are some communities, such as the Kuna people, more politically active than others?
- Would participatory budgeting work in your community? Why or why not?
- Are there other areas besides budgeting where participatory policy making could be effective?

ADDITIONAL READING

American Enterprise Institute: Mexican Lessons for Election Reform. http://
www.aei.org/article/foreign-and-defense-policy/regional/latin-america/
mexican-lessons-for-election-reform/.
Brookings Institute—Election Reform Project. http://www.electionreformproject.org/Topic/6/
r1/Archives.aspx.

Center for Strategic and International Studies—The Coming Elections and Mexico's Reform Paralysis. http://csis.org/blog/coming-elections-and-mexicos-reform-paralysis.

CSIS—Mexico's Recent Electoral Reform: A Change for the Better? http://csis.org/node/12422/multimedia.

IDEA—Costa Rica: A Powerful Constitutional Body Case Study. http://www.idea.int/publications/emd/upload/EMD_CS_Costa_Rica.pdf.

IDEA—Electoral reform in Costa Rica. http://www.idea.int/americas/electoral_reform_costa_r.cfm.

Mexico's 2007 Election Reforms: A Comparative View. http://digitalcommons.law.yale.edu/cgi/viewcontent.cgi?article=1363&context=fss_papers.

CHAPTER FOUR

DEMILITARIZATION AND PEACE PROMOTION

INTRODUCTION

At the height of the Cold War and the Latin American debt crisis in 1981, U.S. Ambassador to the United Nations Jeanne Kirkpatrick accused the embattled Costa Rican president Rodrigo Carazo Odio, who served from 1978 to 1982, of communist subversion and informed Costa Rica that further U.S. economic aid would be predicated on the recreation of a professional army (Black 1986, 186). Kirkpatrick further chided the nearly bankrupt Costa Ricans, telling them that "Costa Rica is not a viable country because it has no military."[15] Are countries viable without militaries?

Through the prism of recent history in Latin America that included civil wars and military dictatorships, it may seem natural to assume that Latin American countries have always had powerful military institutions, from the wars of independence in the first half of the nineteenth century until today. This assumption is false at best when one uses the broadest definition of "military institution," and completely inaccurate for nearly the entire region if we more narrowly define a military to be an institution concerned with protecting the country from armed external enemies. Once we accept that militaries are not always present in modern countries, several questions emerge. Do countries need militaries? What type of security do they need? Does military aid benefit recipient countries? The experience of militarization and demilitarization in Latin America provides important lessons on militarization and its effect on development and security. In this chapter we analyze demilitarization and militarization in

---

15   Kirk Bowman's interview with former Costa Rican president Oscar Arias Sánchez, San José, Costa Rica, November 1997.

Costa Rica and Honduras in the 1948–54 period, and the results of demilitarization in Panama after 1989–90.

4.1. WARMAKING AND MILITARIZATION

The foundation for understanding militarization and demilitarization in Latin America is the absence of interstate wars in the region. Simply put, Latin American countries do not wage war against each other. The observation of an absence of interstate wars between countries in the Western Hemisphere is not new. In Andreski's (1954) classic on militarization, Latin America was singled out as a region with a particular military mission: "The military function has become introverted in Latin American republics; with few opportunities to fight for their countries, the soldiers remained preoccupied with internal politics and the search for personal and collective advantage" (211). Andreski goes on to note that in Latin America there are too many soldiers for a proper police function, and too few for waging interstate wars: "A very important factor here (in Latin America) was the absence of the need for a united effort in a common struggle against foreigners" (198). Andreski persuasively argues that the benefits of militarization to a developing country are determined entirely by the nature of the enemy. In those countries where the military's mission is to protect the country and its citizens from credible external threats, militarization is necessary because it can benefit the country. However, in those countries where the military's long-term primary mission is rooted in fighting both internal enemies and fellow citizens, the effects of militarization are strongly negative.

Many scholars, including Bowman (2002), LaFeber (1984), and Janowitz (1964), have noted the uniqueness of the Latin American military and the largely internal nature of their missions. Erich Weede (1986, 229) singles out Latin America as a region that "seems to have suffered from parasitic praetorians more specialized in bossing, exploiting, killing, and torturing civilians than in fighting other nations' armed forces." Latin America is characterized by having a military that functions as a militarized police force, with their principal enemies being fellow citizens and not external threats. This introverted military has none of the state-making capacity identified by Tilly (1990) and Centeno (2003) and weakens the state by wasting scarce resources that could be used for citizen security and development. This cannot be overemphasized: a military facing a credible external threat can have multiple positive societal and developmental externalities; a military facing no credible external threat, in contrast, generates multiple negative externalities or unanticipated costs.

Is there empirical evidence to support the proposition that Latin American militaries rarely fight interstate wars? The 1996 Correlates of War project (COW) data set yields the following evidence. Between 1816 and 1992 there were 11,158 total country-years in the world; 24.4 per cent of those country years were in Latin America. There were 75 interstate wars with 1,000 or more battlefield deaths globally. Of those 75, only nine were wars between Latin American countries. Latin America represents 24.4 per cent of the country years but a mere 12 per cent of the wars. Of those nine Latin American wars, only three had more than 2,000 deaths, and four barely met the COW standard of 1,000 deaths. The median number of battlefield deaths in Latin American interstate wars is 1,300. The median for the other 66 non–Latin American wars is 11,550. In contrast, Latin America is overrepresented in civil wars, with 32 per cent of all global civil wars (48 out of 151) in the COW data set (Correlates of War 1996).

There have only been three wars of any significance in Latin America: the War of Triple Alliance (1865–70) between Paraguay on the one side and Argentina, Brazil, and Uruguay on the other; the War of the Pacific (1879–83) between Chile on the one side and Bolivia and Peru on the other; and the Chaco War (1932–35) between Bolivia and Peru. The paucity of wars not only had effects on state making and other social factors, but it also led the existing militaries to become far different in form and function from current definitions of armed forces, military, troops, and so forth.

4.2. COSTA RICA AND HONDURAS IN THE FIRST HALF OF THE TWENTIETH CENTURY

4.2.1. THE ABSENCE OF MILITARIZATION BEFORE 1948

The absence of institutionalized militaries is notable in Central America in the first half of the twentieth century. While there were episodes that saw a surge in military activities and political participation, these episodes reveal the military to be more of an amorphous group of disorganized gangs than an organized institution. Established militaries and large numbers of troops would arrive only with the Cold War in the middle of the century. In 1922, when Costa Rica's troop numbers were at an all-time low, on a per-capita basis these numbers were in fact very similar to the other, more populated Central American republics. The oddity was not Costa Rica, but rather Honduras, which was the least militarized nation of Central America between 1850 and 1950.

Even these tiny numbers of soldiers overstate the realities. General Tiburcio Carías (1876–1969) is portrayed as a military dictator during his time as president of Honduras (1932–49). In fact, Carías was an attorney, farmer, algebra professor, and long-time political militant in the National Party. In the 1923 elections, Carías won a plurality but was 3,681 votes short of the necessary majority. After intervention from the United States and months of political violence, Carías agreed to let his running mate take the presidency. Carías ran again in 1928 and was the surprise loser to Liberal

Table 4.1 Numbers of Full Time Soldiers in Army, circa 1922

Country	Population	Soldiers	Soldiers per 1,000
Costa Rica	430,000	300	−70
El Salvador	1,220,000	900	−74
Guatemala	1,370,000	1,000	−73
Honduras	770,000	300	−39
Nicaragua	650,000	500	−77

Source: Muñoz Guillén 1990.

Vicente Mejía Colindres. Carías finally won in 1932, with more than 50 per cent of the vote. The opposing Liberals revolted but were quickly defeated. Carías remained in the presidency until turning over power to his handpicked successor in 1949.

Carías quickly gave himself the title of general, but he was a general without an army. He had little reason to build a military institution: "In a very deliberate manner, Carías was able to keep the military non-professional . . . . This was so, because he distrusted, and the facts tend to confirm it, an autonomous and well-organized military, with the requisite amount of power in its hands to become the arbiter of Honduran political life" (Argueta 1988, 123).[16] Funes (1995) notes that Carías "was not interested in forming an army because . . . it would be dangerous" (145).

In both Costa Rica and Honduras, the military simply did not exist in any institutionalized form after the Tinoco military government fell in 1921 and during the entire first half of the twentieth century in Honduras. The 1948–58 period was a critical juncture in these two countries, however, as the response to the effects of the Cold War and a newly constructed view of the place of militaries in a modern state drastically altered debate and policies around militarization.

4.2.2. THE CRITICAL JUNCTURE IN COSTA RICA AND HONDURAS, 1948–58

The 1940s was a decade of extreme instability and violence in Costa Rica that culminated in the fraudulent elections of 1948 and the ensuing civil war that was won by José Figueres (1906–90) and his band of young local fighters and mercenaries from the Dominican Republic, Guatemala, and Nicaragua—known collectively as the Caribbean Legion. Figueres took power on May 8, 1948, in a climate of polarization, violence, and instability.

By December 1948, the Figueres regime faced domestic and international threats. It was the minister of security, Edgar Cardona, who proposed not to strengthen the security apparatus but to abolish the armed forces. According to Cardona:

> I spoke to Figueres about the dissolution of the army. I could not speak publicly because it was not proper for an official of the armed forces. I told him, "Look, Mr. President, the press is attacking us and the minister of education for spending too much money on education; we should spend even more. We can tell them that it is necessary to spend money on education in the country and with the abolition of the army we can spend even more money on education. Let us abolish the military, for with a civil guard we have sufficient security." Figueres thought for a while, and he said yes, it seemed like a great idea.[17]

Once Figueres had decided that abolishing the military was desirable, the actual act was simple, as the junta ruled by decree, the career military officers had been trounced

---

16 There was in fact an air force in Honduras, which consisted of U.S. planes flown by U.S. pilots. Cárias could use this to put down any rebellions by regional *caudillos*. Carías also had contracts with the commercial airliners so that they would drop bombs instead of delivering mail if he requested.

17 Interview with Edgar Cardona, San José, Costa Rica, December 20, 1997.

and exiled during the civil war, and there was no organized opposition to the idea. The *Book of Official Acts of the Founding Junta of the Second Republic* notes on November 14, 1948, that "[t]he plan of the suppression of the army, presented by the Minister of Security, is authorized and accepted" (Cardona Quirós 1992, 49). On December 1, 1948, the decision to abolish the military was announced to the country in a public ceremony at the Bella Vista fort, as the diminutive Figueres symbolically smashed a wall of the military facility with a sledgehammer.

The most interesting element of the abolition of the military was the utter lack of incredulity or shock on the part of Costa Ricans. There were no alarms of negative consequences from journalists, editors, politicians, and citizens. The junta was abolishing something that barely existed, the Cold War was not in effect yet, and international treaties and cooperation could deal with threats from neighbors such as the Somoza regime in Nicaragua. Demilitarizing was not unthinkable, exotic, or radical; it was a policy that could be seen as appropriate and normal within the context of Costa Rica or Honduras before 1950.

In the ensuing decades, the absence of a military changed the calculus of politicians in Costa Rica. Without a military to intervene as an insurance policy against an unhappy populace, politicians and elites had the incentive to provide education, health care, human rights, and jobs to the Costa Ricans. And without the burden of a defense budget, Costa Rica had far more resources for human capital and economic development than did the militarized neighbors of Central America.

However, the belief that an institutionalized military was a necessary part of a Latin American country began to emerge in the 1950s. The United States extended the 1949 Mutual Security Program to Latin America in 1951 because it feared that communism would spread to the region, and building powerful military institutions became a core component of the war against communism. The first bilateral pact was signed with Ecuador in January 1952. In 1953–54, mutual defense agreements were signed with Honduras and Nicaragua in preparation for the overthrow of Guatemalan president Jacobo Arbenz. In 1955, Guatemala under Castillo Armas became the twelfth Latin American country to sign (Lieuwin 1965, 91–92). Indeed, the United States even exerted considerable influence in an attempt to militarize Costa Rica: as noted by former Costa Rican politician Gonzalo Facio, "We received great pressure from the United States so that we would form a modern army here. They wanted to give us equipment and training and everything. We said no."[18]

Timing would not be so fortuitous for Honduras. Instead of 1948, the crucial decisions on the military were made in 1954, well after the start of the Cold War. In the annals of Honduran history, 1954 will always be a critical year of watershed events that shaped the future of the country: the great banana strike of 25,000 workers on the north coast, the use of Honduran soil by the CIA to launch the invasion against Arbenz in Guatemala, and the signing of the Bilateral Treaty of Military Assistance with the United States.

Honduran president Juan Manuel Gálvez (1887–1972) permitted the use of Honduran soil for the U.S.-inspired invasion of Guatemala. The negative impact of

---

18 Interview, San José, Costa Rica, December 1, 1997.

Honduran involvement in this antidemocratic action goes far beyond the stain of shame for the country and the Gálvez regime. Indeed, on May 20, 1954, in a quid pro quo for Honduran support for the U.S.-supported Castillo Armas invasion and as a continuation of the U.S. policy of military assistance treaties, the United States and Honduras signed a Bilateral Treaty of Military Assistance. The agreement called for U.S. military aid in exchange for free access to any "raw and semi-processed materials required by the United States of America as a result of deficiencies or potential deficiencies in its own resources" (Ropp 1974). U.S. Ambassador to Honduras Whiting Willauer provided the following analysis of the 1954 agreement, foreshadowing the view of Jeanne Kirkpatrick three decades later: "The Bilateral Treaty of Military Assistance, celebrated between Honduras and the United States, is important for achieving the peace. A country that relies on a weak military force can never carry forward a plan of internal and international security. What is necessary is an organized military power that can respond to the techniques and exigencies of national and international security" (quoted in Velásquez Cerrato 1954, 2).

The First Infantry Battalion was organized by the United States on July 20, 1954—less than one month after the fall of Arbenz—and remained under U.S. jurisdiction until August 1956. With alleged communists in neighboring Guatemala and Leftists striking on the banana plantations, the United States wanted insurance for its interests. In 1950, American diplomat and political scientist George Kennan detailed future U.S. strategy for Latin America: "The final answer might be an unpleasant one, but . . . we should not hesitate before police repression of the local government. This is not shameful since the Communists are essentially traitors. . . . It is better to have a strong regime in power than a liberal government if it is indulgent and relaxed and penetrated by Communists" (quoted in Smith 1996, 126). The United States had previously encouraged militarization in the country. The Lend-Lease Program was used by Carías to buy airplanes, and in 1952 the U.S. helped found the Francisco Morazán Military Academy to train professional officers. And finally, at the height of the Cold War in Central America, U.S. actions in 1954 officially established a military institution that would prove capable of "repression of the local government" and "strong" enough to topple any "indulgent" "liberal government."

Unlike the situation with demilitarization in Costa Rica six years earlier, there was an impressive public debate about the need for a military in Honduras. The Honduran press liberalized greatly during the Gálvez regime, and political debates in the various newspapers became common.[19] The level of sophistication of the arguments is at times quite impressive and at other times eerily prophetic. The open discussion began with a piece about the military agreement with the United States:

---

19 *El Cronista* was a Tegucigalpa-based newspaper that was published regularly from 1953–81 and had an estimated circulation of 10,000. In the 1950s, Honduras was largely illiterate, and so *El Cronista*'s impact was mainly among Tegucigalpa's intellectual elite and literate rural merchants and landowners. Nevertheless, this was the "dean" of Honduran newspapers and is regularly used by scholars such as Funes to document the 1950s. It is also important to note that the paper provided both sides of the militarization debate an ample public forum over a three-year period and that the participants in the public dialogue were from as far away as Copán in the far west of the country.

the spectacular notice that invites us to laugh that Honduras and the United States of North America will soon sign a military pact, and it makes us laugh because Honduras has never fought with anybody and has no one to fight with. . . . and to think that we could be invaded by the Russian Soviets, this causes even more laughter because truth be told . . . it is easier to believe that we will be invaded by those that are now making treaties to protect us. . . . we should seek another position . . . one misplaced comma can lead us to complete enslavement [by the U.S.]. (Antonio Gómez Milla, *Acción Democrática*, May 22, 1954)

An official spokesperson for the Liberal Party provided a different opinion shortly thereafter:

among the stipulations figures or is specified the sending of an American military mission to Honduras with the goal of organizing a small army that truth be told, the country does not have outside of some militias under command of a few officials. . . . we believe that for some time the Honduran armed forces should be technically organized, with substantial modernization. . . . (Brown Flores, *Acción Democrática*, May 22, 1954)

A year later the debate heated up with a long series of editorials and letters in *El Cronista* that appeared from May 1955 through June 1957. These commentaries illustrate the absence of a military institution in the country and a keen understanding of the potential dangers of militarization:

A few days ago I read in a certain newspaper from the capital something that appeared as a plan for a school of advanced military studies, which according to the announcement, should be established shortly in Honduras. In government circles and even amongst the public opinion it appears that there exists a favorable climate for this factory of creole "Junkers." This would be the masterwork of our ignorance. . . . it would be a stupendous measure if the government would eliminate the defense minister, and with him all the commanders and soldiers in the country and establish in their place an efficient civil guard, and a mounted police to insure individual security in a civilized manner. (Alvarado, *El Cronista*, May 9, 1955)

René Zelaya Smith, an army captain, responded with a phrase that would be heard for decades in the country: "If you want peace, prepare for war. . . . The armed forces are necessary to oversee the order and tranquility of the country" (*El Cronista*, May 30, 1955).

Néstor Alvarado continued the dialogue on June 13 with a most interesting argument, similar to the one made to author Kirk Bowman some four decades later by Gonzalo Facio in Costa Rica. The United States, he said, is the hegemon in the region, so Honduras would be safer and have more money in the bank if it free-rode on the United States and the security guarantees that the Panamerican system provided. After several more articles by Alvarado and other defenders of the military, Andrés Alvarado Lozano, a schoolteacher from the Copán region, entered the fray:

> If there is one thing that Honduras has in common with Costa Rica . . . it is in the absence of a military caste which weighs on the politics of its people. . . . from this national army, from this military academy that Señor Alonzo asks for, there will emerge an insolent military clique, that over time will become the great headache for Honduras for many years. It is better to be like Costa Rica with an army of teachers than to expose yourself to the creation of a military caste, which has caused bitter tears throughout the Caribbean. (*El Cronista*, July 7, 1955)

Captain Espinoza countered that modern militaries were not like those of old, but were pro-democratic and non-political. And, added Espinoza, Costa Rica had 20,000 well-trained men (*El Cronista*, July 9, 1955).[20] A few days later, another pro-military argument appeared, its key point being that the construction of a military is the core essence of a state: "In Honduras a professional army is not only necessary but urgent. The truth is that we have no military. And since we have no military, it is doubtful that we have a state. This is the truth. The military does consume the budget. With a military other services will be reduced. But the military guarantees the state" (*El Cronista*, July 21, 1955). A week later, J. Simeon Alonzo of the military academy confidently expounded pro-military arguments that he would later come to regret:

> The Republic of Chile is one of the most civilized and cultured nations of South America, it has an armed forces that is a source of great pride, a complete democracy lives there, our first military mentors were from this exemplary nation and even today the teachings of the Chilean soldiers flow in our environment. If in Chile there has never been and there will never be the military caste that you so greatly fear, why can't Honduras structure a similar armed forces? (*El Cronista*, July 18, 1955)

Such public debate on the pros and cons of militarization confirms the assertion that Honduras lacked an institutionalized military at the mid-point of the twentieth century. It also reveals that the development of a professional armed force did not happen unopposed and automatically. To have a strong military or to follow Costa Rica in only having a civilian-controlled police force was one of the dominant issues in the leading independent press in the 1954–57 period. The articulate and far-sighted opponents of militarization presented a sophisticated and well-founded defense of the then-visible and viable Costa Rican model: a military consumes too many resources; with the United States as the hegemon, little Honduras should free-ride, as the U.S.

---

20 Andrés Alvarado responded that Costa Rica did not have a military but only appeared to have lots of soldiers when teachers and volunteers took up arms to fight Nicaragua's Somoza and former Costa Rican presidents in exile in Nicaragua (*El Cronista*, July 19, 1955).

will not permit serious threats to regional stability on the isthmus; the Panamerican institutions such as the Rio Treaty could ensure the existence of the Honduran state; the founding of a professional military would evolve into a monster and would be a great headache for the country; and civilian leadership could never fully develop as it would be smothered by the power of the military. The proponents voiced the emerging intersubjective[21] idea that a strong military is a necessary condition of a viable country. Looking back at these arguments 50 years later, one can see that the opponents to the militarization project were absolutely correct. With the United States actively pushing the militarization project, however, the debate was moot and the development of a military caste forged ahead.

The debate about militarization continued in Honduras for several years. The 1963 election featured Modesto Rodas Alvarado (1921–79), a charismatic politician who ran on a platform of following the Costa Rican example and disbanding the military. On October 3, 1963, a mere ten days before the election that Rodas Alvarado was expected to win, the military staged a pre-emptive coup. Cognizant of the support of civil society and students in the previous coup attempt, the military unleashed one of the most violent coups in the history of Central America. Scores of civil guards were killed as they slept, and violence against civilians continued for days. Attempts by students and Liberal Party supporters to challenge the overthrow of democracy were met with brutal reactions by the armed forces.

The 1963 coup finalized the ascent of the Honduran Armed Forces as the dominant political actor in the country and buried the opportunity for political and social progress in the country. Most importantly, the coup ended any national conversation around the idea of demilitarization. The dominant intersubjective belief that Honduras needed a military was now firmly entrenched. The next three decades of development in Honduras were, in the words of one commentator, "a tragedy irredeemably converted into farce" (Meza 1981, 128).[22] In the 1980s and after the dramatic shift in U.S. policy under the Reagan administration that demanded elections in the region, electoral democracy returned to Honduras in a strange hybrid regime where the military still called the shots and human rights violations surged. Nearly 200 students and labor leaders were "disappeared" by U.S.-trained Honduran soldiers during the "lost decade."[23]

---

21 Intersubjectivity comes from constructivism and is a shared understanding among individuals based on common assumptions, interests, and communication.

22 In 1972, a short-lived reformist military regime emerged, led by the ever-unpredictable Oswaldo López Arellano (1921–2010). In Meza's words, "The timid appearance of a reformist military on the national scene was reason enough so that the dumb, in an excessive and condemnable extirpation of enthusiasm and optimism, easily forgot the political past of the army and began to elucidate diverse theoretical interpretations of the new role of the Armed Forces in Latin America. . . . they pretended to see in the army an ideologically reformed body . . . This error inevitably led to other more serious errors and thus there emerged a whole chain of erroneous interpretations, divorced from reality and based more in desires than in facts" (Meza 1981, 173).

23 In 1996, it was confirmed what many observers had long believed: The United States was training Latin American military officers to use executions, torture, blackmail, and other forms of coercion against civilians (*Washington Post*, September 21, 1996). A figure of 200 disappeared may appear low next to numbers for Argentina and Chile, but it is nonetheless very high in the Honduran context.

By 1982, when "democracy" returned to Honduras, the military institution had grown
to such a degree that

> . . . for reasons of "National Security," the Honduran Armed Forces are in
> charge of the police, the merchant marine, customs, immigration, civil aviation
> and airports, and also the national telephone company. The military exercises
> administrative control of extensive regions in the interior of the country.
> Military officials constitute a power elite, with their own government, their own
> judicial court, and in a growing manner their own economic sector. Making use
> of the resources of the Military Pension Institute (IPM) . . . the military insti-
> tution has accumulated a large group of holdings: their own bank (that offers
> a credit card to the public); an insurance company; many factories including
> the largest cement factory in the country (which was purchased from the civil-
> ian government as part of a "privatization" . . .); a car distributorship; a radio
> station; a public relations firm; large tracks of coastal properties designed for
> tourism development; and—in an ironic example of what an economist would
> call "vertical integration"—a first class funeral parlor. (Comité de Abogados
> por los Derechos Humanos 1994)

With a military in charge of a country during the Cold War, it is not a surprise
that Honduran development stagnated in the second half of the century. Honduras
fell further behind Costa Rica in human development, poverty eradication, health,
education, democratization, and other dimensions. For example, Figure 4.1 shows
Costa Rican and Honduran economic development in real purchasing power parity

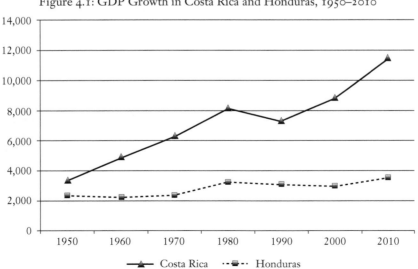

Figure 4.1: GDP Growth in Costa Rica and Honduras, 1950–2010

Source: Data from Penn World Table. https://pwt.sas.upenn.edu.

dollars over six decades. While Costa Rica's per capita GDP was only 45 per cent greater than Honduras's in 1950, it was 221 per cent greater in 2010.

4.3. THE CASE OF PANAMA

As described in depth by former Panamanian vice-president and minister of government and justice Ricardo Arias Calderón (2007), Panama became increasingly militarized throughout the period ending in 1989. Without entering into the pros or cons of the invasion of Panama by U.S. forces in 1989 to overthrow the Manuel Noriega regime, one can tell that an outcome of that invasion was the elimination of both a military clique and the militarized Panamanian Defense Forces. The Panamanian Defense Forces were dissolved in 1990 and permanently abolished in the 1994 Constitution.

In the years since that time, the Panamanian Public Forces have emerged, comprising the National Police, the National Borders Service, the National Aeronaval Service, and the Institutional Protection Service. While there is some warfare capacity within the Panamanian Public Forces, the police forces fall far short of a military organization, are apolitical, and are much closer in training and capacity to their northern neighbors in Costa Rica than to their southern neighbors in Colombia. The early results of demilitarization in Panama suggest that this change coincided with an impressive growth of the economy. The absence of a military clique extends time horizons without the threat of military coups, is good for investment, deepens democracy, and provides funds for increased investments in human capital.[24]

The real constant GDP growth of the economy of Panama is presented in Figure 4.2. In the 20 years after the abolition of the military, Panama's economy grew at an average annual rate of 5.6 per cent, more than double the historic rate from 1950 to 1990. Panama followed the path that all similar countries should take, and one that

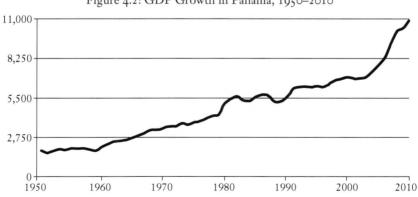

Figure 4.2: GDP Growth in Panama, 1950–2010

Source: Data from Penn World Table. https://pwt.sas.upenn.edu.

---

24 The huge success of Panamanian control of the Panama Canal and the increase in traffic through the canal are also important components of Panama's economic growth.

Costa Rica pioneered more than six decades ago. In the absence of credible threats of invasions from external enemies, the costs of militarization are too high and the benefits of demilitarization are significant.

CONCLUSIONS

Whenever we visit Honduras or Uruguay, we always ask cab drivers, shoe-shiners, waiters, and other people we interact with the following question: Wouldn't it be great if your country had no military and used the money for better police, education, and health care? Invariably the response is one of disbelief: How is it possible for a country not to have a military? This widespread, constructed belief that all countries have institutionalized militaries is relatively recent.

In this chapter, we have demonstrated that in the first half of the twentieth century, Costa Rica was more militarized than was Honduras. Costa Rica demilitarized both in practice and in its constitution in the 1948–49 period. Timing was crucial, as the U.S. Cold War response of militarization of the region did not begin until after 1950. In the mid-1950s, the United States supported and facilitated the militarization of Honduras as part of the Cold War strategy. The idea that viable countries possessed institutionalized militaries was not fully in effect at this time, as demonstrated by the intense public debate over militarization in the Honduran press.

The Cold War, anti-communism, and U.S. training and propaganda contributed to the construction of the intersubjective belief that a military is necessary and normal. The construction of this idea was aided by the academic fields of comparative politics and international relations and the assumption that national power and viability are measured or ensured by militarization.

Over 40 years ago, as Honduras debated the pros and cons of establishing a military, a schoolteacher from Copán predicted that the establishment of a military would become a great headache for Honduras for many years. Another Honduran wrote to the newspaper, exclaiming that "now that the budget is in tatters, now when it would be wise to be economical with government expenditures, it would be a stupendous measure if the government would eliminate the defense minister, and with him all the commanders and soldiers in the country and establish in their place an efficient civil guard, and a mounted police to insure individual security in a civilized manner" (*El Cronista*, May 9, 1955). In 1963, Costa Rican officials visited Honduras in the height of the election campaign, urging the country to follow the Costa Rican example of demilitarization. Things might have been very different in that country if this view had prevailed.

In the six decades since Honduras chose militarization, the economy has stagnated, violent crime has escalated, and democracy has sputtered. The military emerged as such a dominant force and a staging ground for armed actions against the Sandinistas that it was referred to as the USS Honduras, a giant battleship for the United States. By contrast, with the political, psychological, and economic advantages of demilitarization, Costa Rica grew at a faster rate than its neighbors, reduced poverty, diversified its economy, enhanced human capital, and maintained one of the strongest democracies in Latin America.

In 2001, Costa Rican President Miguel Angel Rodríguez visited the Southern Cone with the same demilitarization message as the country had been spreading for decades. In Argentina, Rodríguez asserted that the elimination of the armed forces was a great "blessing, because it stopped the existence of a separate caste. We do not have this enormous and unproductive military expenditure. And we do not suffer from the temptation to use this power. We have seen how militaries use this power in Latin America."[25] He told the Uruguayans to transfer military resources to education, infrastructure, job creation, and health: "The countries of Latin America should eliminate their armies because we are poor and we need these resources to develop human capital."[26] The colonels bristled, but many citizens cheered.

Of course, to some, the very idea of demilitarization is sheer foolishness, nothing more than a pipe dream. No civilized country could eliminate the defense minister, destroy the tanks, and close the barracks. Yet, some 38 years after the proscription of the armed forces in his country, speaking to the U.S. Congress just weeks before receiving the Nobel Peace Prize, Costa Rican President Oscar Arias reported the results of his country's pipe dream:

> I belong to a small country that was not afraid to abolish its army in order to increase its strength. In my homeland you will not find a single tank, a single artillery piece, a single warship, or a single military helicopter. In Costa Rica we are not afraid of freedom. We love democracy and respect the law. . . . We have made considerable progress in education, health, and nutrition. In all of these areas our levels are comparable to the best in Latin America. Although we are poor, we have so far been able to reach satisfactory social goals. This is largely because we have no arms expenditures and because the imbedded practice of democracy drives us to meet the needs of the people. Almost forty years ago we abolished our army. Today we threaten no one, neither our own people nor our neighbors. Such threats are absent not because we lack tanks, but because there are few of us who are hungry, illiterate, or unemployed. (Speech to U.S. Congress, September 22, 1987)

LESSONS LEARNED

- Latin American militaries largely have had an internal focus and have not been used often for fighting external wars.
- Costa Rica was able to demilitarize in 1949 because the Cold War was not the regional organizing principle.

---

25 *Clarín*, 16 August 2001.
26 *La República*, 2 August 2001.

- Militarization has significant trade-offs.
- Demilitarization is not a pipe dream but can actually occur.
- Global powers should encourage and assist in the demilitarization process in smaller countries.

DISCUSSION QUESTIONS

- Can a state really exist without a military? Is a military a necessary condition of a viable country? Can demilitarization only take place in small countries?
- Do you think that there is a causal relationship between demilitarization and strength of economy?
- What benefits are there in downsizing their militaries for countries that have external threats?
- What part does culture play in the military debate?

ADDITIONAL READING

Arias, Enrique Desmond, and Mark Ungar. 2009. "Community Policing and Latin America's Citizen Security Crisis." *Comparative Politics* 41 (4): 409–29.
Høivik, Tord. 1981. "Demilitarization in Costa Rica: A Farewell to Arms?" *Journal of Peace Research* 18 (4): 333–51.

WEBSITES

A Bold Peace movie. http://aboldpeace.com/.
Brookings Institute—Guatemala after the Peace Accords. http://www.brookings.edu/research/books/1999/guatpea.
International Peace Bureau. http://www.ipb.org/web/.
Noam Chomsky, Militarizing Latin America. http://www.chomsky.info/articles/20090830.htm.
Correlates of War dataset. http://www.correlatesofwar.org.
Envio Digital—Demilitarization and Other Challenges. http://www.envio.org.ni/articulo/2519.
Fellowship of Reconciliation. http://forusa.org/content/demilitarizing-life-land.
Center for International Policy—Open the Files: A Chance to Aid Demilitarization in Honduras. http://www.ciponline.org/research/html/open-the-files-a-chance-to-aid-demilitarization-in-honduras.
Rand Corporation: Latin American Institutional Development. http://www.rand.org/pubs/reports/R0586.html.

PART TWO

CULTURAL RIGHTS: RACISM, DISCRIMINATION, AND MULTICULTURALISM

CHAPTER FIVE

THE AWAKENING OF INDIGENOUS CULTURE: THE CASE OF BOLIVIA

INTRODUCTION

On 18 December, 2005, Evo Morales (b. 1959) became the first indigenous person in the history of Bolivia to be elected president. This event is even more important than an African American being elected President of the United States in 2008. African Americans of Barack Obama's parents' generation were not allowed to go on the same sidewalk as whites or get on the same buses, to name but two of the many segregation regulations imposed in the South. Likewise, Evo Morales' mother could not go into the Plaza Mayor in La Paz, the capital of Bolivia, because it was off limits to indigenous people, who had always been segregated from society. But today her son is the first citizen of the country, and the Aymara Indians can go anywhere in La Paz. Regardless of whether or not one agrees with Morales' policies, anyone who cannot grasp what an astonishing revolution this is in Bolivia must be blinded by sectarianism or an absolute lack of historical perspective. Morales won his first election with a comfortable 52 per cent of the votes, and this was another historic event as a clear majority meant he did not have to make alliances in Congress. As soon as his victory was announced, he said, "It is a great honor to be the first indigenous president . . . a stage in history has come to an end."

The ex-president, Carlos Mesa, commented, "The country needed an indigenous president." With Evo Morales as the first president of Aymara origin, the process of indigenizing Bolivia is going strong. However, there are enormous risks because the country has an indigenous majority: instead of continuing along the conciliatory road to multiculturalism and reciprocal recognition, it might fragment into groups of whites, Aymaras, Quechuas, and mestizos (mixed race). In this chapter we will analyze how Bolivia's indigenous population achieved political power, visibility, and recognition for its cultural identity.

Several South American countries have reformed their constitutions since the 1990s, and in Bolivia this involved explicitly incorporating the Aymara and Quechua populations into the state. These are the most numerous indigenous groups, but throughout history they were segregated from the rest of the population and not recognized as nations with the right to their own culture within the Bolivian state. The constitution was reformed in 1994, and Bolivia was defined within it as a "free, independent, sovereign, multi-ethnic and pluricultural" country. It was also laid down that the state would promote bilingual education in the Aymara, Quechua, and Guaraní languages, would support the resolution of disputes in line with indigenous customary law, and would recognize collective rights in land ownership. Article 1 of the new Constitution of 2009 reads as follows: "Bolivia is constituted as a unitary social State of plurinational community law, free, independent, sovereign, democratic, intercultural, decentralized and with autonomous regions. Bolivia is founded on political, economic, legal, cultural and linguistic pluralism, within the integrating process of the country."

We will also briefly analyze the indigenous Bolivians' rise from total exclusion to the pinnacle of political power, and discuss what it is to be an indigenous person in that country in the twenty-first century. Bolivia has advanced further along this path than any other Latin American nation, but it is not an isolated case. Some of what is happening in Bolivia is also occurring elsewhere in the Andean region. From Mexico all the way to Argentina, indigenous populations have won many rights and have become increasingly important actors in the political arena.

5.1. THE CONSTRUCTION OF MULTICULTURALISM IN BOLIVIA

Before the Spanish conquered the Inca Empire, the Aymaras, Quechuas, and other indigenous cultures in the Andean region were organized in a multi-ethnic confederation of states called Tahuantinsuyo and united by the Inca central power. This empire covered parts of what are today Colombia, Ecuador, Peru, Bolivia, and Chile. During the colonial period all these indigenous populations were segregated from society and marginalized because of their "natural inferiority," and they were sometimes used as slaves. Some groups were set apart in pseudo-evangelized "Indian villages" (Yrigoyen 2002). When independence came, things changed very little because the new nations were built in the image of white, Western, Catholic European countries, and there was no place for the original native populations. This explains why the national identity of these countries did not include indigenous people or their rights. What emerged were regimes that did not recognize Indians and were preoccupied with constructing a state with a homogeneous population made up of mestizos (Stavenhagen 2002). At the beginning of the twentieth century, the Bolivian Alcides Arguedas wrote:

> The Aymara Indian is a surly savage with a hard character, arid sentiments, an absolute lack of aesthetic sensibility, no ambitions, he doesn't seek anything,

he doesn't aspire to anything, he lives without enthusiasm, without desires, as passive as an animal. . . . When the exploitation in its most aggressive and brutal form gets too much and the suffering is so extreme that he reaches the breaking point the Indian rises, forgets his manifest inferiority, loses his instinct for self-preservation and, harking to his hate-filled spirit, gives rein to his passions and robs, kills and murders with atrocious fury. (Arguedas 1909, 212–16)

This was the prevailing perception when the Bolivian state was established, and the goal was to negate the Indians and Europeanize the country under the guidance of the white elite, who were also mixed race but more European.[27]

The movement called Indigenism began in Bolivia in the 1930s. This term should be clarified, because it is apparently so similar to the current process of indigenization. In the first decade of the twentieth century there was an Indigenist policy that featured good rhetoric about the Indians, but it was really aimed at turning them into citizens who would be useful for the development of the country. The state implemented communication and education strategies, as well as integration policies geared to assimilating indigenous people and molding them to the requirements of economic progress; however, in spite of the label of Indigenism, the term "peasant" was used to refer to the Indians, and very little of their culture was recognized or considered inspiring (Marroquín 1972).

The current mobilization of indigenous populations in the Andes region began to gather strength in 1992 at the time of the celebrations to mark the 500th anniversary of Columbus's arrival in the Americas. With support from NGOs and international financing, native Indian organizations advanced from making demands oriented toward a leftist political agenda to making demands centered on matters of ethnicity and autonomy, cultural as well as territorial. This shift can be seen as a move away from assimilation and toward multiculturalism. In Bolivia in particular, "[a]fter the 1952 Revolution, the MNR-run[28] state used the *sindicato* (peasant union) model to incorporate highland Indians into the national economic and political schemes. In essence, this model was assimilationist in character, using and eliding the traditional land-holding patterns and forms of social organization to make the varied Indian groups into *campesinos*, a group defined by class rather than ethnicity" (Postero 2000, 3). In the indigenous peoples' struggles since the 1990s, on the other hand, ethnicity rather than class has been stressed, along with culture and political ideology.

In the 1970s, indigenous Aymaras in La Paz and Oruro founded the Katarista Movement. In their ranks were considerable numbers of university students, who had played an important role defending workers and unions at the time of the military dictatorship. This movement came to the peak of its power when its leader Victor Hugo Cárdenas made an alliance with Sánchez de Losada's MNR political party

27   In South America, the preferred expression is Indigenous Peoples; however, Indians is often used too, even by the Indigenous Peoples themselves.

28   MNR stands for the Movimiento Nacionalista Revolucionario (Revolutionary Nationalist Movement).

and they were elected vice-president and president, respectively, for the period 1993 to 1997.

The Sole Labor Union Confederation of Peasants Workers of Bolivia (CSUTCB) was founded in 1979, and it gradually became increasingly Indigenist in nature. Its main leader from 1998 to 2003 was an Aymara named Felipe Quispe (b. 1942), who subsequently started his own political party, the Pachacutec Indigenous Movement (MIP), which has since been dissolved. As leader of the Confederation, Quispe blockaded La Paz in 2003 and forced President Sánchez de Losada to resign; he was also important in the indigenous mobilization that forced President Hugo Banzer from power in 2001, and then ousted President Carlos Mesa in 2005. Quispe's political rhetoric shifted from a Marxist stance that included defending the traditional Andean communities (the *ayllus*) to a separatist platform that made his faction one of the most radical indigenous movements in Latin America. His political ideology was heavily influenced by Fausto Reinaga (1906–94), a theoretician who proposed that the Quechuas and Aymaras should unite and establish a social system based on their ancestral religions and cosmology. Reinaga was bitterly criticized by the left, who accused him of playing the right's game against the workers' unions, and also by the right because they saw him as promoting interracial strife.

At the end of the 1980s, the coca farmers' movement came to prominence and Evo Morales became a popular leader. The United States pressured the Bolivian government to suppress coca production and promised in return to provide economic assistance so that the Indians and peasants could devote themselves to other crops. But there was widespread discontent when it was realized that the income from these alternative crops was far less than they could earn from planting coca. Morales capitalized on this discontent and became the "coca workers' leader."

Coca is an ancient traditional plant that can be used for many purposes apart from making cocaine, but in modern times some of the farmers' revenues have indeed come from selling the leaves to drug traffickers. When we analyze this controversial subject, including the issue of eradicating coca production as a way of eliminating the scourge of drugs, we must bear in mind that cultivation of the coca plant is one of the fundamental elements in how the indigenous peoples of the Andes see the universe. For hundreds of years their whole metaphysical system and understanding of the world has been linked to this plant, and this applies to everyone from the humblest Indian right up to the shaman or chief. One has only to visit the excellent collections at the Museum of Gold in Lima or Bogotá and look at the *poporos*, i.e., the receptacles for transporting the lime that makes the coca leaf ferment more quickly in the mouth. These artifacts were made in wide range of designs, some delicately worked in gold for the elite and other simpler ones for common folk. The hallucinations that consuming some coca preparations can induce are associated with myths, art, and sexuality. It has to be understood that since pre-Columbian times the coca plant has been one of the core elements in Andean cosmology, which is still very much alive, albeit in a hybrid form and mixed with Western influences. To propose eradicating coca among the Andean people of Bolivia is tantamount to wanting to take the cross out of Christianity; both are essential religious symbols around which everything else revolves.

A key precedent for the Bolivian indigenous movement's success and for the rise of the Aymara cultural identity was the Patriotic Conscience Party (CONDEPA). This was founded in the 1990s by Compadre Carlos Palenque (1944–97), an Aymara leader from La Paz. Palenque started out as a singer and later went into radio and television. He became so popular that he found a political party which, like his broadcasting, appealed to the Indians who had settled in La Paz. He spoke in a mixture of the Aymara language and Spanish, and his message included indigenous religiosity and traditional cultural references. He drew attention to the plight of desperate, forgotten Indians, who had been expelled from their lands and driven into poverty, and he echoed their mistrust of the mainstream political parties and the old-style rhetoric. CONDEPA grew quickly, and within a few years Palenque's wife, Mónica Medina, was elected mayor of the city of La Paz. An associate, Comadre Remedios Loza, who always wore typical Indian clothes, was elected to Congress. The CONDEPA movement was the result of "media politics" (Castells 2000): it was opportunist and populist, it did not have a clear message, and it fell apart when Palenque died. Nevertheless, it was important because it was one of the few times that someone had appealed to a displaced sector of indigenous Bolivians in their own language, showed them their own images, and understood their most intimate problems and feelings. Palenque established great empathy with the Indians and with their daily struggle in a society that pushed them into the margins, where they lost their dreams, their names, and their history. CONDEPA also identified itself with the mestizos in the middle class and with the sometime dictator President Banzer.

The party was rejected by radical indigenous groups, however, and the Pachacutec Indigenous Movement founded by Quispe emerged at that time as the most important Aymara voice. Over the centuries Aymara culture has remained relatively untouched by European influence because its center is located in the highlands around Lake Titicaca, 4,000 meters above sea level, in an area called the Tibet of the Americas (www.aymara.org). Under Quispe's influence the movement built an identity based on resistance. It defines itself in terms of ethnicity and race, and its declared enemies are the white population, the Catholic Church, the Bolivian state, capitalism, and globalization. It practices its own traditional religion, which is centered on the sun (Inti), the earth (Pachamama), and the mountains (Apus), and it has its own calendar that is now in the year 5,521. It wants to separate from Bolivia and set up an independent state, with its communities operating without a money-based market economy and outside globalization. In the 1990s, Quispe also founded the Tupak Katari Guerrilla Army, an action for which he was punished with five years in prison. Alvaro García Lineras, a member of this armed movement, later became President Morales' vice-president.

The Confederation of Indigenous Peoples of the Eastern Region of Bolivia (CIDOB) appeared on the political scene in 1990, something that subsequently turned out to be highly significant. CIDOB organized a 70-day march by indigenous people from the lowlands in the east of the country; this march included more than 30 different ethnic groups, including the Guaraní. These Indians had not taken part in previous Aymara mobilizations, and their history is very different from that of the indigenous population of the Andes region. However, when they got to the *altiplano* highlands they were welcomed by the other indigenous groups and together they marched on

La Paz. Their main demand was enshrined in the march's name: the March for Land and Dignity. This was a response to new settlements that threatened to drive indigenous people off their ancestral land, and thus the specific demand that land tenure be regularized was included for the first time with some force on the political agenda: "Indigenous people and their demands for territory and recognition as part of the nation caused an immediate response. President Paz Zamora met with the people, created seven indigenous territories by presidential decree, and *territorio* became an icon of indigenous-state relations" (Postero 2000, 4).

An event that made an enormous impact not only in Bolivia but throughout the indigenous movement in Latin America and the world was International Labor Organization (ILO) Convention 169 concerning indigenous and tribal peoples in independent countries. This Convention was a turning point in several crucial respects. First, it established that people ". . . are regarded as indigenous because they are descended from original populations from before the conquest and colonization, who totally or partially manifest their linguistic and cultural characteristics and social organization, and as a fundamental criterion to determine who is considered indigenous, consider themselves to belong, or ascribe themselves to, a specific indigenous people" (CEPAL 2005, 18). In addition, the Convention establishes that indigenous rights must be put on the same level as human rights, with the corresponding rights to a people's original territory, the use of land, culture, language, self-identification, and self-determination in accordance with their own customs. Article 7 states that "[t]he peoples concerned shall have the right to decide their own priorities for the process of development as it affects their lives, beliefs, institutions and spiritual well-being and the lands they occupy or otherwise use." The Bolivian state signed the Convention in 1991, and in so doing incorporated these provisions into the country's body of laws. Almost all countries in Latin America had signed this Convention by 2013.

In 1994, during President Sánchez de Losada's administration, the Constitution was reformed, with modifications to 35 dispositions concerning indigenous peoples. This was a definitive step toward the creation of a multicultural country. In Article 1 of this charter it is stated that Bolivia is "free, independent and sovereign, multiethnic and pluricultural . . . ." Moreover, the state committed itself to promoting bilingual education in Aymara, Quechua or Guaraní; to respecting the uses and customs of the indigenous populations in settling disputes; and to safeguarding collective property rights. In Article 171 it is explicitly stated that "[t]he social, economic and cultural rights of the indigenous peoples who inhabit the national territory shall be recognized, respected and protected in the framework of the law, especially with regard to their original communal lands, safeguarding the use and sustainable exploitation of natural resources, their identity, values, languages, customs and institutions." These new constitutional dispositions "were the foundational language for multiculturalism in Bolivia, and they were followed by legislation that gave specific rights to indigenous peoples" (Postero 2000, 2).

The year 1994 saw the passing of the Popular Participation Law whereby, for the first time, genuine decentralization of power was established in the country, as 20 per cent of the national budget was allocated to local municipalities, which have autonomy in the way this money is used. This new distribution of public funds has been an unprecedented injection of resources for the rural sector. The new law also stipulated that grassroots organizations (OTBs) would have the power to allocate the municipal budget. These OTBs include three kinds of institutions: neighborhood councils in villages and urban centers, indigenous villages, and peasant communities. There is a precise definition of what an indigenous person is, and this matches almost exactly what the CIDOB proposed in 1991 for the bill for the Indigenous Peoples Law and ILO Convention 169. The 1994 law defines indigenous peoples as follows:

> The human community that is descended from populations settled before the conquest and colonization, and that are within the current borders of the State, have history, organization, language or dialect and other cultural characteristics whereby its members are identified, recognized as belonging to the same socio-cultural unit, and maintain a territorial link in function of the administration of their habitat and their social, economic, political and cultural institutions. In accordance with the above definition the following are considered indigenous grassroots organizations: settlements, official zones, councils, Indigenous Peoples of the East, *ayllus*, indigenous communities and other forms. (Art. 1)

This law provided a strong stimulus for Indians to participate in public and municipal affairs because now their decisions could make a real impact on public works and on how state resources were used.

This local participation has been increasing even more thanks to a new law promulgated in 1997 that reformed the electoral system. According to political scientist René Antonio Mayorga (2002), with this reform "of the electoral system of double constituencies and personalized proportional representation, which has been in force since 1997, the democratic system has shown it can promote inclusion and has strengthened the trend toward autonomous representation for indigenous population sectors and peasants. It has enabled social movements to become political movements." In fact, as a direct consequence of this reform, indigenous representatives were elected to Congress for the first time. There were nine in that first batch, and one of them, a certain Evo Morales, thus began his giddy rise to the presidency.

In 1997 there was another reform, the so-called INRA Law, which was introduced by the Sánchez de Losada government. This law recognizes for the first time in Bolivia the right of indigenous peoples to own their original community land. Article 3 states: "The rights of indigenous and original peoples and communities to their original community lands are safeguarded, and this covers the economic, social and cultural implications, and the use and sustainable exploitation of renewable natural resources." We should bear in mind that a good proportion of this land has very high economic value because of its forestry potential, possible mineral resources, strategic location or suitability for livestock rearing. It has not been easy to establish the legal right to collective ownership of these lands, but the fact that these indigenous peoples' rights have received official and constitutional recognition is a very significant step forward.

A group of social scientists, influenced by the American anthropologist Charles Hale (1994), expressed serious doubts about the Bolivian state's adoption of multiculturalism.

They were incredulous that the Sánchez de Losada administration, with its very orthodox neoliberal economic model, would pursue multicultural policies that were so beneficial for the indigenous population. The only way they could reconcile these apparently contradictory positions was to suggest that the government's multicultural stance was just a façade to mask neoliberal policies to privatize public enterprises and comply with Washington's macroeconomic recipes. From this point of view, multiculturalism in Bolivia would have been a kind of political co-opting of the indigenous people to demobilize them and thus avoid more radical opposition to the government's economic program. It was interpreted as an essential part of a new type of domination of the indigenous majority by the white elite. Nancy Postero took this view in 2000 when she wrote:

> Multiculturalism is the current idiom of that struggle, what Roseberry calls a "language of contention". . . . This does not mean that multiculturalism is merely a sham, or that indigenous people have been fooled. Rather, it points out that the arena of struggle has changed in Bolivia. Previously marginalized indigenous peoples who could never even speak to political officials, now find themselves in battles in municipal meetings, fighting over school room budgets or in vice ministries, arguing over regulations for land titling legislation. Some things have changed; some have not. (Postero 2000, 11)

This perspective, which prevailed before Morales became president, was very cautious in its evaluation of the country's multiculturalism and always tried to link it to neoliberalism. It was unable to appreciate that Bolivian multiculturalism fed back into the indigenous movement, which was multi-faceted and harbored contradictory interests but was strengthened in all its various parts by the multicultural trend (Mignolo 2006). Critics from a Žižek-style pseudo-radical left-wing position dismissed what they regarded as a mere cultural veneer and failed to comprehend the immense impact that multiculturalism would have. They underestimated it because they were still imprisoned in an ideology that did not have a theory of culture in its full dimensions and did not understand that power struggles are also culture battles.

In April 2004, the same year in which the Cinta Larga Indians killed miners on their tribal land in Brazil, there was trouble in the small town of Ilave, near Puno, a Peruvian city on the border with Bolivia. Members of the Aymara community there killed the mayor in a street demonstration that turned ugly, and three other people were seriously injured in the violence. This action was supported by Aymara communities in Bolivia and Peru, who blocked roads in a show of solidarity. Like many border towns, Ilave is on a smugglers' route, and the value of the goods transported along these dusty roads every year has been estimated at $200 million. The murdered mayor, Cirilo Robles Callomamani, was himself an Aymara, but now that these indigenous communities could democratically elect their own mayors, they held them accountable for their actions. They accused Robles of corruption and he fled the city, but when he found out he was going to be formally dismissed from office he returned. The enraged crowd dragged him out of his house and through the streets and beat him to death, his lifeless body found under a bridge the following morning. One of his rivals was arrested for the crime, and in 2012, nearly five years later, he and another person were found guilty of the murder and sentenced to 30 years in prison.

This killing took place within the Aymara community and was not against officials of a different ethnic origin. It was important because the formal legal system hardly operates in this remote part of Peru, and members of the local indigenous community dealt out their own justice. Nor was it the first time that the Aymaras have acted in this way. In October 2003, near a small town called Pucarani on the banks of Lake Titicaca, some Aymara followers of Felipe Quispe caught two people who had been rustling and beat them to death. When the killers were arrested they claimed they had acted in accordance with their indigenous traditions. Quispe and his followers supported them with a massive show of force by blocking roads and confronting the police, and in the ensuing violence several people on both sides were killed (*The Economist* 2004a, 2004b).

The indigenous movement has also acquired international mobilization and co-ordination. In 1997 the co-author of this book, Felipe Arocena, spent several weeks in Peru. On the slopes of one of the mountains that encircle the city of Cuzco he saw a large sign, constructed like the famous Hollywood sign, and it had an inscription: PACHAKUTEK. He asked the locals about it and they said it had been put up by an indigenous movement whose main aims included preserving and reconstructing Inca pride and the Inca identity. Pachakutek (also known as Pachacuti or Pachacutec) was one of the best-known Inca emperors, and in the Quechua language the word also means to revive or be reborn. On that same trip Arocena witnessed a non-violent street demonstration against the mayor of the city, and most of the people taking part were indigenous. Until a few years ago there was in Peru, and in Bolivia too, another small radical political faction called the Pachakutek Movement for the Liberation of Tahuantinsuyu (MPLT). Their principal goal was to reconstruct the ancient Inca community of Tahuantinsuyo and free themselves from the oppressive nation of Peru, which is perceived as a continuation of the old Spanish colonial regime dominating their religion and culture. There are no big indigenous political parties in Peru, but nevertheless more and more Indians have managed to establish themselves in politics. According to a study by the anthropologist Ivan Degregori, in 1966 in the department (province) of Ayacucho, only one municipality in ten had a mayor who spoke Quechua, but 30 years later ten mayors spoke the language, six had Quechua names, and seven were of Inca origin (*The Economist* 2004a, 2004b). Today there are also indigenous movements in Ecuador that use the name Pachakutek, and in recent elections they won positions of power in various cities and provinces. In addition, they helped ex-president Lucio Gutiérrez win the national elections and force the incumbent, Jamil Mauad, from power. Subsequently they turned against Gutiérrez because they felt he had betrayed them by signing an agreement with the International Monetary Fund and trusting in support from the United States, and they compelled him to resign as Mauad had done.

Similarly in Bolivia, the Bolivian Pachacutec Indigenous Movement, whose leader is the Aymara Felipe Quispe, played a part in the fall of the last two presidents, Gonzalo Sánchez de Losada ("Goni") and Carlos Mesa. It was one of the most powerful indigenous political movements and it obtained 6 per cent of the votes in the 2002 elections. Its ultimate objective was to set up a new sovereign country, the Republic of Quillasuyo, named for one of the four regions of the ancient empire when the Aymaras were conquered by the Incas. As Quispe himself explained, "The Indians are a majority in Bolivia (between 60 and 80 percent of the population), and as a historical majority we are determined to govern ourselves, establish our own laws, replace the Constitution of the State with our own Constitution, abandon capitalism, restore our own community system, and replace the Bolivian flag of three colors with our own flag which has seven colors" (*La Jornada* 2003). According to Quispe, this new republic will have its own national anthem and its own symbols, and since it will be organized without money there will be no economic inequality, which is "quite like the way we are living in some of our communities now."

Figure 5.1: Evo Morales Receives the Staff of Office at the Sacred Site of Tiwanaku.
Credit: Jaime Razuri/AFP/Getty Images.

Along with Quispe, after he was elected to Congress Evo Morales became one of the two most influential Aymara leaders. In 2002, Morales felt the time had come to make a bid for the presidency. He did not win, but he did not do too badly because his candidacy stopped the election being decided on the first ballot. He was only defeated on a restricted vote in Congress, and "Goni" became president again. The years following Morales' first presidential attempt saw perhaps the greatest mobilization of the indigenous people up to that time: they staged marches, mass demonstrations, and strikes; they blocked roads and blockaded the city of La Paz; and eventually they forced the elected president, and then his successor Mesa, to resign. Indigenous people's rhetoric became increasingly indigenist under the influence of the radical Quispe and the ideologist García Lineras, and it became increasingly reminiscent of Fausto Reinaga's indigenist vision. They achieved complete victory in 2005 when Evo Morales was elected president, and this time he had an absolute majority of the votes so he did not have to consult Congress at all, something that had never happened before in the history of Bolivia.

Since that triumph, Morales has become increasingly dominant politically. He made intermediate electoral gains, and in 2009 he won a second term as president in an overwhelming victory at the polls, with a two-thirds majority on the first ballot. He completely vanquished the economic elite of Santa Cruz and avoided a rupture in the country. He also defeated Felipe Quispe, his Aymara rival for the presidency, who disappeared from the political map leaving his party, the MIP, without legal status. Some years ago Isaac Bigio (2002), a specialist in Bolivian conflicts at the London School of Economics, said that some people thought that the MAS (Movement Toward Socialism), Morales' party, would try to make tentative reforms and would seek to conciliate the whites (*blancoides*). Others believed that there was a multicultural plan of action that was feasible in the context of an increasingly interconnected capitalist world. According to Bigio, Morales could become the new indigenous Nelson Mandela and put an end to racial apartheid in the Andes. However, he equally well might become the leader of a bloody uprising, like the insurrection that took place 50 years ago. So far he has avoided the latter extreme, even in situations when it seemed Bolivia was heading for civil war as a result of the vast gap between the very rich white minority in the east and the enormous majority, the poor indigenous people. Some 97 per cent of the land in Bolivia is still owned by a minority that amounts to 3 per cent of the population and are all white, while 93 per cent of the population, including all the indigenous peoples, possess only 7 per cent of the land.

5.2. WHO ARE THE INDIGENOUS PEOPLES IN BOLIVIA?

According to the census in 2001, only a small minority of the population of Bolivia is white, while most, some 66 per cent, are indigenous. The most numerous of these are the Quechua (50% of the indigenous population) and the Aymara (40%), and there are also the Chiquitano (3.6%), the Guaraní (2.5%), and around 30 other groups that each amount to less than 2.5% (CEPAL 2005). Intersecting these two categories (whites and indigenous) is a whole population group that could be defined as mestizo. It is interesting to note how, over time, the proportion of indigenous people, instead of decreasing, has grown. In the 1900 census only 46 per cent of the population were registered as indigenous, compared to 63 per cent in the 1950 census and 66 per cent today. The explanation for this evolution lies in how people respond to the census questions: it is no easy matter for people to decide if they should consider themselves indigenous. On the one hand there is a set of legal criteria, but there is also a series of operative criteria that may be used in censuses or surveys.

For example, in the 1900 census someone was classed as indigenous if he or she spoke native languages and dressed in Indian clothes. But the numbers of indigenous people the census registered in their communities of origin were subsequently used to calculate the tax this community paid. For this reason many indigenous people migrated to the big cities, stopped wearing traditional clothes, and passed themselves off as mestizos so that their community would pay less tax. An official report that analyzed those census findings concluded at the time that "[a]ccording to the laws of statistical progression the indigenous races will either disappear from national life completely or shrink to a tiny minority" (CEPAL 2005, 16). In fact this conclusion was nothing less than the old wish on the part of the Bolivian state to make the Indians "disappear." Curiously, there is not much difference between this vision and the ideology of the revolution of 1952, which supposedly promoted agrarian reform to benefit the indigenous populations but avoided calling them by that name. This coincidence came about for the following reason:

> In the nationalist ideology of the party that carried out the revolution there was an attempt to construct a crossbreed nation resulting from the fusion of the indigenous tradition and its history with the Iberian culture and heritage. The label Indian was expressly rejected as it was considered negative and loaded with racial content, and it was replaced by the label peasant. However, although they were formally considered citizens with the same rights and obligations, their situation as a people was invisible. This continued until the Constitutional Reform of 1992; up to that time Bolivian judicial economics did not contain the term indigenous people or territory. (CEPAL 2005, 17)

It should be no surprise that the 2001 census registered the greatest percentage of indigenous people in a century, because it was carried out at a historic point in time when the ideology of mestization (racial mixing) was being replaced by that of new indigenism. Being Indian was changing from being a source of shame to a cause for pride, and the state already included indigenous people in its judicial framework, political rhetoric, and the Constitution of the Republic itself. This radical cultural transformation in the country did not solve the operative difficulties involved in the question we examined at the start of this section. At the present time, regardless of juridical and legal definitions, three different operative criteria came into play when identifying people as indigenous, and two of these involve language. The first criterion is the language the person can speak at the present time, the second is the language he or she learned to speak as a child, and the third is whether he or she identifies himself or herself as indigenous. The results presented in Figure 5.2 reflect the ethnic and linguistic combination of these three questions. After that, those who define themselves as indigenous are asked which tribe or group they belong to or identify with. In its 2009 Constitution, Bolivia recognizes 37 official languages, of which the main ones are Spanish (the biggest group), Quechua, and Aymara. Besides being defined as pluricultural and multiethnic, the Bolivian state also stresses that it is plurilingual, and it explicitly mentions *interculturality* as an integrating principle among its different nations.

The methodology used in the census has been criticized in subsequent studies that promote being of mixed blood (mestizo) as the main sign of identity for a Bolivian. A study in March 2009 carried out by the Bolivian Foundation for Multiparty Democracy found that 68 per cent of the population "considered themselves mestizo," 20 per cent "indigenous" or "original," 5 per cent "white," 2 per cent "*chola*," and 1 per cent "Afro." Furthermore, 44 per cent "consider themselves to belong to an original people" and 53 per cent do not. Most people in the country identify themselves as mestizo, but the proportions vary widely in different regions. In the so-called Bolivian "West," a greater proportion of the population feel they belong to some or other original group than in the Bolivian "half moon," which is the Santa Cruz area of influence and the center of economic power. To research the weight of sub-national identities, the above-mentioned survey included the following question: "Is it more important to be of Bolivian nationality or to belong to an indigenous people?" A huge majority, some 76 per cent, said Bolivian nationality, 8 per cent chose the indigenous option,

Figure 5.2: Bolivia: Population by Indigenous Condition, 2001 Census

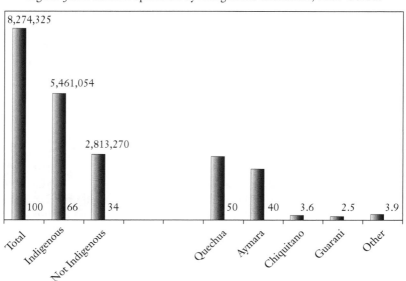

Source: Authors' calculations, based on data from the 2001 Census and CEPAL 2005.

and 13 per cent thought that both were equally important. These results reflect the general will of the people: 89 per cent want the country to remain united and not fragment into separate parts in spite of its internal differences, while 9 per cent think the country should divide. Lastly, the feeling of belonging to Bolivia is almost universal, as 92 per cent of its citizens "are proud to be Bolivians," taking into consideration the bad as well as the good. However, the fact that the population is so diverse yields divided opinions. Some 48 per cent think that "there are many different kinds of people in the country and due to this we cannot progress," but on the other hand 44 per cent believe that "having different kinds of people in the country can help us progress."

The idea that the population has become so mixed in recent centuries that now there are no pure identities and everyone is of mixed blood is both important and, in a sense, accepted. But this notion that the national identity is of mixed blood served in the past to annul the indigenous identity. There is a parallel situation in Brazil, which has various races and has long seen itself as a mixed-race country, but one in which this image of racial harmony has in fact perpetuated discrimination against the Afro-Brazilians. The Brazilian self-image as a racial democracy was contemporaneous with a parallel myth that saw Hispanics as a "cosmic race," which was popularized in 1925 by the Mexican José Vasconcelos in his book *Raza Cósmica: Misión de la Raza Iberoamericana* (1948).

The idea of a Bolivian mixed race sounds good and has a certain justification from historical experience, but it has led to the indigenous people being negated. The white part of the mix always predominates, and all indicators show that the Indians suffer discrimination because they are indigenous. As was mentioned briefly above, when the idea of mestization held sway, Evo Morales' mother couldn't go into the main square in La Paz, her people did not have the right to education in their own language, and they were not considered to belong to the country. In the 1990s, a woman who tried to have tea with her friends in a café in La Paz was refused admission because she was indigenous. In fact she was the wife of Vice-President Cárdenas, but only when the managers of the café found this out did they apologize and let her in. Mixed-race Bolivia has always been a mirage for the Indians, who were trapped in poverty and humiliated in their own land for being indigenous.

5.3. MULTICULTURALISM AND NATIONALISM

Brazil and Bolivia are clear examples of how difficult it can be for a country to strike a balance between multiculturalism on the one hand and unity and national identity on the other. More than anything else a nation is a cultural definition; it is a collection of facts, values, ideas, and shared customs that over the years acquires common significance as it constructs a history that is perceived as different to that of other countries. This is the cornerstone of cultural identity, and in the modern world it usually crystallizes in the nation-state. However, national boundaries are becoming more and more blurred as globalization threatens states' sovereignty from outside, and local communities find themselves challenged inside the borders of their own country. This has given rise to new nationalisms; some are supranational and others subnational, but either way they usually do not coincide with the country's borders. If this problem is not resolved it may cause violent conflicts whose ideological foundations are erroneous ideas of cultural or national identity (as in the case of the extreme racism that broke out in the former Yugoslavia), or political and developmental solutions that take the wrong approach (such as ethnic, cultural or religious fundamentalism). Will the current multicultural strategies of different ethnic communities in Brazil and Bolivia affect these countries' national unity? Will they be able to survive as unified states? Will multiculturalism, along with this new call to ethnic consciousness, evolve toward a positive regeneration of ideas of mestization, like those of Gilberto Freyre (see Chapter 6) or José Vasconcelos's (1948) ideas of Latin American mestizos as a "cosmic race"? Is there a risk that this new multiculturalism might lead to fundamentalist positions and solutions?

After the fall of the Berlin Wall, old nations disintegrated and new countries emerged, but in this new political geography there were various groups that felt they were no longer represented by the state. This happened in Europe with Yugoslavia and Czechoslovakia, with several republics from the old Soviet Union, and also in Africa with Eritrea and in Asia with East Timor. Up to now no Latin American state has split apart, but this does not mean it could not happen.

In the 2004 UNDP Report *Cultural Liberty in Today's Diverse World*, the central theme is the need to construct multicultural democracies, as well as the difficulties this involves. Respect for cultural diversity must be considered one of the main aims of development itself, and in this sense it is an ethical matter. But embracing diversity also has a very practical consequence because it is probably the only way to reduce conflicts between ethnic and religious communities that are confronting each other violently in the world. According to the UNDP, the report

> makes a case for respecting diversity and building more inclusive societies by adopting policies that explicitly recognize cultural differences—multicultural policies. But why have many cultural identities been suppressed or ignored for so long? One reason is that many people believe that allowing diversity to flourish may be desirable in the abstract but in practice can weaken the state, lead to conflict and retard development. The best approach to diversity, in this view, is assimilation around a single national standard, which can lead to the suppression of cultural identities. However, this Report argues that these are not premises—they are myths. Indeed, it argues that a multicultural policy approach is not just desirable but also viable and necessary. Without such an approach the imagined problems of diversity can become self-fulfilling prophecies. (PNUD 2004, 2)

The "myth" this statement refutes is that multiculturalism necessarily undermines a nation's capacity to remain united. In many states a multicultural policy may be the only way to maintain unity and avoid fragmentation. While there is some truth in this claim, neither of the two horns of the dilemma is that simple.

First, we should recognize that there is a degree of tension between multiculturalism and national unity: the tension of the philosophical aporia between parts and the whole, the tension involved in pursuing integration in diversity. Clearly there are various ways of trying to resolve these tensions, and the solutions may be positive or negative, but whichever path is taken the tension could well continue to exist. Second, multicultural policies may be good for helping marginalized populations that deserve compensation and may even partially remedy the effects of past discrimination. But these policies run the risk of becoming unconstitutional because they could all too easily violate the principle of equality before the law, or stray into reverse discrimination, which sparked the current debate about affirmative action. Brazil recently adopted a quota system for Afro-Brazilians, while in the United States the use of a similar system to compensate for past discrimination has been banned, a measure that has raised doubts about its functionality as a strategy to promote diversity.

Bolivia, on the other hand, has not implemented quotas or affirmative action. Brazil's adoption of this policy was a historic moment in South America as it was the first time specific measures had been taken to alleviate the effects of discrimination against indigenous populations and people of African descent. These groups know perfectly well they had to mobilize if they wanted the government to intervene to protect their cultures and safeguard equal rights. In some cases, such as the Quispe movement, there are signs of extremism, which raises doubts about what gains might be made. It is not hard to understand indigenous people's frustration, which stems from the cruel discrimination they were subject to for such a long time. This is precisely why multicultural policies in Bolivia must be strengthened, and quickly, as they are the best defense against separation and radicalization. Racial mixing has not succeeded in bringing about integration, and assimilation theories are one step away from sweeping the problem under the carpet. Grandiose ideas like a cosmic race, racial democracy, and ethnic mixing have not helped indigenous or Afro populations in the fight against poverty, lack of education, exploitation, or inequality. When Evo Morales came to power in 2006, he said, "Indigenous peoples are a majority in Bolivia. Of the population 62.2 percent are Aymaras, Quechuas, Mojeños, Chipayas, mulattos, Guaraní, etc. Throughout history these peoples have been marginalized, humiliated, hated, despised, condemned to extinction. . . . Forty, fifty years ago we didn't have the right to go in the Plaza San Francisco, the Plaza Murillo; our ancestors didn't have the right to walk on the sidewalk." To grasp how great the change has been we only have to recall the terrible epithets Alcides Arguedas hurled almost exactly a hundred years ago: these indigenous "savages," "surly," "without feelings," and "lacking in aspirations or aesthetic sense."

CONCLUSIONS

There is serious debate in Bolivia about the problem of discrimination against the Aymara, the Quechua, and the dozens of other ethnic groups whose cultural roots go back to pre-Columbian civilization. These populations are organizing in a powerful movement built around defending their indigenous cultures and rights. Some factions in this great mobilization reject a multicultural integration strategy and are pursuing segregation and demanding their own new nation-state. This would be the first time a Latin American nation has broken apart since the United States separated Panama from Colombia by force in 1903. The vague notion of national fragmentation in Bolivia is beginning to look more likely to come true, however, because the white elites in the east are also making threatening noises about splitting off from the country.

It is no coincidence that in the past ten years the strategy of assimilation through mixed blood has been seriously challenged in both Brazil and Bolivia, in spite of their different social, historical, and demographic contexts. At the present time, multiculturalism (in Bolivia this concept is called interculturalism or the plurinational state) is becoming the main strategy to merge the different cultures in the country. In Bolivia this move toward multiculturalism had led some ethnic groups, which have suffered terrible discrimination, to reconstruct their own identities in opposition to the dominant Westernized white elites, and even in opposition to the democratic goal of mixing races and cultures. These new identities are based on various systems of symbols derived from ancient ethnic heroes such as Pachacutec, alternative religious beliefs such as Pachamama and pre-Columbian myths, territorial autonomy, music such as Andean rhythms, and physical appearance such as skin color and phenotype. These trends are bringing about profound changes in the national identity of Bolivia, a nation of nations, a country that is trying (with no route maps) to construct a new multicultural and multiethnic democracy. This scenario has been set out in the latest round of constitutional reforms, in which the pluriethnic and multinational nature of the country is recognized. This is a great step forward, and it should be followed by practical solutions to reduce the appalling poverty among the indigenous populations.

LESSONS LEARNED

- Bolivia is the first Latin American country to define itself as a plurinational state (rather than a nation-state) so as to integrate the diverse nations that live in the land but were previously not considered part of the Bolivian state.
- Bolivia is also the first Latin American country to elect an indigenous president.
- The indigenous movements in Bolivia have made good progress toward securing their cultural rights. The same is happening in other Latin American countries, in which indigenous movements (which are diverse and contradictory like all mass social movements) are emerging as important political actors.
- These changes have generated severe social and political tensions in countries where indigenous populations suffered harsh discrimination under the Spanish Empire and then under ruling elites in nation-states.

DISCUSSION QUESTIONS

- What does it mean to be indigenous in the twenty-first century in Bolivia and in Latin America?
- What rights are the indigenous populations in Bolivia demanding, and what rights are recognized in the new Constitution of 2009?

- Can a modern country be governed by indigenous people?
- How can traditional indigenous culture be made compatible with the organization of a modern state?

ADDITIONAL READING

The Economist. 2000. "Bolivia: Inca Nation." October 26.

Instituto Internacional para la Democracia y la Asistencia Electoral. 2010. *Miradas. Nuevo Texto Constitucional de Bolivia.* Bolivia, Vice presidencia del Estado Plurinacional de Bolivia, Universidad Mayor de San Andrés.

Sieder, Rachel (ed.). 2002. *Multiculturalism in Latin America: Indigenous Rights, Diversity and Democracy.* New York: Palgrave Macmillan.

Ströbele-Gregor, Juliana. 1996. "Culture and Political Practice of the Aymara and Quechua in Bolivia: Autonomous Forms of Modernity in the Andes." *Latin American Perspectives* 23 (2): 72–90. http://dx.doi.org/10.1177/0094582X9602300205.

Wade, Peter. 1997. *Race and Ethnicity in Latin America.* New York: Pluto Press.

WEBSITES

Confederation of Indigenous Peoples of Bolivia. http://www.cidob-bo.org.

International Work Group for Indigenous Affairs. http://www.iwgia.org/index.php.

Aymara Uta. Una lengua, una cultura y un pueblo. http: //www.aymara.org.

Fondo para el desarrollo de los Pueblos Indígenas de América Latina y el Caribe. http://www.fondoindigena.org/drupal/es/.

CHAPTER SIX

BRAZIL: WHERE WERE THE BLACKS?

INTRODUCTION

In Brazilian intellectual circles, with very few exceptions, there used to be a systematic refusal to acknowledge the fact that the country had a problem with discrimination against people of African descent or Indians. Quite the contrary in fact: the accepted view was that, unlike in the United States, in Brazil the different races that made up the bulk of the population—Portuguese, Afro-Brazilians, and Indians—were harmoniously integrated. Only in 1995, when Fernando Henrique Cardoso was president, was it publicly recognized that the country had a serious problem with racism. Since that sincere confession, which was supported by an abundance of empirical data showing the stark reality of the problem, Brazil has determinedly taken the path of affirmative action. In this chapter we will analyze this radical change from the long-lived conception of the country as a racial democracy to the Statute of Racial Equality, which is a law that questions the previous version of history and officially establishes affirmative policies to combat racism. This legislation was passed in the Senate, and its proposals and content were somewhat watered down before it was finally enacted by the *Diputados* (Representatives), but what really matters is that it still contains instruments for the promotion of multiculturalism and thus the pursuit of greater racial equity and better intercultural relations.

Our discussion includes an analysis of how the myth of Brazilian racial democracy was constructed, an examination of how the Afro-Brazilian movement developed and then grew powerful enough to challenge the vision of racial harmony that was so dominant in the twentieth century, and lastly an overview of Brazil's most recent laws to improve opportunities for people of African descent.

6.1. THE MYTH OF RACIAL DEMOCRACY[29]

At the start of the book *Casa grande y senzala*, Gilberto Freyre writes:

> When the civil and economic aspects of Brazilian society were organized in 1532, the Portuguese had already had a whole century of contact with the tropics; in India and in Africa they had already demonstrated their aptitude for tropical life. There was a change in the nature of their colonization in San Vicente and Pernambuco when their easy mercantile approach was largely replaced by agriculture, and their colonial society was organized on more solid foundations and under more stable conditions than in India or at their factories in Africa, and here the Portuguese gave definitive proof of this aptitude. (1989, 4)

So the Portuguese were not making a mistake when they began a process of definitive colonization. On the contrary, they were one of the European peoples best suited to handle the problems of a tropical climate, and this is very important because, as Freyre points out, the Anglo-Saxons had failed in their attempts to establish themselves in the tropics. One of the main Portuguese colonization strategies was miscegenation, a mixing of races both with the indigenous Indians and with the African slaves, and this was no error either. One of the most important arguments of *Casa grande y senzala* is the idea that mixing races does not produce inferior individuals or regressive hybrids.

Before Freyre, there were two main opposing views in Brazil about the racial mix of Portuguese with Indians and people of African descent. One was that the population had to be whitened by the slow predomination of the white Aryan race, which was superior and would eventually impose itself on the other inhabitants. As the Indian and the Afro populations were thought to lack the capacity to develop the country into a modern Western state, this supposition that the white race would prevail pointed the way forward, and within one or two centuries at most Brazil would be white and civilized. The opposing view was more realistic, but equally racist and even more pessimistic: the notion that Brazil had no future because the mixing of races created hybrid individuals who were inevitably doomed to extinction. Freyre was against both theories, and in response he created the modern conception of Brazil, namely that it must be seen as a mixed-race country; he stressed that this is not prejudicial but rather—when the physical and social environment is not too hostile—yields positive results that should be valued.

6.2. THE DECONSTRUCTION OF THE MYTH

Is Brazil really a racial democracy? Has its ethnic integration been successful? Is the economic performance of people of African descent and mulattos worse than that of

---

29   Material in this section is taken from Arocena's book *Muerte y Resurrección de Facundo Qurioga* (1996).

whites? And, if it is, is this a matter of socioeconomic class or is it the result of racial discrimination?[30] The great revolution in ideas that Freyre started made a virtue out of something that was perceived as a problem. He thought it was precisely this mixing of races that gave Brazil its great potential and unique cultural identity. The mixture of indigenous, Afro-Brazilian, and Portuguese races and cultures provided the foundations on which modernization and the nation's future would be built.

It was relatively easy to maintain this view when there was almost no cultural input from an Indian or Afro-Brazilian perspective, but today the situation is changing, and these communities are organized and building their own cultural identities, which mostly do not coincide with the idea of a nation that Freyre so successfully elevated to a dominant position. One very significant sign of this change in national consciousness is that Afro organizations have selected as their ethnic symbol a man named Zumbi, who lived over 300 years ago (1655–95). Zumbi was the recognized leader of Palmares, the biggest of the *quilombos*, the communities of escaped slaves who lived apart and resisted white domination. The Afro-Brazilian movements' national holiday is the anniversary of Zumbi's death, November 20, a date that has also become Black Consciousness Day. In fact, these movements identify more with this date than with May 13, which was the day in 1888 when slavery was abolished and is now the official day against racism. Another important sign of a change in national consciousness is the way in which some heroes of Brazilian history, such as the Duke of Caxias (1803–80), are now heavily criticized for their negative attitude toward people of African descent.

For decades, it was widely believed that the reason why blacks achieved so little had nothing to do with their color; it was because they were mostly poor. But a series of studies have shown that blacks' deepening poverty and society's increased discrimination are more related to variables of race and ethnic characteristics than to socioeconomic class. Afro-Brazilian communities are now building their defenses on racial and ethnic foundations. As one of the movement's most respected leaders, Abdias do Nascimento (1914–2011), explained, "Of course anything that goes against the status quo is running a risk. But blacks are running a risk from the moment they are born. They aren't afraid of the epithet 'black racist' because the result of intimidation is docility. Our historical experience teaches us that anti-racist racism is the only way that we can eliminate race differences" (do Nascimento 1968). This was written 80 years after slavery was abolished in Brazil in 1888. Do Nascimento was very aware of the civil rights movements in the United States at that time, but people did not listen to him because most Brazilian intellectuals thought there was no problem of racism in the country. For this very reason he was accused of importing segregation problems and Jim Crow laws from the United States, where the situation was completely different. At the time of the dictatorship, do Nascimento had to go into exile because he opposed the authoritarian regime, and it was not until quite recently that he became a crucial voice to be able to better understand race and ethnicity in the country. His ideas have been revived and vindicated in

---

30 In the following sections we have used parts of an article by Arocena and Elfstrom (2008), and material from Arocena (2008) and Arocena (2012).

several black-pride movements, such as Olodum in Bahía, Rio Negro, and the Black Brazilian Women's Group.

As we shall see below, there has never been a single unified Afro-Brazilian social movement. In the 1970s, in fact, there were 600 institutions that included the fight against racism in the causes they pursued. There were religious, sporting, music, and cultural organizations, as well as grassroots associations. In 1978, the Unified Black Movement was founded with the aim of gathering these uncoordinated forces together and providing the Afro-Brazilians with a political voice (UNDP Brazil 2005). This attempt to unify the various movements failed, but its effect in the country was widespread and it stimulated the disparate efforts with renewed energy. More recently other institutions have appeared, such as the National Alliance of Black Groups (ENEN), founded in São Paulo in 1991, the National Coordination of Black Groups (CONEN), and the National Coordination of Quilombola Communities (CONAQ). More recently there was a mobilization in connection with the World Conference against Racism that was held in Durban, South Africa, in 2001. While Brazil was preparing to take part in the conference, racism was hotly debated, and this was echoed in the public arena at the First National Conference against Racism and Intolerance in Rio de Janeiro. Moreover, after Durban, the government set up a National Council to Fight Discrimination. These movements and institutions raised new awareness about racial problems, and they were supported by concrete information that laid bare the truth about racism in Brazil.

The question about racial identity was removed from the 1970 national census, and even though it was included again in the 1980 census, the findings were not made public until two years later for fear of damaging the idea that the country was ethnically harmonious. In fact, the results showed that average earnings among Afro-Brazilians were only 35 per cent of a white person's income and that mulattos earned only 45 per cent as much as whites (Skidmore 1992). Recent data have confirmed this inequality in various ways. Only 4 per cent of Afro-Brazilians go to university, compared with 14 per cent of whites. The University of São Paulo is one of the most prestigious educational institutions in the country, but in 1994, out of a total of 50,000 students, only 2 per cent were of African descent. In the 2001 Human Development Index, Brazil ranked 65th out of 175 countries, but the real situation was very different. If whites and Afro-Brazilians had been considered separately, the white Brazilians would have ranked 46th in the world but the Afro population would have been in 107th place (Paixão 2003). This same study showed that average income among whites was 2.64 times the minimum wage but that people of African descent earned a mere 1.15 times the minimum. Life expectancy among whites was 72 years but among Afro-Brazilians only 66 years. The literacy rate among people over 15 years old was 92 per cent for white Brazilians but only 82 per cent for Afro-Brazilians. According to data from the Health Ministry's Information System on Mortality and the Brazilian Institute of Geography and Statistics (IBGE), the homicide rate among white men aged 20 to 24 is 102.3 per 100,000 inhabitants, but among young Afro-Brazilians it is 218.5 (UNDP Brazil 2005).

The myth of racial democracy in Brazil, which was fomented by Freyre's writings and supported by the fact that racial segregation is not institutionalized and was partly based on the mixture of blood through inter-ethnic sexual relations, was rejected in 1950 by the sociologist Florestán Fernández and some militant Afro-Brazilians. They recognized there was some truth in what Freyre said, but they claimed that Brazil had a strong informal system of discrimination against people of African descent and indigenous populations. However, these rumblings against the myth of a racial democracy were suppressed by the military dictatorships that ruled the country from 1964 to 1985.

Once democracy was restored, discussion of the myth re-emerged in the public arena. The Constitution was reformed in 1988, and in the new version cultural and ethnic diversity was acknowledged for the first time, and the government committed itself to protecting the various cultures and incorporating them into the nation's identity. This new Constitution contained two unprecedented measures: racism was classed as a non-bailable offense, and affirmative action policies were established. These policies included providing special scholarships for indigenous people and Afro-Brazilians to enable them to prepare for competitions for state jobs, setting quotas for jobs in the public sector and at universities, and providing financial assistance to help people study for entrance exams at public universities. Some states, Bahía for example, went as far as to introduce quotas in the advertising industry, something that is very important because Afro-Brazilians are severely underrepresented in the media. A study showed that in 59 hours of peak-time broadcasting on 3 of the main TV channels, only 39 people of African descent appeared in advertisements, they spoke in only 9 of these advertisements, and featured in a central role in only 4 (UNDP Brazil 2005).

The census organized by the IBGE in 2000 featured a question about self-definition by skin color and gave four options: white, mulatto, black, and other. It turned out that 54 per cent of Brazilians defined themselves as white, 39 per cent as mulatto, 6 per cent as black, and only 1 per cent as "other." These findings are absurd because, according to these percentages, Uruguay, one of the Latin American countries that had fewest slaves and the highest proportion of immigrants from Europe, would have a greater percentage of people of African descent than Brazil, the country that had the most African slaves. The latest official data in Uruguay from the 2011 census show that eight per cent of the people in that country are of African descent, which is three percentage points higher than the official census figure for Brazil at that time. Where are the blacks in Brazil? The answer is only too obvious: they have been made invisible and negated in the cultural history of their own country.

The findings of the Brazilian census of 2000 are extremely interesting for several reasons. First, they clearly show that even in the twenty-first century most of the population feel that being of African descent is a problem. It is not true that only six per cent of the population is in this category; the real percentage is much higher, but people do not want to be perceived as black. This is probably due to the general perception that being white means being located toward the upper end of the socio-economic scale. Many of the mulattoes would be considered black in other countries, just as many of the whites would be seen as mulattoes. But because these findings were based on self-definition by skin color, the key dimension is precisely how people see themselves in terms of ethnicity. One of the Afro-Brazilian movement's main aims is to

Figure 6.1: Skin Color in Brazil, 2000 and 2010

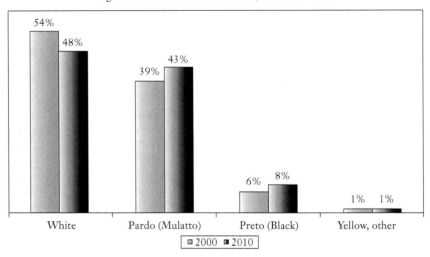

Source: Brazilian Census.

create a consciousness whereby people of African descent stop being ashamed to define themselves as such, and this has reached the point where there are now t-shirts with the slogan "100 percent negro." In the 2010 census a new term, "Afro-Brazilian," was used for the black and mulatto categories combined, and it turned out that this group outnumbered the whites. Therefore, for the first time in its history, Brazil officially confirmed that it has more people of African descent than whites. This might not seem terribly important, but it will have far-reaching repercussions for how the country sees itself, because it is clearly not a white-majority country. The long-cherished idea that the population would gradually become whiter can no longer be maintained because, with the emergence and greater visibility of the population of African descent, it is clear that exactly the opposite has happened.

Brazil has the biggest population of African descent outside Africa, and it was the last Western country to abolish slavery (in 1888). These two factors alone suggest that the question of racism and discrimination against Afro-Brazilians is crucial (Roberge 2006). There has been a sudden wave of lawsuits involving the system of race quotas, and Brazil has been profoundly shaken by a debate about race that had been ignored for decades (da Silva Martins, Medeiros & Nascimento 2004). The general view in Brazilian society is that the country is a racial democracy (Lloyd 2004a), but this is highly ironic given the obvious contradiction between affirmative action and legal wrangles over race on the one hand, and the old rhetoric about racial harmony on the other (da Silva Martins, Medeiros & Nascimento 2004). Can it be that Brazil has finally come full circle and is now, as Skidmore (2003) suggests, resorting to the very measures that were once considered inappropriate in a racial democracy?

The main inspiration for the ideology of a racial democracy was provided by Gilberto Freyre in his master work *Casa Grande y Senzala*, and after that the concept became the basis for a self-proclaimed Brazilian heritage in which racial conflict had ostensibly been resolved. From this perspective, the country was educating its population in the processes of mestization and cultural assimilation. Both processes were expected to have very positive results and to show that different populations and cultures had been assimilated. One implication of this ideological stance was that "color doesn't matter," because these processes had eliminated racial differences (Skidmore 1992). The Brazilians decided there was no racism in their country because there was no racial hatred or formal segregation as there was in the United States, and this meant that a new Brazilian identity, one that was uniform and of mixed blood, would emerge. Because of this lack of interest in the race problem, the government did not even think it important to include questions of ethnic origin in censuses until the 1980s. Even when the Afro-Brazilian movement gained strength in the 1990s and managed to draw attention to "the race question," their demands were angrily rejected and they themselves were labeled racists (da Silva Martins, Medeiros & Nascimento 2004). When we consider that the self-image of racial harmony "has been at the center of the country's identity[,] . . . if the proponents of a new racial policy gain ascendancy this whole idea may change" (*The Economist*, 2006).

Those who still uphold the notion of racial democracy claim that affirmative action is not feasible because the population is so completely mixed that nobody can know for sure who is an Afro-Brazilian and who is not. If the criterion of "one single drop" is adopted, as it is in the United States (i.e., a person with even one single drop of African blood in his or her veins is classed as being of African descent), then affirmative action would make no sense. It would mean almost the whole population would be classified as Afro-Brazilian, since the overwhelming majority could claim some Afro-Brazilian ancestry if this was to their advantage (da Silva Martins, Medeiros & Nascimento 2004). Against this argument, Senator Paulo Paim—one of the most active supporters of affirmative action and a major force in promoting the Racial Equality Statute—commented, "This is the first excuse they come up with. When we talk about the problematic side of society they easily identify the blacks, but when we come to the matter of giving them compensation nobody knows who is really black!" (Htun 2005a, 1). Those who defend affirmative action claim there is a simple criterion: people who define themselves as Afro-Brazilian should be considered as such. But this has its problems, because studies have found there are as many as 143 popular terms that Brazilians use to define themselves by skin color, and it is not easy to say exactly what makes someone *pardo* (mulatto) or defines them as black (Lloyd 2004b).

José Luis Petrucelli, a statistics specialist in Brazil, has analyzed how races are classified in censuses and national surveys in the country. The first public statistical survey in Brazil that inquired into color or race was in 1872, and the categories it used were "white," "black," "*pardo*" (which was replaced by "mestizo" in 1890), and "*caboclo*" (i.e., a mix between Indigenous and European). In 1940 the category "yellow" was added, and only in 1991 did "indigenous" appear. But when interviewees were asked to state their color or race in an open way with no pre-set categories, as was the case in 1976 and 1998, the numbers of different terms used were 136 and 143, respectively. This sparked widespread debate. Many people argued it was not possible to know for certain who is black and who is not, and so it was impossible to decide who should benefit from affirmative action. But, in fact, of the 143 different terms used in 1998 more than half appeared once only, 10 per cent referred to regions in the country, and almost 15 per cent are different ways of calling oneself "white." Some 97 per cent of the answers fell into just seven categories, and some of these are regional synonyms such as "*morena*" for a mixed-race (mulatto) person in Recife, and "*pardo*" for the same color in the south.

It is surprising that the notion of racial democracy had such an impact and has been so persistent. On the whole, Brazilians are proud that there is no racism in their society, and they rarely perceive the close connection between racial divisions and the enormous gap between the wealthy and the poor. We should remember that Brazil has one of the highest inequality ratings in the world, and although this lamentable situation has improved considerably in the past ten years, it still ranks among the most unequal. The data are so conclusive that "[t]here can be no doubt that color is highly correlated with social stratification in Brazil. No sensible Brazilian would have denied this in 1900 and no sensible Brazilian would deny it today. The question is why" (Skidmore 1992, 9). It is true that defining who should benefit from affirmative action programs is problematic, and the reason is that in spite of irrefutable statistical evidence of inequality, in daily life the Afro-Brazilian identity is still masked behind the supposedly cordial relations between races. People who criticize the current state of race relations in the country just say that racism is everywhere and it will not disappear unless something specific is done to tackle the problem. However, the statistical information clearly establishing the connection between race and poverty only began to reach the general public quite recently, and society is still confused and uncertain as to how it should handle this new reality. As Skidmore (1992) asks, can the white Brazilians possibly accept data that so crudely expose discrimination and support compensatory action?

Afro-Brazilians make up approximately half the population, but are they organizing themselves to press for new laws? Recent action against racial discrimination in Brazil has been largely modeled on United States legislation, and at one end of the scale we find a former Brazilian ambassador to the United States, Juracy Magalhães, maintaining that "[w]hat is good for the United States is good for Brazil" (*Veja* 2006). *Veja*, one of the most important magazines in Brazil, also commented, "In a country that was always dazzled by American inventions like blue jeans, Coca-Cola and Disney, it was inevitable that affirmative action initiatives would be adopted" (*Wall Street Journal* 1996). The histories of both countries are stained with racism and slavery, and the will to confront past—and present—discrimination has only just emerged in Brazil and has done so in a very heterogeneous way (Toni 2004). If we briefly compare three countries with racial histories that have certain points in common—the United States, South Africa, and Brazil—we can see that Brazil is probably the one where the ceiling of equality is most difficult to reach. This is because the race question emerged into public consciousness only very recently after many years of denial, and the population of African descent is not sufficiently mobilized (Ikenberry 2002). Academics often make direct comparisons between the United States and Brazil, but things are not that simple because obviously many aspects of the two countries—social, cultural, ideological, and economic—are drastically different. The mistaken parallels between United States scenarios and Brazil that are employed to either support or oppose the need for affirmative action seem to be complicating rather than helping the debate about race and public policies.

There is no denying that the U.S. experience has been instructive, because Supreme Court decisions in that country can help us understand how affirmative action programs have been designed (Toni 2004). However, the U.S. is not at all like South America, and one difference is that the early colonists in North America brought their families with them and did not mix sexually with the indigenous population or the slaves, at least not in high numbers. Furthermore, Brazil never had anything like the terrible Jim Crow laws that gave racism a legal basis, so U.S. elites have far more of a sense of guilt than do their Brazilian counterparts. When it comes to developing affirmative action, therefore, Brazil needs to look within and design programs in accordance with its own situation.

There are two areas in which the Afro-Brazilians have achieved great success and are widely accepted: music and sport. But there are also important examples of positive change in other fields, as when Joaquim Benedito Barbosa Gomes became the first person of African descent in the country's history to join the Supreme Court. Before he was appointed by President Lula da Silva, Barbosa Gomes was asked about his chances of getting the post, replying, "I'll never make it; it's impossible for someone black." Another outstanding example of individual achievement is Beneditta da Silva, who was born in a *favela* (shanty town) in Rio de Janeiro. In 1986 she was elected to the House of Representatives, in 1994 she became the first woman senator, and later she became Governor of Rio de Janeiro and Minister of Social Action in the Lula government. There was also Gilberto Gil, an Afro-Brazilian from the northern state of Bahía, who came to fame as a singer and was later appointed Minister of Culture by Lula. Although the majority of the population is Afro-Brazilian or mulatto, the country has still not had a president from this sector of the population. Sooner or later this will probably change, as it did recently in Bolivia, where for the first time an indigenous president was elected in a country where a solid majority of the voters are Indians (see Chapter 5).

We shall now turn our attention to the indigenous population in Brazil. The original peoples living within the borders of the country were systematically driven from their lands and almost exterminated, and only a few still survive. Today they are divided into small tribes and amount to less than one per cent of the total population. In numbers and in history they are very different from the Afro-Brazilians, but their situation today is similar with respect to cultural survival. Many of the indigenous tribes do not identify with modern Brazil or with the mixing of races but rather with their own people, myths, and historical epics. In April 2004, in a remote part of the Amazon jungle in the state of Rondonia bordering on Bolivia, members of the Cinta Larga (Broad Belt) tribe killed 29 diamond miners. This occurred in an area that had been declared a reservation for this indigenous population by the FUNAI (the public institution in charge of protecting indigenous people's rights). The Cinta Larga claimed they had killed the miners in self-defense and in accordance with their ancestral customs. Thus the state was trapped in the dilemma of trying to enforce the law without violating indigenous people's rights to autonomy and cultural diversity. These particular tribes had their first contact with white civilization in 1960; most of them still live from hunting and fishing, and although they speak Portuguese and wear Western clothes, their living conditions are very rudimentary.

Most of the Indians in Brazil live on reservations, where the state allows them to run their own economic affairs but holds the rights to sub-soil resources. Parts of these lands are extremely rich in minerals and have to be defended from illegal mining. Besides, in some places these lands are threatened by development projects to establish agriculture and build infrastructure. This is the problem today in a reservation in Roraima, a northern state on the border with Venezuela. The Lula government adopted a policy of "disoccupation," which has meant displacing non-indigenous people from several towns and relocating large-scale rice plantations to other areas. This policy is opposed by the non-Indian people involved, who claim it is not a viable way to defend the small tribes in Roraima or to protect the Amazon jungle. The big agriculture enterprises argue that development is being impeded, and the state authorities are worried because they fear they might end up governing a weak state with a small population and most of the land controlled by autonomous indigenous tribes. In 2004, members of the Raposa-Serra Do Sol Indian community, which had been occupied by gold miners (*garimpeiros*) and agriculture enterprises for decades, blocked the roads and all access to their lands and appeared on TV wearing typical Indian costume and with their bodies painted in the traditional way.

It has to be said that the Brazilian government has made a huge effort to protect the indigenous peoples. They make up only 0.4 per cent of the population, but the FUNAI has set aside 13 per cent of the nation's land for their reservations. The reason for this disproportionate allocation is that the Indian tribes still live by hunting, fishing, and a little agriculture, and they need vast swathes of forest so that they can move from one region to another when these resources begin to run low. But 10 per cent of the surface area of a country as vast as Brazil is an awful lot of land, and so this policy is bitterly criticized by those who argue that the nation cannot afford the luxury of maintaining such a huge area outside the productive development process. Defenders of the policy reply that this land belongs to the indigenous people; they maintain it as a nature reserve and without it they would die out.

The indigenous and Afro-Brazilian populations are both basing the defense of their identities on multicultural strategies. In other words, they are pushing to promote the coexistence of cultures and claiming that all must be treated equally but have their independence and differences recognized. This is very different from the idea of mestization, which has held sway in Brazil for decades and became its trademark as a nation. Ethnic conflict in the country has not yet reached the stage of massive political violence, but confrontations have been many and frequent and may go on. The challenge facing Brazil today is how to change into a genuine racial democracy in which cultural diversity is respected while national unity is maintained.

6.3. THE PATH TOWARD AFFIRMATIVE POLICIES IN BRAZIL

Unlike the United States, Brazil has never had a strong social movement fighting for civil rights. The fact that there has not been a united front against racial discrimination is partly a consequence of the long period of dictatorship from 1964 to 1985 in which all forms of social protest were suppressed. And even when opposition managed to rear its head, the political movements did not include the race question on their agendas because all their energies were focused on securing a return to democracy. They wanted to be united against the dictatorship, and they felt that demands for racial equality were a bothersome detail that would sap their strength. But in spite of all the resistance against even admitting there was a race problem, the time to act finally came at the end of the twentieth century.

We shall now focus on part of the difficult path that Afro-Brazilian organizations have trodden in their efforts to mobilize against racial discrimination, and on the progress they have made in their demands. In this overview we have used information provided by da Silva Martins, Medeiros, and Nascimento (2004) and Medeiros (2004) to assist with the construction of the timeline that follows.

1931	The Brazilian Black Front was founded. It was censured and banned by the dictatorship in 1937.
1941	Abdias do Nascimento, one of the main Afro-Brazilian leaders, founded the Black Experimental Theater (TEN). His aim was to fight racial discrimination in general and particularly in the world of theater, by reconstructing the African cultural heritage and promoting the country's Afro-Brazilian identity.
1945–46	After the fall of the dictatorship, an offshoot of the TEN called the Afro-Brazilian Democratic Committee was set up, and Afro-Brazilian national conventions were organized in São Paulo (1945) and Rio de Janeiro (1946). These meetings bore fruit in the "Manifesto of the Brazilian Nation," which contained six demands, including subsidies for Afro-Brazilian students who entered public or private secondary schools or universities.
1950	The TEN organized the First Black Brazilian Congress in Rio de Janeiro to discuss the problems Afro-Brazilians faced, their backwardness in education, the protection of their rights, and the defense of the black identity.
1964	The dictatorship violently repressed any discussion of racism, and do Nascimento had to go into exile, but he continued to preach from Africa.
1968	The dictatorship issued a decree banning the public discussion of racism.
1978	The few activists left in the Afro-Brazilian movement met at the São Paulo Municipal Theater, in defiance of the military, and founded the Unified Black Movement (MNU).

1982	It was decided that the Third Latin American Black Culture Congress would be held in São Paulo, and this was a milestone in the international history of the consciousness of the African diaspora. The Marxist wing was severely criticized for maintaining that racial discrimination in Latin America was a class problem and not specifically a race problem. This congress gave rise to a package of demands geared to promoting public policies to directly combat racial discrimination.
	Abdias do Nascimento managed to get elected as a federal representative in the first direct legislative elections under the military dictatorship. He submitted a bill, number 1.332/83, to establish compensatory measures for Afro-Brazilians to promote equal opportunities. This scheme was based on subsidies and incentives for private firms that adopted initiatives to promote diversity. It stipulated that 40 per cent of all scholarships and subsidies at the prestigious Baron de Rio Branco Institute of Diplomacy would be awarded to Afro-Brazilians, and that all teaching institutions had to put the history of Africa and of people of African descent on the curriculum. Congress never voted on the bill, and it was criticized for promoting and inciting racism instead of fighting it. However, 20 years later many of its provisions became law.
1984	The Olodum Cultural Group was founded in the city of Salvador, Bahía. This group first emerged in 1979 as a carnival act and subsequently evolved into a key institution in the Afro-Brazilian movement with its cultural and social work promoting the cause, and it reached the international stage through its samba-reggae.
1986	The National Committee to Combat Racism emerged from the ranks of the Methodist Church, providing a big boost to raising awareness about the racial inequality problem.
1988	For the first time, some of the Afro-Brazilian movement's demands were included in the Constitution: racism was classed as a non-bailable crime; the *quilombos* that still existed had their lands officially registered, Brazil was redefined as a "multicultural nation," and Afro-Brazilian demonstrations were guaranteed protection.
1988–89	November 20 was designated "National Black Consciousness Day" to commemorate the death of Zumbi, the leader of the Palmares *quilombo* and the Afro-Brazilians' greatest historical hero. The previous official day, May 13, which marked the anniversary of the abolition of slavery, now became merely a day for reflection about how the "freedom" that came with the abolition had turned out to be an illusion.

1991	The Rio de Janeiro state government set up the Extraordinary Secretariat for the Defense and Promotion of Afro-Brazilian Populations (SEAFRO), the first institution to adopt specific public policies to defend Afro-Brazilians.
	The National Meeting of Black Organizations took place in São Paulo. Its goal was to unify and coordinate all the separate efforts, but it fell short of success.
1993	In a review of the five years for which the new Constitution had been in force, Senator Florestán Fernández proposed an amendment that included a complete chapter devoted to compensation for racial discrimination, and advanced the principle of affirmative action for the first time. Congress did not pass the amendment, but it was still a key step toward discussion of the subject.
1994	SEAFRO was closed down by the legislature after accusations of inverse racism.
1995	An official report by the delegates of the United Nations Human Rights Committee stated that although there was no official racism in the country, "it is necessary to adopt research measures and policies to break the vicious circle of discrimination, and the denial that inequality is racial in nature." These conclusions directly contradicted the complacent perception that Brazil was a racial democracy.
	Thirty thousand people took part in a demonstration in Brasilia to present a "Program to Overcome Racism and Racial Inequality," which became a synthesis of the Afro-Brazilian movement's demands for affirmative policies.
	Senator Beneditta da Silva introduced Constitutional Amendment 14/95, which established a quota of 10 per cent for indigenous people and Afro-Brazilians in higher education, but it never came to a vote.
1995	On November 20, President Fernando Henrique Cardoso issued a decree to set up the Inter-Ministerial Working Group for Valuation of the Black Population (GTI). In this unprecedented measure, the Brazilian state for the first time officially recognized that racism existed and proposed to fight it with public policies. The GTI promoted a series of national seminars to discuss affirmative action policies, and in an international forum 46 policies against racial discrimination were formulated.
	Senator Paulo Paim introduced bill number 1.239/95, which refers to "the moral and material debt the Brazilian State owes the Afro-Brazilian population due to the slavery regime and the lack of integration measures after it was abolished."

1996	The National Coordination of Quilombolo Communities (CONAQ) was founded in the state of Bahía on the initiative of members of old *quilombos*, who demanded communal ownership of the lands they inhabited.
	The tenth United Nations Human Rights Report was published in Brazil. It contained a recommendation that the state should implement positive action to promote equality and public policies to help the Afro-Brazilian population gain access to tertiary education.
2000	Reports containing conclusive data that racial inequality persisted in the country were published by the Institute of Applied Economic Surveys. These had enormous repercussions in the press and in public opinion, and the evidence was so overwhelming that the state could no longer remain deaf to discussions of the race question.
2001	The World Conference on Racism took place in Durban, South Africa. It had a big impact in Brazil, and its results served to catalyze affirmative action policies.
	No fewer than 14 different bills establishing various kinds of quotas in federal institutions were introduced in Congress. Acting independently, the state of Rio de Janeiro adopted a quota of 40 per cent for Afro-Brazilian at the state universities. The states of Bahía and Minas Gerais adopted the same policy.
2002	The new president, Luis Ignacio "Lula" da Silva, appointed Joaquim Barbosa to the Supreme Court. He was the first Afro-Brazilian in history to occupy this post. When he heard the news, Barbosa said publicly he had thought no person of African descent would ever ascend to such a position. Lula also appointed four Afro-Brazilians to posts in his new cabinet and set up a Ministry for Racial Equality.
2003	The new Special Secretariat for Policies to Promote Racial Equality (SEPPIR) was set up in the realm of the Ministry for Racial Equality. Its most important task was to carry out studies into how racial equality in education could be secured. The results were published as the "National Policy for the Promotion of Racial Equality." The study vehemently emphasized the need to implement affirmative action.
	In the courts there was a series of appeals against the quota laws, and this provoked a massive campaign in favor of the quotas. Several heavyweight institutions took part in this mobilization, and organizations in the Afro-Brazilian movement took action against the appeals as *amicus curiae* (persons outside the litigation process who provide the judge with information they consider relevant)

and submitted sociological and political material supporting the principles of affirmative action.

2004   In September, President Lula, frustrated with the prolonged debates about the quota proposals in Congress, issued a decree compelling private universities that enjoyed tax exemption to reserve a percentage of their places for students of African descent.

2008   The Representatives passed a racial quotas bill (number 73/99), which was originally submitted by Senator Tarso Genro. This stipulated that all public tertiary-education institutions had to allocate half their places to students from public education, and this 50 per cent had to be distributed in accordance with the relative weights of the racial populations in the state where the institution was located. This measure is not yet a federal law, but many universities have already implemented these quotas in their admissions structure.

2010   In 2005 the Senate had unanimously passed the Racial Equality Statute, a 35-page bill introduced by Senator Paulo Paim of the official party. This document proposed affirmative action at all levels in public institutions. This legislation, with many limiting changes, was finally passed by the Representatives in 2009 and came into force as law in 2010.

Figure 6.2: President Dilma Rousseff and Supreme Court President Joaquim Barbosa.

This timeline—which is inevitably incomplete—indicates the main events that eventually led to a total transformation of the race question in Brazil. The Afro-Brazilian movement rarely managed to mobilize large numbers of people, but in the long run it was very successful in raising awareness about racial problems by employing solid arguments based on conclusive empirical data, and this has been a key factor behind legislative progress in recent years. In this book we consider the Afro-Brazilian movement as an umbrella term for all the organizations—cultural, religious, economic, and political—whose aim is to defend and promote the Afro-Brazilian population's rights (UNDP, 2005). Some of these institutions have a higher profile and greater impact than others, and as a movement they are not very efficiently coordinated, but they have managed to make the general population aware of racial discrimination in the country, and, equally important, they have succeeded in getting concrete affirmative action policies passed into law.

6.4. A RADICAL LAW

As the timeline above shows, the bill for the Equal Rights Statute was first introduced in Congress by Senator Paulo Paim of the Workers Party in 1998. Seven years later, in 2005, it passed unanimously in the Senate, in 2009 it passed in the Chamber of Representatives (albeit in very diluted form), and 12 years after the process began it finally came into force as law in 2010. In recent years the race question has been discussed intensely in Brazil, with a huge number of articles in the major newspapers, numerous academic studies, and public figures and celebrities taking one side or the other in the public opinion debate. What is interesting is that there is nearly as much support for the initiative as against it, and highly qualified people have lined up on both sides. It is no surprise that this new legislation should have caused such a stir, because the 85 articles in the original bill outline a profile of society radically different from the vision that prevailed throughout the history of Brazil, which is the youngest republic in South America. One of the most far-reaching changes is that the official definition of the population now includes the new category of "Afro-Brazilian," which comprises "persons who classify themselves as such or as Negroes, blacks, *pardos* (mulattos) or some analogous definition" (Art. 2, III). This new classification combines two categories that were separate in the censuses—mulattos and blacks—and by this definition Afro-Brazilians now amount to 51 per cent of the population. Many of these people defined themselves as mulattos (*pardos*) because of the negative associations of being black and because of the allure of the idea of whitening—reducing the black proportion in the population—that was held so dear in Brazil's history. Besides this redefinition of the Afro-Brazilian population, the law also establishes measures to fight racial discrimination, which is defined as "all distinction, exclusion, restriction or preference based on race, color, descent or national or ethnic origin . . ." (Art. 2, I). Discrimination underlies racial inequality, which is defined as "all situations of differentiated access to the enjoyment of goods, services and opportunities in the public or private sphere" (Art. 2, II). It is clear that this new image of Brazil, with half the population Afro-Brazilian and with racism acknowledged, is completely different from what many Brazilians previously believed.

This new vision of the country is reflected in a recent book by Ali Kamel entitled *Nao somos racistas* (We Are Not Racists): "When we wake up we are frightened. Or at least I was frightened and I suppose many other people were frightened too. So we are a racist people, are we? . . . A nation of whites and blacks in which the whites are oppressing the blacks. Another shock: that country is not my country" (Kamel 2006, quoted in *Veja* online, Aug. 16, 2006). Kamel cannot believe in the image created by the Afro-Brazilian movement and by sociologists such as Florestán Fernández and Fernando Henrique Cardoso, an image that is very different from his own image of the country. Kamel criticizes the use of the category "Afro-Brazilian" in the redefinition of race because it divides most of the population into two large groups as in the United States, whereas in fact the Brazilian context is very different, thanks to its exuberant mixing of races. He also criticizes the new Statute and claims it is simply wrong to say that Brazilian society is racist. No wonder Kamel was shocked, because the bill threatens to overturn one of the country's great myths: that of Brazilian racial harmony, white coffee, a mulatto country, a happy welcoming country, the country as seen by Gilberto Freyre. But once Brazil perceives itself in this new way, new instruments will have to be used in order to better understand it and to tackle its new old problems.

The version of the Statute that passed in the Senate contains ten long chapters about the Afro-Brazilian population: I) rights to health services, II) rights to education, III) freedom of belief and religious cults, IV) financing for racial equality initiatives, V) the rights of Afro-Brazilian women, VI) land ownership in the *quilombos*, VII) the job market, VIII) quota systems, IX) the media, and X) specific bodies to investigate reports of discrimination. These ten chapter themes give an idea of how wide-ranging the new law is.

We will briefly examine two concrete measures in the text of the original bill that stand out, not because they are more important than the others, but because they reflect how important this proposed legislation is for understanding Brazilian society. In the first chapter, about rights to health care, it is laid down that all health institutions shall be required to apply the race classification when compiling information about their users. At first sight this might seem odd, but it is vital because there are some illnesses that affect mainly people of African descent, such as sickle cell anemia, which is transmitted genetically and can be detected if the right analyses are incorporated into standard clinical practice. Up to now these tests have never been done, simply because the people prone to medical conditions such as these did not have a voice in society. Another measure worth highlighting is that television channels would have to have at least 20 per cent of the prominent roles in their advertisements and films played by Afro-Brazilians. The logic of this is very simple: in the Brazilian racial democracy this group is not shown in the media, and the overwhelming majority of actors and featured personalities are white. However, in the end neither of these two measures was included in the legislation that was passed into law.

Still, the final version of the Statute does state that all unjustified differences in access or opportunities that are based on race, ethnic descent, or national origin constitute racial inequality. Moreover, it explicitly defines racial discrimination as any distinction, exclusion, restriction, or preference based on race, ethnic decent, or national origin. The law goes on to stipulate that primary- and secondary-level schools must teach African history and the history of the population of African descent in Brazil. It also requires the government to implement programs to ensure that some middle- and higher-level positions in federal institutions are reserved for Afro-Brazilians, but does not specify quotas for this. In the area of jobs, the law proposes tax incentives for businesses with more than 20 employees that have a workforce containing at least 20 per cent Afro-Brazilians. It provides incentives for rural productive enterprises to employ people of African descent. It prohibits employers from requiring job applicants to have a good appearance or to have to attach a photo to their CV. In the sphere of sport, it recognizes capoeira[31] as a sport and makes it incumbent on the government to allocate funds to develop it. In terms of religion, it again recognizes the right to the free exercise of religious cults of African origin. It sets a punishment of up to three years in prison for racism on the Internet. In the political realm, at least 10 per cent of the candidates that political parties put on their voting lists have to be Afro-Brazilian (in the original bill this was set at 30 per cent). It guarantees the *quilombos* the right to preserve their customs under state protection and makes special public financing lines available for them. It stipulates that a permanent system be set up to defend the Statute and monitor its implementation. In addition, the state shall adopt measures to reduce police violence against people of African descent.

The Statute is a big step forward, but it does not meet all the Afro-Brazilians' demands, and reactions to it in the movement are divided. A member of the National Coordination of Black Groups (CONEN), Flávio Jorge, sees the law as "the crowing triumph of the black movement's long fight to have public policies enacted and to overcome racism. It is the achievement of thirty years of struggle." On the other hand, Ricardo Bispo of the Unified Black Movement (MNU) believes, "The Statute was the most criminal regression the black movement has seen. We are the majority in a country that obstinately denies us visibility" (Noblat 2009).

A total of 114 well-known public figures in Brazil signed a manifesto against the Statute and the bill for quotas in universities. The signatories included social scientists such as Gilberto Velho, Luiz Werneck Vianna, Bolivar Lamounier, and Wanderley Guilherme dos Santos, the musician Caetano Veloso, and the poet Ferreira Gullar, and it is no coincidence that all those signatories who were highlighted in the press are white. The fact that so many prominent personalities have lent their weight to a public declaration opposing the Statute demonstrates how controversial the law is. Werneck Vianna sums up their concern as follows: "We are faced with the possibility that we have enacted legislation that might leave a very unhappy mark, a racial scar, on our country's history."[32] And Caetano Veloso (2006) rejects it because it "sets up a definition of a Brazilian citizen that is based on the concept of race. But we shouldn't

---

31   An Afro-Brazilian dance mixed with fighting movements of the body and legs.
32   Intellectuals Sign Manifesto Against Law of Equality. http://www.ufcg.edu.br/prt_ufcg/asses soria_imprensa/mostra_noticia.php?codigo=2417.

imitate systems from the United States. Brazil has something much more interesting: a long tradition of coexistence without racial conflict. We consider any discrimination, above all racial segregation, as an aberration, and this tradition is our cultural treasure."

There was also a rival manifesto supporting the two laws, signed by a similar number of people who, while not being as well known as the anti-Statute signatories, were still influential. These included university professors such as Kabenguele Munanga from the University of São Paulo, Nilma Lino Gomes from the Federal University of Minas Gerais, José Jorge from the University of Brasilia, the sociologist Emir Sader, and the playwright Augusto Boal. Their argument echoed the one promoted in the Statute: that it is not possible to go on insisting there is racial harmony when the data make it so starkly evident that the people of African descent in Brazil are second-class citizens, even though there is no law that defines them as such, and that general policies are not sufficiently effective to solve this problem.

CONCLUSIONS

In this chapter we have called into question the image of Brazilian society as a racial democracy in which the positive integration of the three main races that formed the country—Indians, Portuguese, and people of African descent—would have complemented each other harmoniously. There has been increasing criticism of this view over the past ten years, based largely on an emerging mass of reliable statistical information that lays bare the brutal economic and social inequalities afflicting the Afro-Brazilians. The conclusions of these studies are only too clear: Afro-Brazilians are unable to improve their lot in society, not because they are the poorest sector, but because of the color of their skin. The average pay of an Afro-Brazilian is far less than that of a white person with the same educational level. And we should call this discrimination by its real name: racism.

The Afro-Brazilian movement has played a key role in the effort to deconstruct the myth of a racial democracy by making slow but persistent progress in a struggle that has lasted decades. This movement has been unable to mobilize mass support among the population or organize itself into one single united force, but we must recognize that the efforts of a range of different institutions with the common aim of combating discrimination have been crucially important in redefining the country's national identity. And to the historic process we have analyzed in this study we must add another factor, the opening of the state itself. In 1988, for the first time in the country's history, racism was officially classed as a crime. This state opening to progress continued with public affirmative action policies in some states and at the federal level, and setting quotas for Afro-Brazilians has been one of the key elements in this effort.

The two most important laws in this sphere are the bill to implement quotas in education and the Racial Equality Statute. The former requires that half the places at federal public universities be allocated to students from the public education system, and that this must include a percentage of people who declare themselves to be Afro-Brazilian or members of indigenous populations proportional to the weight these groups have in the region where the university is located. The Statute is a much more far-reaching document, as it redefines the population of African descent, which was previously divided into blacks and mulattos, as Afro-Brazilians, and establishes affirmative policies to benefit them.

The passing of this Statute into law must be seen as a great victory for the Afro-Brazilian movement. There are three very simple reasons for this: first, it has raised the population's awareness of the question of race; second, it has generated enough information to prove beyond doubt there is structural racial discrimination in society; and third, for the first time the state has taken positive action by implementing public policies to fight racism effectively.

LESSONS LEARNED

- Brazil is an example to the world for the ways in which it has brought its main population groups—Indians, Portuguese, and people of African descent—closer together physically as well as culturally.
- Although it might seem contradictory, the country's integration did not save Afro-Brazilians from discrimination or racism in the period since slavery was abolished.
- In the last decade, Brazil has enacted a series of laws and public policies to combat racism and pursue greater inequality in society.

DISCUSSION QUESTIONS

- How is it possible, in a country where interracial relations are so intense, for racism against people of African descent to have gone on so long?
- In what ways has the Brazilian state tried to reduce discrimination against Afro-Brazilians?
- What are the virtues and criticisms of affirmative action to reduce discrimination that has gone on for centuries?

ADDITIONAL READING

Levine, Robert, and John Crocitti. 1999. *The Brazil Reader*. Durham, NC: Duke University Press.

Page, Joseph. 1995. *The Brazilians*. Cambridge, MA: Da Capo Press.

Ramos, Alcida Rita. 1998. *Indigenism, Ethnic Politics in Brazil*. Madison: University of Wisconsin Press.

Santos, Gevanilda y da Silva, Maria. 2005. *Racismo no Brasil: Percepções da Discriminação e do Preconceito Racial do Século XXI*. San Pablo: Editora Fundação Perseu Abramo.

Skidmore, Thomas E. 1976. *Preto no Branco. Raça e Nacionalidade no Pensamento Brasileiro.* Río de Janeiro: Editora Paz e Terra.
Telles, Edward Eric. 2004. *Race in Another America: The Significance of Skin Color in Brazil.* Princeton, NJ: Princeton University Press.

WEBSITES

Cultural and Music Organization in Rio de Janeiro. http://www.afroreggae.org.
Mundo Afro Brazil. http://mundoafro.atarde.uol.com.br.
Portal Olodum. http://olodum.com.br/.

CHAPTER SEVEN

LATINO IMMIGRATION INTO THE UNITED STATES: A PARADIGM SHIFT FROM ASSIMILATION TO MULTICULTURALISM

INTRODUCTION

In 2010 the most recent census in the United States confirmed that a real demographic revolution has been building up for several decades. Today there are around 50 million Latinos living in the country; they make up 16 per cent of the total population, nearly three times the proportion of 30 years ago. The "Latino" or "Hispanic" categories used in the census are based on the person himself or herself, or one of his or her ancestors, being of Latin American or Spanish descent. This criterion is not based on race or citizenship, so a Latino may be of any racial group and may be a U.S. citizen by birth or through legally acquiring nationality. Between 1970 and 1980, this population grew by 50 per cent, between 1980 and 1990 it increased by 53 per cent, between 1990 and 2000 it rose by 58 per cent, and even if in the first decade of this century the rate slackened somewhat, there was still a 43 per cent increase. This explosion makes Latinos the biggest ethnic minority in the country; they even outnumber African Americans. The United States now has the third biggest population of Latin American origin in the world; it has overtaken Colombia and Argentina, and only Brazil and Mexico have more.

Latino immigration into the United States has gone against the theory of assimilation that supposedly set the paradigm for the various migratory waves that came into the country. One famous American myth was that the country would be a "melting pot" and that new arrivals' identities would dissolve as they rapidly adopted "the American way of life," but in the case of the immigrant Latinos this has not happened. They still speak Spanish, they have developed a sense of dual identity, they have maintained strong links with their countries of origin, and their family life and daily existence are very different from "the American way." A good explanation for this phenomenon is the theory of multiculturalism, whereby culturally diverse societies are analyzed from the perspective of the cultural rights of minorities or subordinate population groups.

In this chapter we will examine the impressive evolution of the Latino or Hispanic population in the United States, which in 30 years of uninterrupted immigration has become the biggest minority in the land. We will then analyze the consequences this mass migration has had on the country, and argue that the theory of multiculturalism provides a better interpretation of it than does the theory of assimilation.

7.1. THE EVOLUTION OF THE LATINO POPULATION

In 1960, Latin Americans comprised only 9 per cent of the foreigners living in the United States. By 1990 this had risen to 44 per cent, and in 1997 they accounted for 50 per cent. Half of them are Mexicans; the next biggest group is from the Caribbean, followed by Central Americans and then South Americans. The populations of Latino origin are concentrated in well-defined geographical areas. Half of the Mexicans live in the Los Angeles, Texas, and Chicago regions; the Caribbeans are grouped in Miami and New York; and the Central and South Americans are concentrated in New York and Los Angeles. But now the Latinos are moving into new areas, such as the vast region made up of Alabama, Tennessee, Georgia, North Carolina, and South Carolina, where their numbers have increased considerably in the past ten years. The wave is spreading.

There are some big differences between the recent Latin American influx and previous immigration flows. Several studies have shown that immigrants at the end of the nineteenth century and early years of the twentieth developed a strategy of trying to assimilate into what they perceived to be the model of U.S. citizenship. For example, the Jews, Italians, and Irish who arrived quickly melted into the majority, and consequently the second generation usually did not learn their parents' language—which was lost—and tended not to develop links with their parents' homeland. The third generation was completely assimilated and did not consider the land of their forefathers an important dimension in their self-perception or identity.

The population of Latin American origin, on the other hand, seems to be developing in a different way. Far from adopting a policy of mimesis, the Latinos have made a great effort to maintain their customs and traditions in their daily lives. The most noticeable difference is that they still insist on speaking Spanish and hence have become bilingual. Another equally important difference is that they cultivate links with their countries of origin, which is easier not only because these countries are nearer but also because of the development of rapid transport and communications. A third difference is that they tend to congregate in specific geographical areas, which facilitates cultural and social ties inside the community through trade in specific foodstuffs, their own restaurants, and a network of services geared to a population numerous enough to make this profitable.

A key factor in the difference between the Latino experience and previous arrivals is the period in history when immigration from Latin America boomed. In the 1960s there was a social revolution that involved combating racial segregation and defending African Americans' rights to be treated equally, and this had a huge impact in terms of redefining what it meant to be a U.S. citizen. The African Americans demanded not only their rights, but also their own history and recognition of their contributions to building the nation in spheres such as music, language, the economy, sport, religion, and war. They succeeded in establishing the idea that a person did not have to be white, Protestant, and Anglo-Saxon to be a U.S. citizen. In harmony with this new multicultural climate, the Latin American population in general, and particularly the Mexicans and Cubans, have undergone an integration process that involves preserving their identity and their memory of and links with their homelands, while at the same time taking on the rights and obligations of their new situation as residents or citizens of the United States. In addition, most Latinos could not follow the assimilation strategy of the immigrants from Europe even if they wanted to, because their physical appearance is different. An Irishman or a Pole can pass unnoticed in the lonely crowd on the subway in Manhattan, but a Mexican with indigenous Zacateca ancestry or a Mayan from Guatemala does not find it so easy.

If the growth rates of the past 30 years continue, and everything indicates that they will, by 2050 the estimated population of Latino origin will be a 150 million, which means the United States will undoubtedly have become a bilingual society. In the first decade of the twenty-first century, the remittances that Hispanic workers sent back to their countries of origin amounted to more than $300 billion, which works out at around $30 billion a year, and these remittances already constitute one of the main sources of foreign investment for the Central America countries. For example, Mexicans in the United States send billions of dollars per year back to their country, and this constitutes Mexico's third-largest source of income, behind only tourism and the oil business. The same applies to Cuba: the Cuba Study Group reports that nearly half the Cubans in Miami, some 48 per cent, regularly send money home. Total remittances vary from $600 million to $950 million a year, which is a massive injection of cash for Cuba's economy. In fact, this figure could go even higher if conditions for sending money improve (Solimano and Allende, 2007).

In addition, relations between the United States and Latin America are no longer unilateral, because new veins of opportunity have opened in the north. Not only is the long-standing transfer of wealth from the south to the north finally tilting toward a fairer balance, but the north's cultural influence in the south (mainly through films) is being partly returned in an inverse process whereby the United States is being gradually Latin Americanized.

In the United States, this process of Latinization has provoked, and will continue to provoke, reaction and resistance. Some Americans, such as the ultra-conservative Pat Buchanan, who once ran for the presidency, believe that the new migratory wave is the main reason for his country's decline. And many of his fellow citizens agree with him, judging from the fact that his book, *The Death of the West*—which carries the eloquent subtitle "How dying populations and immigrant invasions imperil our country and civilization"—was a best-seller when it was published in 2001. His thesis is very simple: "The Mexicans do not only come from another culture, millions of them are of another race. History and experience have taught us that different races find it much more difficult to assimilate. The sixty million people of German descent are completely assimilated in our society whereas the millions who came from Africa or Asia are still not really part of it" (Buchanan 2001, 125). Buchanan reaches an eminently practical conclusion: immigration must be stopped in any way possible, or it will end up sinking the United States.

Figure 7.1: United States: Population of Latino-Hispanic Origin and Percentage
of Total U.S. Population by Year

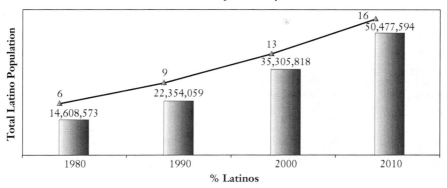

Source: Authors' calculations, based on data from the United States Census Bureau.

Figure 7.2: United States: Population of Latino-Hispanic Origin, 2010

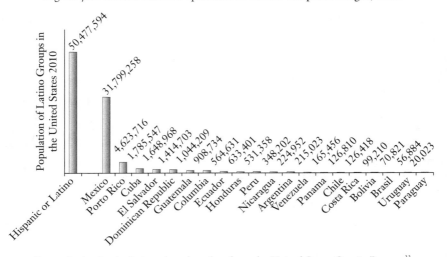

Source: Author's calculations, based on data from the United States Census Bureau.[33]

---

33 http://www.census.gov/2010census/data/2010-census-briefs.php. This is the link for *Census Brief 2010, The Hispanic Population 2010.* In this report there is a serious mistake concerning Brazil. First, it has been omitted from the list of countries, and second, because of this oversight the number of people in the category "Other South American Populations" is said to decline between 2000 and 2010. But in fact the Brazilians were not included in the latter calculation. The number of Brazilians shown in the chart is taken from a 2006 estimate by the Census Bureau itself and should be very near today's actual figure.

7.2. WHO ARE WE?

This question was used by Samuel Huntington as the title of his last book, which was published in 2004. Weighing in at nearly 500 pages, it was a great effort to define the U.S. national identity, and that is what the question above refers to. Asking who I am has to do with my personal identity, but asking who we are involves a group identity, and the former question cannot be answered without reference to the latter. As this whole section is devoted to Huntington's analysis in the above-mentioned book, we would like to make it clear at the outset that we disagree completely with his main conclusions. However, our aims and our interests do not stop us appreciating that his book is probably one of the most complete publications on this subject in recent years. What is more, the author was an excellent social scientist and in the book he builds his arguments with concepts and theories that have been indispensable for our own ideas, although we frequently reach conclusions exactly opposite to his.

Huntington's main conclusions can be summed up as follows: the national identity of the United States of America can be characterized in a reasonably concrete way; it is important for the country's continued existence that this identity be preserved in the present and strengthened in the future; and the Latino immigration of recent decades is one of the most serious challenges to the U.S. national identity. It follows that Latinos must be assimilated as rapidly as possible through effective policies, so that the Mexicans and their descendants will stop identifying themselves as such and become proud U.S. citizens.

According to Huntington, the main historical components of the American identity have been the Anglo-Saxon race, ethnicity, politics, and culture. This race was the determinant factor from the first colonization until the civil rights revolution of the 1960s. This ethnic group was key to Americans' self-perception up until World War II, but after that it became unimportant. The country's political ideology has been and still is a cornerstone of the American identity. The fourth component, Anglo-Saxon culture, has been a central part of the vision that Americans have of themselves since the Founding Fathers. We shall now look in greater depth at what Huntington believes each of these four components represents in the U.S. identity, what each signifies, and how each one came into being and functioned over time.

According to Arthur Schlesinger, Jr., "For much of its history the United States 'has been a racist nation.' Historically white Americans have sharply distinguished themselves from Indians, blacks, Asians, and Mexicans, and excluded them from the American community" (Huntington 2004, 77). Huntington goes on to say that, in the early years, relations between the first Anglo-Saxon colonists and the native Americans deteriorated rapidly and, justifying themselves with an ideology of white supremacy and the God-given mission to found a new Promised Land, the newcomers attacked the indigenous peoples and exterminated them or drove them out of their enclaves along the Atlantic coast. These "uncivilized savages" could not be part of the nation. When there were no more Indians available, African slaves were brought in with the same justification, and this trade continued until 1808. So many slaves were brought that around the end of the eighteenth century they amounted to 20 per cent of the population, although of course they lived segregated lives. When slavery was abolished, some who were free were sent back to Africa where a country, Liberia, had already been set up for them in 1821. When President Lincoln received the first group of freed slaves at the White House he told them it would be better for everyone if they went to Africa. There was no place in the United States for colored people, not even for the Indians. It was the same story when workers came from China to provide cheap labor building the railroads. When they became too numerous the Act of Exclusion was passed to turn off the tap, immigration from Asia stopped, and those already in the country were sent back to their homelands because they could not be assimilated and posed "a menace to our civilization. . . . For all practical purposes America was a white society until the mid-twentieth century" (Huntington 2004, 56).

Ethnicity is central to the American identity, and its significance can be properly understood by examining the period when the migratory deluge from Europe arrived. The Greeks, Irish, Poles, Germans, Italians, and Jews were met with resentment on the part of the Anglo-Americans, who felt threatened by these millions of newcomers who did not speak English or who were predominantly Catholic and had different customs and habits. The solution was to Americanize the immigrants, and they had to assimilate quickly to be accepted. Thus was born one of America's most cherished myths: the melting pot in which all the various ethnic groups and cultures were merged into one. The toughest test that proved this strategy had succeeded was World War II, in which immigrants and their descendants stood shoulder to shoulder with Anglo-Americans and fought and died alongside them. The United States thus incorporated a new component into its identity: it came to see itself as a multi-ethnic society that worked so well that it was able to defeat the Nazis and save the West. But this multi-ethnic society that dissolved ethnic differences in a melting pot and had a common language was in fact subject to a dominant culture whose most important component, according to Huntington, was the Anglo-Saxon tradition.

The "key elements in this culture" are the following: the Protestant religion and Christianity, the English language, the basic values of the work ethic and individualism, the responsibilities of governments, citizens' rights, and the rule of law. The United States has been built with this dominant culture since the first colonists arrived, and this culture has remained as the backbone that gives sense to being American. This "nation with the soul of a Church" has always surprised foreign visitors and social analysts. Alexis de Tocqueville was among the first to note the importance of the Church when he said we should never forget that to understand a country we must always look at its religion first. But political freedoms and individual rights very often clash with religious sectarianism. American culture is built on the Protestant principles of exalting the work ethic, the regular practice of religion, valuing small communities over the institutional centralization of Church or State, the simplification of the opposing forces of good and evil with no gray areas, and faith in individual ability to succeed in life. This vision gave rise to the specific components of the American creed, which is very different from the ideology of the French, for example, or even that of the English. This culture is what gave form to the melting pot in which, in theory, all the cultures are fused. But in fact they did not all lose their previous identities because one of them—the Anglo-Saxon Protestant element—has always predominated, and the others had to adapt themselves to it. All current indicators show that Americans are still among the most religious people in the Western world; they devote more time to work, which constitutes an important part of their identity; they reject leisure more; and they systematically oppose Spanish becoming a second official language in the country.

However, in recent decades the dominance of this Anglo-Saxon Protestant culture has come under threat. This is because "the salience and substance of this culture were challenged by a new wave of immigrants from Latin America and Asia, the popularity in intellectual and political circles of the doctrines of multiculturalism and diversity, the spread of Spanish as the second American language and the Hispanization trends in American society" (Huntington 2004, xvi). Why should Latino and Mexican immigration pose such a threat to the predominance of Anglo-Saxon culture? What makes this kind of immigration so different from the previous waves of immigrants that it has become a danger to Anglo-Saxon Protestant culture? Why is multiculturalism undermining the U.S. national identity?

To answer the first two of these questions we must examine the United States' immigration model. Huntington talks of three ways in which we can describe this process, and all three are based in a culinary metaphor: the melting pot, the tomato soup, and the salad bowl. The best known is the melting pot, whereby each incoming culture is melted into the mix until it loses its original characteristics. The second metaphor expresses the idea of a dominant culture, the American Way, and other lesser cultures are added but do not change its essential nature, just as tomato soup is still tomato soup even when other ingredients are added. In the third model there is no dominant culture, as in a salad where all the ingredients are on the same plate but separate. As Huntington himself explains, the first model corresponds to "racial mixing," the second is "cultural assimilation," and the third is "cultural or ethnic pluralism." He thinks the second model is the one that "more accurately . . . describes the cultural absorption of immigrants until the 1960s" (Huntington 2004, 129). Both the melting pot and the salad bowl are unsuitable terms because the predominance of Anglo-Saxon culture has never been challenged or put in doubt. The proof of this assertion was the demand that all immigrants who came into the country had to be assimilated and "Americanized."

However, both Hispanic immigration in general, and that from Mexico in particular, are unprecedented in the United States and seem to contradict the theory of assimilation whereby the third generation of immigrants would be completely Americanized and adopt the patterns of U.S. identity. This different evolution is sustained by a dozen characteristics that make Latino immigration different: territorial contiguity, numbers, illegality, regional concentration, persistence over time, historical presence, language, education, types of occupations and income, dual citizenship, mixed marriages, and identity.

Let us briefly survey some of these specificities of Latino immigration. First, no other immigrant group came into the United States across a land border three thousand kilometers in length; previously they all arrived by plane or sailed from countries thousands of miles away across the ocean. The land border between a rich country and a relatively poor one like Mexico is a permanent incitement to cross, and this has given rise to a trans-border area with almost all the migration going one way. Second, with respect to numbers, never in the history of U.S. immigration has there been an influx of so many people from the same country and speaking the same language. At the present time nearly one-third of all foreigners entering the country are Mexicans (and if we add in all the other Latin Americans the total of Latinos is more than half the new arrivals). The next largest national group is the Chinese, but they amount to a mere five per cent (although all Asians together comprise one-quarter). The third characteristic on the list, illegality, is a recent phenomenon in U.S. immigration history. It is partly due to territorial contiguity, because people arriving on the docks or at an airport are much easier to control. The illegal Mexican population in the country is thought to amount to several million, and it has aroused general unease because "nothing comparable has occurred previously in the American experience" (Huntington 2004, 226).

As to the fourth characteristic, Latino immigration is strongly concentrated in California (Mexicans), Florida (Cubans), and New York (Puerto Ricans and people from the Dominican Republic). The censuses in 2000 and 2010 revealed an accelerated rise in Latino expansion into other cities and regions such as North Carolina, Georgia, and Connecticut, for example. This high density of Latinos in specific areas has led to the formation of genuine enclaves in which the dominant language is Spanish, and where English is hardly used at all. The immigrants and their children can find marriage partners, friends, and even employers of the same origin, which fosters socialization inwards into the group rather than mixing outside it. The fifth characteristic is that immigration from Mexico has been very persistent over time; it has been going on for 30 years and is still increasing. In the past, immigrants from Europe came to America to escape economic crises or wars and then stayed and lost their identities, but there are no signs that the Latinos will follow the same pattern. Quite the contrary, in fact, because the continuous flow of Latino immigrants tends to renew the use of Spanish and keep people's links with their countries of origin updated. Hence "the Spanish speaking population is being continually replenished by newcomers faster than that population is being assimilated" (Huntington 2004, 229). A sixth difference between Mexicans and other immigrants is that nearly half the United States was once part of Mexico. One and a half centuries ago the states of Texas, New Mexico, Arizona, California, Nevada, and Utah belonged to Mexico, and they were conquered in a war or purchased for next to nothing. That whole area is stamped with a strong Mexican culture. This situation has been compared to that of the largely French-speaking Canadian province of Quebec, which has long been separated from its motherland, but the Latino connection is more intense because Mexico is just across the border while France is an ocean away. Huntington concedes, "History shows that serious potential for conflict exists when people in one country start to refer to territory in a neighboring country in proprietary terms" (Huntington 2004, 230). Canada's approach to this problem was to adopt multiculturalism and bilingualism, but Huntington rejects this solution and claims that multiculturalism could cause conflict in the United States, even though exactly the opposite happened in Canada, where peace was consolidated and secession avoided.

The six characteristics analyzed above that distinguish Mexican immigration from any preceding wave—contiguity, number, illegality, regional concentration, persistence and historical presence—"pose problems for the assimilation of people of Mexican origin into American society" (Huntington 2004, 230). What is in play at the present time is a question of acceptance. From the multicultural perspective, an individual should be accepted in a new society without having to surrender his or her original culture, without becoming completely assimilated, and certainly without having to pass a Lord Tebbit kind of test.[34]

7.3. MULTICULTURALISM AND RECENT LATINO IMMIGRATION

The concept of multiculturalism we are working with in this book is very like the definition proposed by Will Kymlicka and Charles Taylor. According to Kymlicka, liberal multiculturalism means "that the state should adopt various group-specific rights or policies that are intended to recognize and accommodate the distinctive identities and aspirations of ethnocultural groups" (Kymlicka 2007, 61). A good reference on this subject is the book *Multiculturalism in the United States*, edited by John Buenker and Lorman Ratner (1992). The volume contains a specific study of the contributions to the country made by, and the integration strategies of, different cultural communities including African Americans, the descendants of Native Americans, German Americans, Irish Americans, Swedish Americans, Polish Americans, Jewish Americans, Italian Americans, Chinese Americans, and Mexican Americans. In many of these communities there was internal disagreement about the best way to integrate culturally into U.S. society, and the proposed strategies were sometimes mutually contradictory due to tension between those who wanted to cling to their original culture and those who favored rapid assimilation. The new cultural rights Kymlicka talks about are of course additional to the defense of citizens' civil, political, and social rights as laid down in all liberal constitutions (Arocena 2012).

According to Charles Taylor, multiculturalism is essentially the recognition of groups that suffer discrimination or exclusion because they are ethno-culturally different. Multiculturalism is always a reaction against a homogenizing nation-state dominated by a cultural group that imposes its own "language, history, culture, literature, myths and religion," and "anyone who does not belong to this dominant group is compelled to assimilate into it or be excluded" (Kymlicka 2007, 61–62). This is precisely the situation in the United States, and the multiculturalism in that country has come into being to defend itself against this pressure.

We have seen that Huntington explicitly recognizes that the United States was built by a dominant Anglo-Saxon group that imposed its culture, which included racism and xenophobia; that excluded, exterminated, or segregated the indigenous population; that excluded and segregated African Americans; and that compulsively forced immigrants to assimilate and be Americanized. According to Huntington, this pattern was overturned with the civil rights revolution of the 1960s and 1970s, and

---

34 According to Lord Tebbit, a Conservative politician in the United Kingdom, one could only be considered English if one cheered England in a cricket match against any other national team.

since then neither race nor ethnicity has been part of the national identity of citizens of the United States. He concludes that affirmative action based on ethnicity or race makes no sense and in fact would be prejudicial because it would ethnicize or racialize U.S. culture, whose backbone is the English language, Christian values, the Protestant work ethic, and the American creed, which harks back to the first colonists and their vision to create a free country in a new world.

We will not analyze in any depth the question of native people or African Americans because our focus in this chapter is the Latino population, but it is all too evident from the information available about those groups that they have continued to suffer discrimination since the 1960s. Black urban ghettoes and Indian reservations are pockets of poverty, forgotten territory. All the indicators of education, health, poverty, type of occupation, access to decision-making positions, and daily discrimination are still much worse than for the rest of the population. Multiculturalism has emerged in the United States to narrow this gap, and its adherents denounce the fact that, in spite of what is laid down in the Constitution, these appalling social differences still exist.

The main argument underlying multiculturalism is that we should not be blind to color and race in the world today because these were major factors in how people have been seen for centuries. The effects of long-term discrimination cannot be corrected merely by universal policies to ensure access to jobs based on each person's individual merits. In other words, the negative discrimination that has reigned for centuries can only be corrected with positive discrimination for a limited period. That is to say, the only way to improve long-term unequal levels of opportunity is to implement unequal policies to help population sectors that have been victims of inequality. This is highlighted by multiculturalism, and this is how the Supreme Court interpreted it in 2003 when it ruled in favor of the University of Michigan and allowed it to go on including race and ethnicity among its student selection criteria. The Court added that using race and ethnicity as admissions criteria should be relatively temporary, and it expressed the hope that "within twenty-five years the use of racial preference will no longer be necessary."[35] Affirmative policies were first introduced precisely to compensate for negative discrimination in the past by implementing positive discrimination today, and without these policies much of the successful social mobility that African Americans have enjoyed in recent decades would simply not have existed. Nor would there have been the upsurge of African American energy, courage, and determination to pursue their rights in practice and in the courts, and to overcome what Frantz Fanon reminds us are the feelings of inferiority and shame that subjugated people are afflicted with. It is true that in some cases affirmative action went too far and became inverse racism, which must be severely censured, but without multiculturalism and affirmative policies the progress that various ethnocultural groups have made toward securing their rights would simply not have happened. And Barack Obama would not have become the first African-American president in the country's history. But let us be clear about this: the fact that Obama has "joined the establishment" and been elected president does not show that multiculturalism is wrong; on the contrary, it is precisely

---

35   2003 Split Ruling on Affirmative Action in Michigan Case. http://www.npr.org/news/specials/michigan/.

because multicultural policies have been in force for decades that his election was possible. Huntington sums it up perfectly when he says that multiculturalists

> promoted programs to enhance the status and influence of subnational racial, ethnic, and cultural groups. They encouraged immigrants to maintain their birth country cultures, granted them legal privileges denied to native-born Americans, and denounced the idea of Americanization as un-American. They pushed the rewriting of history syllabi and textbooks so as to refer to the "peoples" of the United States in place of the single people of the Constitution. They urged supplementing or substituting for national history the history of subnational groups. They downgraded the centrality of English in American life and pushed bilingual education and linguistic diversity. They advocated legal recognition of group rights and racial preferences over the individual rights central to the American Creed. They justified their actions by theories of multiculturalism and the idea that diversity rather than unity or community should be America's overriding value. The combined effect of these efforts was to promote the deconstruction of the American identity that had been gradually created over three centuries and the ascendance of subnational identities. (2004, 142).

The quotation above is an excellent account of multiculturalism in the United States. Huntington criticizes all these aspects and condemns them as prejudicial, but we beg to differ. We feel these changes amount to a great step forward, just as important as when liberal thought gradually took on board the leftist socialist program of pursuing workers' social rights in the closing years of the nineteenth century and at the start of the twentieth.

We now turn to the question of multiculturalism in the United States and its connections with Latino immigration. According to Huntington, immigration is the main threat in the modern world to "societal security," which is "the ability of a people to maintain their culture, institutions, and way of life," or "the sustainability, within acceptable conditions for evolution, of traditional patterns of language, culture, association, and religious and national identity and custom" (Huntington 2004, 180). He sees Latino immigration in the United States as the biggest menace to "societal security" because it could lead to a system of "two languages, two cultures and two peoples." We agree that the languages are different—that is obvious—but it is not so easy to prove that one culture is better than the other, and to assert they are two separate peoples is to reject that people can have juxtaposed nationalities, or the feeling of belonging at the same time to two countries.

Huntington is against Latino culture because of a whole series of negative characteristics that differentiate it from Anglo-Saxon Protestant culture. These negative aspects include the following: Mexico's Iberian, indigenous, Catholic heritage versus Luther's Protestantism; nihilist attitudes such as *el vale madrismo* ("Whatever . . ."), a lack of commitment as in *ahí se va* ("I don't care"), and not making an effort today because of the so-called mañana syndrome, *mañana se lo tengo* ("Tomorrow will do");

obsession with the past; resignation in the face of poverty; not trusting people who are not family; undervaluing education; lack of individual initiative; not seeing hard work as a means to personal realization; and moral indolence. In drawing up this list he uses expressions from Mexicans such as Carlos Fuentes, Jorge Castañeda, and Andrés Rozental, or Mexican Americans such as Lionel Sosa. According to Huntington, these beliefs, attitudes, and values held by Latinos in general, and by Mexicans in particular, account for Mexico's relative backwardness compared to the United States. And now they are starting to threaten Americans because Mexicans are not only refusing to be assimilated but, under the influence of multiculturalism, are increasingly proud of their own culture and disdain traditional American values. This pride feeds their sense of belonging to Mexico and reinforces their Mexican identity, which includes another series of attitudes, beliefs, and values that we perceive as positive but that Huntington prefers not to mention, perhaps because he too would see them as positive. For example, such a list would include family ties and respect; friendship; the risks involved in emigrating, which is a vivid example of initiative, courage, and the desire to better oneself; solidarity with one's own people and sending remittances home; questioning strict moral fundamentalism; a balance between work and leisure; imagination; and religiosity. Of course, this list of positive aspects of Latino emigrant culture is just as arbitrary as the negative aspects listed above, and we present it here simply because Huntington stresses negative aspects of Mexican culture that he feels are contaminating Anglo-Saxon Protestant culture. He could just as easily have listed problematic aspects of U.S. culture and good points about the Mexicans, but he does neither.

A third aspect of Latino immigration that causes Americans societal insecurity is the newcomers' dual nationality. For a citizen of a foreign country to obtain citizenship in the United States, the Constitution requires him or her "to swear to support the Constitution of the United States; and that he does absolutely and entirely renounce and abjure all allegiance and fidelity to any foreign prince, potentate, state or sovereignty whatever whereof he was before a citizen or subject" (as written in the U.S. Naturalization Act of 1795). Foreigners seeking U.S. citizenship today still have to take this oath, but in practice immigrants are not required to renounce their original nationality.[36] More and more countries nowadays are changing their regulations and accepting dual nationality, and consequently more and more immigrants are entitled to two passports. In 1996 only 7 out of 17 Latin American countries had this dual nationality rule, in 2000 there were 14, and today nearly all Latin American countries allow dual nationality. These changes are in response to a new migration context in which so many of these countries' citizens are living abroad that they constitute a full-blown diaspora. The emigrants' countries of origin are very keen to maintain links with them because the remittances they send constitute a massive source of income, and because they are potential voters who could be influenced as a

---

36 The other requirements to obtain U.S. nationality are as follows: five years of legal residence; not having a criminal record; being able to speak, read, and write English at an 8th grade level; and passing a basic U.S. history and politics knowledge test. In addition, anyone born on U.S. soil is automatically a United States citizen (*ius solis*).

Figure 7.3: Walker Lake Munitions Sign.
Credit: Kelapstick. Licensed under the Creative Commons Attribution-Share Alike license
(CC-BY-SA).

group. There is another sociological factor behind this change: in the modern world, contact between emigrants and their homelands is very intense and fluid thanks to the new information and communication technologies and the fact that travel is now cheaper. Many countries have adapted to these changes and are beginning to consider their nation's population as consisting of citizens who live abroad as well as those who live at home, and have therefore facilitated voting abroad. Emigrants in the United States who have acquired dual nationality have been able to do so because their country of origin does not require them to renounce their nationality, as was previously the case, and because the United States does not insist on exclusive nationality in practice, although strictly speaking this contravenes the letter of the law. These transmigrants do not simply have dual nationality; they also have dual identities, are bilingual, and have values and culture from both sides, as one Latino makes it clear: "People like us have the best of two worlds . . . two countries, two homes. It doesn't make any sense for us to be either this or that. We're both. It's not a conflict" (Huntington 2004, 205).

Huntington opposes this view and maintains that dual nationality, which fosters dual identity, has many negative consequences for the United States. According to him, these new citizens do not develop the same sense of loyalty to the country as previous immigrants, they do not assimilate to the American dream, they are Latinizing large swathes of territory, and like termites in wood they are eating into and undermining the structure of the American identity, which is to say the English language, the Protestant heritage, Christianity, and the political creed.

CONCLUSIONS

Latino immigration into the United States has challenged the theory of assimilation that used to be the standard interpretation of the successive migratory waves that arrived in the country. One of America's myths, "the melting pot" in which the newcomers' identities would be dissolved as they rapidly adopted the "American way of life," has not functioned with the new Latino population. They have clung to their Spanish language, developed a sense of dual identity, maintained strong links with their countries of origin, and have a different kind of family life and daily life. This phenomenon is well explained by the theory of multiculturalism, which approaches the analysis of culturally diverse societies from the perspective of the cultural rights of minorities or subordinate populations.

When one travels by subway in Atlanta, Georgia, the successive stations are announced in Spanish as well as in English, and most of the travelers are African Americans. When you go for a hamburger in Durham, North Carolina, some businesses have their menus in English and in Spanish. For those taking a walk on the streets of Manhattan, New York, many of the instructions are in both languages. Strolling through Miami, you hear more Spanish spoken than English. Traveling in Texas or Arizona, you see more people with ethnic Mexican complexions than Anglo-Saxons. And in Los Angeles you notice more and more cars with Mexican workers on the highways and broad avenues. The United States is being Latin Americanized because there are 50 million Latinos living within its borders. A country that 30 years ago had almost no Latin American immigration and 30 years from now will have a hundred million Latinos cannot remain unchanged; it must have changed already, and the changes will surely go on. There is no doubt that this is a crucial time in history for the Latinos in the United States. In spite of racist xenophobic rejection, they have maintained their culture, transmitted their identity to their children, introduced their cuisine, and made the United States a bilingual country. There is still a long and difficult way to go before the many immigrants without documents obtain their rights, but they will get there.

LESSONS LEARNED

- The 50 million Latinos in the United States of America have contributed significantly to the country's development.
- It is impossible to ignore the fact that the majority of the Hispanics are legal U.S. citizens and have established themselves at all levels of society as governors, judges, sportsmen and women, musicians, scientists, workers, and so on.

- Unlike previous immigration groups, this Latino population has managed to retain the main characteristic of their own culture while integrating positively into American culture. The outstanding example of this is the Spanish language, which is now being adopted by the authorities themselves and by businesses to communicate with the public.
- The fact that there are so many descendants of Latinos in the country is having significant and unprecedented consequences—political, economic, and cultural—for the relations between Latin America and the United States.

DISCUSSION QUESTIONS

- Why is Latino immigration better interpreted by the theory of multiculturalism than by the classic theory of assimilation?
- How is it possible for a person to have two juxtaposed identities: Mexican-American, Cuban-American or Nuyorican?
- What are the main criticisms that Samuel Huntington formulates against Latino immigration into the United States?

ADDITIONAL READING

Augenbraum, Harold, and Ilan Stavans (eds.). 1993. *Growing Up Latino. Memoirs and Stories.* New York: Houghton Mifflin.

Gutmann, Amy. 1994. *Multiculturalism.* Princeton, NJ: Princeton University Press.

League of United Latin American Citizens. http://lulac.org.

Portes, Alejandro, Cristina Escobar, and Alexandria Walton. 2005. "Immigrant Transnational Organization and Development: A Comparative Study." Working Paper No. 05–07. Princeton, NJ: Center for Migration and Development, Princeton University.

Salins, Peter. 1997. *Assimilation, American Style.* New York: Basic Books.

Stavans, Ilan. 2010. "Literatura en Spanglish: Codex Espanglesis." Montevideo: El País Cultural, No. 1061, March 26.

PART THREE

SOCIAL POLICY, INEQUALITY, AND THE BEAUTIFUL GAME

CHAPTER EIGHT

THE DELAYED REVOLUTION AND THE RISE OF THE SOUTH

INTRODUCTION

Brazil was singled out for decades in the annual *Human Development Reports* of the United Nations Development Program (UNDP) as a development tragedy, with the promises of human development in a country with vast resources and rapid economic growth never reaching the masses of poor Brazilians. Brazil's national level of income inequality was the world's highest, and the regional inequality between the south and north was so great that Brazil was often referred to as Belindia: half Belgium and half India. Brazil was the country of the future, and always would be.

The story was quite different in the 2013 *Human Development Report*. Subtitled "The Rise of the South: Human Progress in a Diverse World," Brazil was suddenly a development model: "Brazil is lifting its standards through expanding international relationships and antipoverty programs that are emulated worldwide."

What is the transformation by which Brazil has gone from being the example to avoid to the model of development? Brazil's human development is a story of first adopting an imported model that prioritized growth over distribution, and of following that model for some 30 years. After three decades of disappointment for most Brazilians, the country abandoned that dominant theory of development and implemented innovative home-grown policies for growth with equity: policies that have succeeded and subsequently been copied around the world.

The seeds of Brazil's model from the late 1960s to the mid-1990s are found in Simon Kuznets's watershed 1954 presidential address to the American Economic Association, in which he suggested that income inequality first increases but subsequently decreases as a country industrializes. In subsequent years, a huge body of empirical research confirmed the Kuznets effect for advanced industrial nations and also discovered that the relationship held in developing countries. Some studies have even identified the per-capita GNP turning point in the so-called inverted U curve, which when reached by the "typical" country will provide the expectation of a more equitable distribution to naturally accompany additional economic growth. In policy terms, the Kuznets inverted U-curve is very appealing: a country must concentrate only on economic growth, because economic growth alone will eventually reduce inequality and poverty; a rising tide eventually lifts all boats (Bowman 1997).

While most of the cross-sectional quantitative research supported the Kuznets effect in less developed countries, there were important exceptions and detractors. Some scholars expressed skepticism that the cross-sectional approach would ever generate conclusions about the Kuznets inverted-U effect. What all the studies do agree on, however, is that inequality increases markedly in the earliest phases of industrialization, "[b]ut there is controversy whether a decrease in inequality with development is inevitable (the inverted U-hypothesis)" (Adelman and Robinson 1978, 958–59).

While there existed considerable debate among scholars, the majority of economists and international financial institutions such as the World Bank and the International Monetary Fund believed in the Kuznets inverted U-curve as a near law of economics. Consequently, consultants and advisors in the 1970s and 1980s recommended that developing countries concentrate on growth and not worry about distribution. Moreover, scholars were also able to use advanced cross-national statistics to determine the precise level of economic development whereby additional growth would naturally lead to reduced inequality; for our purposes we should remember that Brazil passed this point in 1971 and Costa Rica in 1961 (Bowman 1997). In Latin America, the Kuznets effect was followed as policy by many, but not all, countries.

While most scholarly debates are of little significance outside of academia, an understanding of the forces that reduce inequality has potentially staggering real-world repercussions. To illustrate, we briefly examine the cases of Brazil and Costa Rica circa 1992. At that time, both of these Latin American countries were at middle levels of development; according to the 1992 *World Development Report*, Brazil's 1990 per-capita GNP was $2,680 while Costa Rica's was $1,900. These countries had similar levels of inequality in the size distribution of income in 1960; the top quintile income share was 62 percent in Brazil and 61 percent in Costa Rica. By 1989 the Gini co-efficient for inequality in Brazil was an astonishingly high 0.663, while the Gini in Costa Rica was a much more moderate 0.4604 (Psacharopoulos et al., 1993). The result is that even though Brazil had a higher per-capita income, 40.9 per cent of its population was in poverty in 1989, compared to only 3.4 per cent in Costa Rica. If Brazil could have only matched Costa Rica's moderate level of income inequality, some 53 million individuals would have been lifted out of poverty!

This chapter examines social and inequality policy in Brazil and Costa Rica. We demonstrate that Costa Rica ignored the Kuznets effect and focused on growth with equity for the past half-century. An important component in this strategy was human capital formation, which was crucial for economic development in recent years. In contrast, Brazil embraced the Kuznets inverted U-curve and policies of growth, without the need for distributive policies and with low human capital formation for many years, hoping that eventually growth would lead to greater equity. That equity never arrived, and Brazil reversed its development policy beginning around 1994. Since that time, the Brazilian state has used daring indigenous policies in welfare, human capital, and the minimum wage, and has experienced one of the greatest growth-with-equity successes of all time.

8.1. THE CASE OF COSTA RICA

Costa Rica in 1950 was a poverty-stricken, resource-poor, and inegalitarian country emerging from the devastating 1948 civil war. However, Costa Rica's total economic growth from 1950 to 2010 has been a solid 338 per cent, a growth that has been accompanied by impressive gains in life expectancy and a reduction in poverty (Heston, Summers, and Aten 2012). Economic growth was accompanied initially by significant but moderate improvements in the size distribution of income, followed after 1984 by a slight increase in inequality. What has been the relationship between income inequality and economic growth in Costa Rica, and what have been the causes of any significant changes in income distribution?

The available data indicate that income inequality as measured by the Gini co-efficient decreased significantly from 1950 to 1984, and then increased slightly with additional economic per-capita growth. The Gini co-efficient over time is presented in Figure 8.1. Most conspicuously, the percentage share of the richest 20 per cent decreased from 60 to 50.6 per cent and then remained somewhat stable. In the World Bank's study of equity and growth in Costa Rica, González-Vega and Céspedes reject the Kuznets inverted-U path as an explanation for Costa Rican development: income inequality has been moderate, and a substantial reduction in poverty was observed during most of the 1950–85 period. Alleviation of poverty was complemented by effective assistance for the indigent and other critical groups. Thus Costa Rica has been an example of growth with equity (1993, 126). What were the causes of this growth with equity? Rapid economic growth was likely one important factor, as GNP was growing at an annual rate of 6.5 per cent during this time (Seligson 1987, 180). Yet country experts also point to political factors.

The seeds of Costa Rica's relative success were sown in the years immediately following the 1948 civil war, when a coalition of intellectual modernizers led by war-hero José Figueres (1906–90) created a social-democratic Latin American–style welfare state. In contrast to Brazil at that time, a key component of the framework was an interventionist and equity-enhancing state as the basis for economic development. At no time, however, did the state advocate the large-scale sectoral restructuring (equity-then-growth) that was used in Japan, South Korea, and Taiwan, but rather emphasized the reduction of poverty and an improvement in social development and education. The stability of this sociopolitical transformation was partially due to the weakened position of the coffee oligarchy, which lost considerable relative power during the 1930s depression and the civil war. In addition, Figueres permanently disbanded the military and rechanneled defense dollars to education and social policies that had a long-term positive effect on economic growth and equity (Bowman 2002). One of the most powerful tools at the disposal of governments that can serve to redistribute is the tax structure. Improvements achieved in Costa Rica came about as a direct result of government policies in the 1950s and 1960s that led to a tripling of income tax revenues (Seligson 1987, 185). With the country lacking an expensive military, these tax revenues were funneled into equity-enhancing educational and social programs. In 1976, 30 per cent of the budget was spent on education, compared to worldwide averages of only 7 per cent (Seligson 1987, 182). As defense spending fell from 25 per cent of the national budget in the late 1940s to 2 per cent in 1958, the percentage of the budget going to health and social services climbed from 20 per cent in 1938 to 45 per cent in 1958. By 1987, a scant 0.6 per cent of GDP was allotted to national defense, while more than 20 per cent of the entire GDP was spent on social services (Proyecto Estado de la Nación 1995, 67). It is estimated that the effective income of the poorest Costa Ricans is doubled due to the extent of the social services. Eighty per cent of all social services are of universal coverage, including health care, social security, and education (Proyecto Estado de la Nación 1995, 22). The growth of social services and poverty amelioration programs are such that levels of poverty declined even during the "lost" decade of the 1980s, when real per-capita GDP declined. Social indicators have improved dramatically.

In addition, the state largely replaced the invisible hand in credit and investment decisions. Figueres quickly nationalized the banks, stating that "[t]he administration of money and credit ought not to be in private hands, any more than the distribution of water and the mail" (quoted in Honey 1994, 77). The four national banks were used not only to spur economic development, but also to encourage co-operatives, exports, and social programs. In addition, the banking system allowed the government to set up or purchase many of the most important industries such as electricity, communications, fertilizers, cement, and petroleum processing. In one state bank, the Gini co-efficient for credit declined from between 0.7 and 0.9 in 1950–60 to 0.39 in commercial credit and 0.41 in rural credit by 1987 (Proyecto Estado de la Nación 1995, 25). This is a case with magnificent success against poverty and mixed success against inequality. Economists often point to human capital as a key factor for national competitiveness in our increasingly globalized world. A highly educated and healthy workforce is a necessary condition for higher paying jobs and economic development. Costa Rica instituted an innovative and cost-effective program to deliver high-quality primary health care to the entire nation. This program is known as the EBAIS (Basic Health Attention Teams).

Costa Rica has long held to several basic health-care principles:

- universality of health care for all inhabitants;
- solidarity, whereby all individuals and employers contribute to the system;
- equity, whereby all citizens have equal opportunity for high quality care;
- subsidy, whereby the state contributes to the health care of the poorest.

With these principles in place, the large public hospitals have long provided major hospital care to the population. For many years, the existing challenge was to provide high-quality primary care for both the urban and rural population. In the 1970s and 1980s, rural community health clinics expanded, and the first EBAIS clinic was implemented in Coronado in 1987. These first EBAIS clinics provided preventative medicine, basic care for children up to age six, maternal care, family planning, and vaccinations. EBAIS clinics also handle obesity, alcoholism, mental health, and minor illnesses. At first the population was wary of these basic clinics, as Costa Ricans were accustomed to receiving all medical care in large hospitals. However, the popularity of the clinics grew, and more and more communities requested their own EBAIS.

In 1994, President José María Figueres Olsen decreed that all primary attention would be handled through EBAIS. At a minimum, each EBAIS would have a medical doctor, a nurse, and a technician and would provide basic health care to between 3,000 and 5,000 people in the community. The technician carries out visits to all individual houses in the covered community. In 1995 there were 242 EBAIS clinics; by 2012, the number of EBAIS had grown to 991, covering 4.197 million people, which is practically the entire Costa Rican population. Patients who need more specialized or advanced care are referred to hospitals. Costa Ricans are served by 29 public general hospitals and 9 hospitals that specialize in specific needs such as psychiatry, geriatrics, women's health, and rehabilitation. The EBAIS serve to keep hospitals from being overrun with routine patients, leaving hospitals free to treat more serious conditions.

What are the benefits of the Costa Rican health system and the EBAIS? The most obvious is very high health indicators that far exceed those expected at Costa Rica's moderate level of economic development. Health care is both universal and relatively inexpensive. In 2012, Costa Rica had the highest life expectancy of any country in Latin America and, indeed, a higher life expectancy than Denmark or the United States.

The human capital gains of health care along with education—Costa Rica has provided universal free education since 1870—has allowed the country to diversify its economy and exhibit strong economic growth over the past two decades. The Costa Rican economy grew by some 56 per cent from 1990 to 2010, adjusted for inflation. This was due largely to two sectors that required high levels of human capital.

The first is the high-technology manufacturing sector. This sector was virtually nonexistent in 1990 but had grown to some 40 per cent of manufactured exports by 2010. Spurred by Intel's 1996 decision to locate a $300-million semi-conductor plant in the country, Costa Rica has developed high-tech clusters and leads the region in R&D spending as a percentage of GDP. Costa Rica's high-tech exports topped $2 billion in 2010 and provide tens of thousands of direct and indirect jobs.

The second pillar of Costa Rica's new economy—tourism—also needed high human capital for real success. Recent research reveals that tourism growth in Latin America in destinations with high levels of poverty and low levels of human capital takes on an enclave form—where tourists stay in self-contained, walled-off resorts—that exacerbates exploitation and inequality and where most of the benefits of tourism leak out of the country (Bowman 2013). In enclave tourism destinations such as the Dominican Republic, a booming tourism industry does little to improve the lives of the population. In contrast, Costa Rica represents a much more beneficial integrated tourism model, where locals and international tourists participate together in tourism activities and where small and medium-sized locally owned businesses benefit from the tourism industry. Low levels of poverty and relatively low levels of crime combine with high human capital (including language skills) to spread tourism and its benefits throughout the country.

Costa Rica has not followed the Kuznets inverted-U; rather, it has exhibited a regular-U since Gini co-efficients became available, with inequality declining from 1959 to 1984 and subsequently rising. Country experts have concluded that Costa Rica is a case of growth with equity. While income growth may have been a contributing factor to periods of inequality reduction, political factors and redistributive measures are more salient for this case. Compared with other developing countries of similar size and resource endowment, Costa Rica has been exceptional. In the long run, this country has been able to sustain an unusual combination of rapid economic growth, substantial improvements in standards of living, political stability, and a strong concern with the wide distribution of the fruits of progress and with the alleviation of poverty (González-Vega and Céspedes 1993, 3). One potentially alarming trend is the increase in income inequality from 1999 to 2010, as the Gini co-efficient rose from .45 to .50. Fortunately, poverty rates have fallen by some 50 per cent over the same time period, but continued increases in inequality could seriously stress the Costa Rican welfare state.

8.2. THE BRAZILIAN MIRACLE, 1960–94

Brazil is an ideal case for an examination of the Kuznets effect and the turning point for emerging economies, as government officials religiously clung to the inverted-U as a developmental policy until 1994, when redistributive policies began to be introduced for the first time. In the past decade, these equity-enhancing policies have produced both high levels of economic growth and historic reductions in income inequality. In Brazil, the relationship between economic growth and inequality can be analyzed in a case with both minimal intervention of government redistributive policies in an early time period and then extensive intervention in the market in favor of the poorest Brazilians.

Brazil's original market-forces approach to distribution is embodied in the work of Carlos Langoni, a University of Chicago–trained government economist who believed that increasing inequality was an inevitable concomitant of economic development, but that eventually the turning point would be reached and income inequality would decline naturally, without any need for government intervention. Following Kuznets, Langoni linked the rise and subsequent decline in inequality to the forces inherent in sector dualism and urbanization (Taylor 1980, 306–13). For Langoni, the role of the government in distribution should be minimal, aside from providing more university education; all the Brazilian government needed to do was continue with the business of growing—and market forces would take care of the equality issue (Hewlett 1982, 332). Langoni and the inverted-U made a considerable impression on Antonio Delfim Netto, the flamboyant architect of the Brazilian economic miracle, who expressed the official position on inequality: "We know 100 percent of the population are getting 100 percent of the national income: the distribution is not important" (quoted in Mittelman 1988, 98). In his preface to Langoni's 1973 book, *Distribuição de renda*, Delfim Netto ridiculed those who favored government policies to reduce Brazil's legendary disparity between the haves and the have nots, accusing them of indulging in "a veritable confidence game which would end up leaving the nation dividing up the misery more equitably" (12). As Hewlett notes,

The "market forces" theory has been adopted as the official interpretation of distributional trends over the recent period for the obvious reason that it absolved the military regime (1964–1985) from any direct guilt in the deteriorating social welfare situation. The theory is extremely convenient in that it precludes the need for any redistributional policies in the future. It also disarms criticism from the advanced democracies. Underlying much of the analysis is an implicit comparison with nineteenth century Europe and North America. If these nations could incur short-run costs in their development processes, why not Brazil. (Hewlett 1982, 332)

The results of Brazil's "market forces" policies from 1960 to 1994 are decidedly mixed. The country experienced tremendous per-capita economic growth of a total of 256 per cent over the 34-year period. Economic power for the country was extensive by 1994. In agriculture, the country ranked as the world's largest exporter of coffee and orange juice. In manufacturing, Brazil's impressive economic machine exported everything from high-tech arms, airplanes, and computers, to low-tech shoes and jeans. Unfortunately, the market never intervened as predicted by Langoni, and the benefits of all of this growth were never realized by most people. By 1994, almost 25 years after passing Randolph and Lott's turning point whereby future growth should result in lower inequality (reached in 1971), Brazil was the world's second-largest market for executive jets, while at least one-quarter of the population went to bed hungry each night and inequality was an epidemic (Brooke 1993, E7). Infant mortality, malnutrition, life expectancy, and other social indicators were at very low levels, given the country's level of per-capita GDP. Poverty levels as a percentage of population approached those of Honduras and Bolivia. In the words of one Brazilian military president, "Brazil is doing fine. It's the people who are doing poorly" (quoted in Brooke 1993, E7). By 1989, the Gini co-efficient was at an astonishing 0.6331, the worst in the world. The richest 20 per cent received 66.5 per cent of the national income, while the poorest 40 per cent received a trifling 7 per cent. The case of Brazil serves as a warning for those who rely on the Kuznets effect and the magic of the market alone to spread the benefits of economic growth to the population.

8.3. THE MIRACLE FOR BRAZILIANS, 1994–2012

The Brazilian Miracle left tens of millions of Brazilians illiterate, desperately poor, and excluded from the economic gains of the previous decades. Brazil transitioned from a military regime to a democracy in 1985, and by 1994 it had transformed into a developmental state where redistribution and poverty eradication became critical national objectives (UNDP 2013, 73). In 1994 Brazilians elected the Social Democrat Fernando Henrique Cardoso, who subsequently served two terms, to the presidency. His policies combined economic liberalization, enhanced taxation, and the implementation of Brazilian-designed social policy. Since that time, the promotion of social cohesion and social integration has been a stated objective of the country. Luiz Inácio "Lula" da Silva, the working-class head of the leftist Workers' Party (PT), followed

Cardoso from 2003 to 2010 and built on policies introduced during the Cardoso years. As more equal societies tend to do better in human development than do unequal societies, Brazil has achieved a virtuous circle where growth with equity has positively affected multiple societal outcomes. This new Brazilian development path is "reshaping ideas about how to attain human development" (UNDP 2013, 2). The policy mix in Brazil reduced poverty from 17.2 per cent in 1990 to 6.1 per cent in 2009 and reduced inequality by previously unseen amounts from 1994 to 2011.

Brazilian social policy is based on three pillars. The first is neither innovative nor daring, but is the idea that primary and secondary education must improve significantly for Brazil to succeed in an increasingly competitive world that demands an educated populace, along with the principle that education levels in the poorer regions of the country must catch up with the wealthier south and southeast:

> State-led investments in education have dramatically improved develop-ment outcomes in Brazil. The transformation of education started with the equalization of funding across regions, states and municipalities. The national Development Fund for Primary Education, created in 1996, guaranteed na-tional minimum spending per student in primary education, increasing the resources for primary students in the Northeast, North and Centre West states, particularly in municipally run schools. Funding "followed the student," providing a significant incentive for school systems to expand enrollment. Similarly, states were required to share resources across municipalities so that all state and municipal schools could reach the per-student spending thresh-old. As a result of this investment, Brazil's math scores on the Programme for International Student Assessment rose 52 points between 2000 and 2009, the third largest leap on record. (UNDP 2013, 80)

The second pillar, and one of the most original and innovative social policies in recent years, is the conditional cash transfer (CCT). This policy innovation was first implemented by the mayor of Campinas, José Roberto Magalhães Teixeira, and Brasilia governor and intellectual iconoclast Cristovam Buarque, and was known as *Bolsa Escola* (school purse). The intellectual roots of the program emerged at the University of Brasilia in the 1980s through Buarque, who was at the time a professor there. *Bolsa Escola* had the objective of decreasing truancy and enhancing human capital while providing necessary resources to poor families with children. The program in Brasilia guaranteed a minimal family income that made attending school more appealing than child labor. The program provided direct monthly resources to poor families with chil-dren between the ages of 7 and 14. However, these monthly payments were conditional and paid only if the children in the family attended a minimum of 90 per cent of school classes. In essence, the Federal District of Brasilia paid families to send their children to school. The results of the program were rapid, impressive, and relatively inexpensive, with school truancy falling from about 10 per cent to less than 1 per cent.

The idea that economic incentives can change behavior is not new, but the use of behavior conditions in exchange for money for poor families was something quite novel. The success of the program led President Cardoso to adopt *Bolsa Escola* at the national level in 2001. Families received 15 reais per month per child (up to 3 children or 45 reais total). By 2002, the program supported 8 million children with coverage in 99 per cent of the municipalities. The total program cost was a mere 12 reais per Brazilian per year (Denes 2003).

When President Lula took office in 2003, there was much speculation as to whether he would continue his predecessor's policy; Cardoso and Lula were serious political rivals. In the end, Lula maintained the conditional cash transfer with some modifications. Lula combined several programs into one conditional cash transfer named *Bolsa Familia*. The combined programs of *Bolsa Familia* include anti-hunger programs and subsidies for energy. To manage the program, Lula founded a new ministry—the Ministry of Social Development and War Against Hunger. The *Bolsa Familia* provides 22 reais (about US$11) per child attending school and receiving regular health check-ups and vaccinations. In addition, pregnant women must make prenatal care visits to qualify for the program. The poorest families receive an additional 70 reais per month. The money is delivered through debit cards known as *citizen cards*, and the cards are generally held by women. The direct payments to individuals through the debit cards reduce both administrative costs and the possibilities of corruption. The result of *Bolsa Familia* has been "substantial declines in poverty and extreme poverty and reduced inequality" (UNDP 2013, 106).

The praise for the program has been extensive. *The Economist* magazine referred to the *Bolsa Familia* as a welfare program "invented in Latin America" that "is winning converts worldwide" (2008). In 2005, the World Bank issued the following summary:

> Brazil's flagship social program, Bolsa Familia, is one of the largest of its kind in the world. Two years after its launch, it is improving the living conditions of eight million poor families throughout Brazil, and the government hopes to achieve universal coverage (around 11.2 million families) by 2006. "Bolsa Familia has already become a highly praised model of effective social policy," said World Bank President Paul Wolfowitz. "Countries around the world are drawing lessons from Brazil's experience and are trying to produce the same results for their own people." (World Bank 2005)

Brazilian President Lula launched the Bolsa Famila Program (BFP) in October 2003 as his government's flagship social program. Like other conditional cash transfers (CCTs) in the region, the program seeks to help:

1. reduce current poverty and inequality, by providing a minimum level of income for poor families; and
2. break the intergenerational transmission of poverty by conditioning these transfers on compliance with key human development objectives, such as school attendance and health visits.

While the state of Brasilia was the pioneer in using conditional cash transfers, the first country to implement these policies was Mexico. The CCT program in Mexico began in 1997 as *Progresa* and was later renamed *Oportunidades*. The program not only requires school attendance and medical checkups but also requires that parents attend community meetings on personal health and hygiene. Like the programs in Brazil, the Mexican CCT is designed to break intergenerational poverty traps. The program distributed some US$3 billion to some 5 million families in 2012. Transfers are provided twice each month to female heads of households. One part of the money is transferred based on conditions tied to preventative medical care. The second part is transferred based on the conditions that children attend at least 85 per cent of classes and do not repeat a grade more than twice. Benefits are higher for female students than for male, as truancy was historically higher for girls (UNDP 2013, 84). As in Brazil, the Mexican program is highly efficient and relatively cheap: "Brazil's *Bolsa Familia* and Mexico's *Oportunidades*, the two largest programs in Latin America, cost less than 1 percent of GDP" (UNDP 2013, 84).

The success of the Mexican CCT program led Michael Bloomberg, then-mayor of New York, to visit Mexico in 2007 to learn about the program and to begin a pilot program in New York: "Mayor Bloomberg acknowledged that the program might not work in the five boroughs. 'But shame on us if we don't have the courage to try things which, if it doesn't work, you will describe as a failure and I would describe as something we should be proud of that we at least tried to help,' he said. 'We should not walk away from any idea that can possibly help'" (Rivera 2007).[37] The New York pilot program lasted for three years, providing funds for students with 95-per-cent attendance, for parent-teacher conferences, for passing regents' exams, for medical checkups, and for job training. While the program did not continue, evaluations showed that the program did reduce poverty and increase school attendance. Mayor Bloomberg's personal assessment is as follows:

> In 2007, the center launched Opportunity NYC: Family Rewards, the first conditional cash transfer program in the United States. Based on similar programs operating in more than 20 other countries, Family Rewards reduces poverty by providing households with incentives for preventive health care, education, and job training. In designing Family Rewards, we drew on lessons from Brazil, Mexico, and dozens of other countries. By the end of our three-year pilot, we had learned which program elements worked in New York City and which did not; information that is now helpful to a new generation of programs worldwide.
>
> Before we launched Opportunity NYC: Family Rewards, I visited Toluca, Mexico, for a firsthand look at Mexico's successful federal conditional cash transfer program, *Oportunidades*. We also participated in a North-South learning exchange hosted by the United Nations. We worked with the Rockefeller Foundation, the World Bank, the Organization of American States and other institutions and international policymakers to exchange experiences on conditional cash transfer programs in Latin America as well as in Indonesia, South Africa and Turkey.

---

37 Some social scientists, such as developmental economists Banerjee and Duflo (2011), argue that the cash of conditional cash transfers matters but not the conditions. Parents would send their children to school voluntarily with the additional money, and do not need the requirements.

Our international learning exchanges are not limited to these cash transfer initiatives; they also include innovative approaches to urban transportation, new education initiatives and other programs. No one has a monopoly on good ideas, which is why New York will continue to learn from the best practices of other cities and countries. And as we adapt and evaluate new programs in our own city, we remain committed to returning the favor and making a lasting difference in communities around the world. (UNDP 2013, 85)

One of the benefits of CCTs is that they can be designed to allow vigorous statistical impact evaluation. For example, the program in Paraguay known as Tekopora has been shown to have significant positive impacts on poverty reduction, health, nutrition, and education without having negative impact on labor supply (UNDP 2013, 83). Along with Brazil, Mexico, and Paraguay, at least 15 other countries have CCTs. These include Argentina, Bangladesh, Cambodia, Chile, Colombia, Egypt, Honduras, Guatemala, Jamaica, Indonesia, Nicaragua, Panama, Philippines, Peru, Turkey, and Uruguay.

The program in Argentina has an additional and specific objective to reduce inequality, and is the cornerstone of the social policy of presidents Néstor Kirchner, who served from 2003 to 2007, and incumbent Cristina Fernández de Kirchner. The Argentine conditional cash transfer program—*Asignación Universal por Hijo*—requires school attendance at a public school, economic need, vaccination and health check-ups, and minimal levels of sanitation in the home.[38] In May 2013, President Fernández de Kirchner announced an increase of 35 per cent in the program, providing 460 Argentine pesos per child (about US$90). Argentina pays much more money per child in its CCT than does Brazil or Mexico.[39]

If education policy was unsurprising and conditional cash transfers innovative, the policy that had the biggest effect on reducing inequality and poverty in Brazil was the most daring—dramatic increases in the minimum wage. In the 15-year period before 2000, Brazilian wages had fallen and stagnated. A large part of the election campaign of Lula in 2002 was the promise of a rapid increase in the minimum wage, far above the rate of inflation or gains in productivity. According to Lula, the Brazilian poor and workers were not getting their fair share of economic output, and while social programs such as *Bolsa Família* could help in social welfare, a job with decent pay was the most favorable path toward development and inclusion.

The election of the Workers' Party in 2002 horrified the Brazilian elite. Lula's promises of raising the minimum wage and living standards of the poor were seen as part of a zero-sum game, whereby gains for the poor would come at the expense of the elites. Economic conservatives around the world argue that large government-mandated increases in the minimum wage will reduce economic activity and job creation.

---

38   Amounts for Conditional Cash Transfers per Child in Argentina. See http://www.anses.gob.ar/asignacion-universal/asignacion-universal-hijo-144.

39   There are several possible explanations for this. The Argentine crisis in 2001 and 2002 was very deep, leaving millions of Argentines unable to feed their families. Chaos resulted and crime escalated. A relatively high conditional cash transfer is therefore seen both as something just and normatively good but also as a source of social peace and lower levels of insecurity.

In fact, the large increases in the minimum wage in Brazil had the opposite effect: "In February 2009, the Brazilian minimum wage was R$465 (approximately US$ 230), almost twice what it was in February 2002, when it stood at R$264 (constant prices for February 2009). During the same period, there was a significant expansion of employment and formal jobs" (Berg 2009, 1).

The official minimum wage in Brazil has extensive effects. It not only fixes the income for formal workers earning the minimum wage, but also for many workers whose income is stated in multiples of the minimum wage. The minimum wage is also a benchmark for unemployment benefits, welfare, and social security pension benefits (Berg 2009, 3). As wages in Brazil are correlated with race and gender, the dramatic increase in the minimum wage has an important effect of reducing the gap between the income of men and women and between white and black workers. "Increases in the minimum wage under President Lula secured him a political legacy that led not only to his reelection in 2006, but also of whomever he picked to succeed him, i.e. Dilma Rousseff," notes economist Luis Alberto Esteves (Tavener 2011).

It was not only the poor who supported Lula at the end of his first term, but a significant percentage of the upper class and elites. The growth of the minimum wage and the reduction in poverty did not lead to greater unemployment and a slower economy, but created a massive and expanding domestic market for manufacturers, the housing market, and other consumption. Brazilian state policies brought tens of millions of people out of poverty, and the entire country benefitted. Even economic liberal publications have conceded that the intervention of the government deep into the market has had positive outcomes. *The Economist* remarked that

> thanks largely to government policy, the poverty rate in Brazil has halved. With this, income inequality (measured by the Gini coefficient) has also fallen, declining on average by 1.2 percent a year. . . . this year Brazil will overtake Britain to become the sixth largest economy in the world. GDP per person, at around $11,000, has been growing at an average annual rate of 1.7 percent since 1990; closing the gap with high-income countries. And income growth is faster among the poorest (comparable to China's GDP per person growth rate). Consequently by 2015 Brazil could reach its Millennium Development Goal of poverty reduction, some ten years early. (*The Economist* 2011)

The secret of Brazil is that there is growth for all, but government policies favor the growth of the poor. As the *Forbes* title calls out, "In Brazil: The Poor Get Richer Faster." The article continues:

> It's a tale of two Americas. One, in the North, has the rich getting richer faster. That's the U.S of course. In South America, Brazil is seeing the opposite happen. The poor are getting richer faster. . . . Wages for Brazil's poorest grew an impressive 29.2 percent between 2009 and 2011, and during the same period, the average income of the general labor force grew 8.3 percent. By comparison, our average income is rising by, what? A penny? Something like that. Brazil is showing the world that it is possible to grow and include at the same time,

and that the inclusion of the poorest contributes to the growth of the country. (Rapoza 2012, n.p.)

The growth of the minimum wage continues unabated, and is currently based on a mechanism that combines GDP growth and inflation. According to the 2011 federal budget, by 2015 the minimum wage in Brazil will be R$815, compared to R$545 in 2011. Nearly 50 million Brazilians earn the minimum wage (Tavener 2011).

If the income of the poor grows significantly faster than that of the rich, then a decline in inequality is expected to follow. Indeed, Brazilian inequality has declined rapidly in recent years. The 2013 government data reveal that the Gini co-efficient in Brazil fell from .585 in 2002 to .5095 in 2012. At the same time, the United States Census Bureau reported that the Gini co-efficient for families grew by 1.6 percent between 2009 and 2010, reaching .477. These two trends led one academic to announce that "[t]he US will become as unequal as Brazil. And that bothers both societies" (Lara 2013, n.p.).

The changes in income inequality in Brazil and Costa Rica are shown in Figure 8.1. No one would have predicted in 1989 that Brazil and Costa Rica would have similar Gini co-efficients in 2012.

The successes in Brazil, however, do not mean that all will go smoothly there. In 1968, political scientist Samuel Huntington published the influential book *Political Order in Changing Societies*. Huntington argues that as societies modernize and economies grow, expectations of individuals grow faster than the capacities of governments

Figure 8.1: Income Inequality: Gini Co-efficient in Brazil and Costa Rica

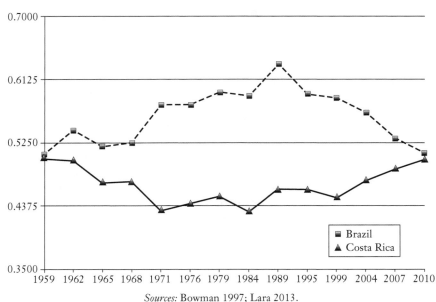

Sources: Bowman 1997; Lara 2013.

and institutions. Stresses develop, and we witness the puzzling and non-intuitive outcomes of political violence and instability in countries that have experienced rapid economic growth and significant upward mobility. Brazilians protested en masse beginning in June 2013. The reasons for the protests were complex and multiple, but they included cost increases in already expensive and often poor-quality public transportation, constitutional changes (PEC 37)[40] that were interpreted as an effort to provide impunity to officials convicted of corruption, and anger over the cost overruns of stadiums for the 2014 World Cup and 2016 Rio de Janeiro Olympic Games. Brazil has made significant progress, yet the country has a long way to go and the road will be bumpy.

CONCLUSIONS

Over the past half-century, Latin America has followed many development strategies. Some, as in Costa Rica, have pursued a growth-with-equity model where an active state intervened in the market to reduce poverty and enhance human capital. Costa Rica's human development has been exceptional and economic growth has been solid. A recent trend toward greater inequality is worrying.

The ideas embodied in the Kuznets effect were imported to Brazil and guided the development model through the Brazilian Miracle from the 1960s to the 1990s. Brazil had exceptional per-capita growth during this period, but the equalizing forces of the Kuznets effect never arrived, and the poor were left behind. After a return to democracy and the election of social democrats and a leftist labor party, Brazil reversed course and no longer relied on the market to lift millions of Brazilians out of poverty.

The Brazilian social welfare state began about 1994. President Cardoso adopted a Brazilian-developed social innovation, conditional cash transfers, to deliver resources to poor families in exchange for families upgrading their human capital. President Lula continued this model with a much more extensive conditional cash transfer program. The program has been successful overall, and has been copied and implemented in countries around the world and in a pilot program in New York City.

Over the past decade, the minimum wage rose considerably in Brazil. The income of poor people has grown much more rapidly than the income of the rich. This has contributed to a reduction in income inequality and the strong growth in domestic consumption. Forty million Brazilians have been lifted out of poverty over the past decade, and Brazilian banks report that they gained 40 million new customers over the same period (Lara 2013). That is the equivalent of adding the total populations of Florida and Texas as new consumers in a single decade!

---

40 The PEC 37 was an attempted constitutional reform that would have stripped all powers from Public Ministry, the fourth branch of government, to investigate official corruption. The passage of PEC 37 appeared assured until the protests derailed the project.

The Brazilian model includes conditional cash transfers, education, and wage increases for the poor. What had the greatest effect on reducing inequality? The effect of the minimum wage on the reduction of the Gini co-efficient was responsible for 73 per cent of the improvement in the income distribution among workers with an income and is the single biggest factor for the reduction of the overall Gini co-efficient. With inequality being a growing problem in much of the world, the success of Brazil and the policies that reduce inequality while also enhancing economic growth contains possible lessons for many.

LESSONS LEARNED

- Reliance on the market alone to redistribute resources has failed in Latin America.
- Conditional cash transfers, originated in the capital of Brazil, are one of the most influential policy innovations and have contributed to development in many cases.
- Brazil's redistribution toward the poor has contributed to long-term economic growth.
- Economic growth and an improvement in standards of living do not guarantee stability but can produce protests and instability.

DISCUSSION QUESTIONS

- Which do you think is better for a country: economic growth or equality of distribution?
- Can Costa Rica and Brazil be compared due to their size differences?
- Do you think that Costa Rica's growth-with-equity model is sustainable?
- Langoni believed that the role of the government in distribution should be minimal. Why do you think he singled out university education for Brazilian government intervention?
- How do you feel about mandated school attendance and medical check-ups?
- Do you agree with the use of economic incentives to change behaviors?
- If you were implementing a CCT program, what would you require?

ADDITIONAL READING

Frankema, Ewout. 2008. "Comparing the Distribution of Education across the Developing World, 1960–2005: What Does the Grade Enrollment Distribution Tell about Latin America?" *Social Indicators Research* 88 (3): 437–55.

Gasparini, Leonardo, Guillermo Cruces, and Leopoldo Tornarolli. 2011. "Recent Trends in Income Inequality in Latin America." *Economia* 11 (2): 147–201.

Kuznets, Simon. 1955. "Economic Growth and Income Inequality." *American Economic Review* 45: 1–28.

WEBSITES

Brookings Institute—Latin America Economic Perspectives: Shifting Gears in an Age of Heightened Expectations. http://www.brookings.edu/research/reports/2011/04/08-blep-cardenas.

Foreign Policy—A Real War on Inequality. http://www.foreignpolicy.com/articles/2012/12/17/a_real_war_on_inequality.

Heritage Foundation—Brazil's Economic Woes Show Limits of State Meddling. http://www.heritage.org/research/commentary/2013/8/brazils-economic-woes-show-limits-of-state-meddling.

Inequality and Economic Development in Brazil—World Bank. http://www-wds.worldbank.org/servlet/WDSContentServer/WDSP/IB/2004/10/05/000012009_20041005095126/Rendered/PDF/301140PAPER0Inequality0Brazil.pdf.

Penn World Table: Downloadable data on per capita GDP and other variables for most countries over 60 years. https://pwt.sas.upenn.edu.

RAND—Center for Latin American Social Policy. http://www.rand.org/labor/centers/clasp.html.

Democracy and the Left: Social Policy and Inequality in Latin America by Huber and Stephens. http://press.uchicago.edu/ucp/books/book/chicago/D/bo13590041.html.

UNE-Wider Inequality Database: http://www.wider.unu.edu/research/Database/.

United Nations—Models of Development, Social Policy and Reform in Latin America. http://www.unrisd.org/80256B3C005BCCF9/(httpPublications)/7E4B8522A609EC67C1256C7C0039C99D?OpenDocument.

CHAPTER NINE

RETIREMENT WITH DIGNITY? LESSONS FROM PENSION REFORM IN CHILE AND BEYOND

INTRODUCTION

The rest of the world has largely ignored a range of innovative public policies from Latin America. Latin America is beneath the United States on the map, the globe, and in governance. There is, however, one striking example of policy innovation that has garnered the attention of the world: privatizing pensions or mandated individual retirement accounts.

There were good reasons for pension innovation to spread. The first public pay-as-you-go (PAYG) retirement system was introduced by Otto von Bismarck in Germany in 1889, providing pensions for workers beginning at age 70. PAYG pensions spread around the world and provided old-age and disability support to generations across the globe. Demographic transformations challenged the PAYG model. A rapidly aging population worldwide, a lower proportion of workers to retirees, and pressures on national budgets led many countries to reassess the traditional PAYG universal public pension plans, where current workers' contributions and taxes pay the benefits of the retired population. Without significant reform, many public pensions faced shortfalls in meeting the promises to growing numbers of retirees. Chile was both innovative and a policy pioneer. Offering a new model to a potentially large global challenge, the Chilean model has been studied, lauded, and subsequently replicated in one version or another in 30 countries. Mainstream newspapers, magazines, blogs, and other media have spread the word of "Chile's Pension System: A Model for the World" (Butler 2011). Joe Klein entitled his influential 1994 *Time* magazine article "If Chile Can Do It . . . couldn't (North) America privatize its social-security system?", wherein

"Pinochet's plan turns workers into big-time investors." Klein further added that the Chilean model "now being emulated or studied in six other Latin American nations— is perhaps the first significant social-policy idea to ever emanate from the Southern Hemisphere."

It is difficult, however, to easily understand the lessons of Chilean pension privatization, as ideological convenience contributed to the spread of these policy ideas and produced incompatible assessments of the program from both supporters and some detractors. The global assessment and characterization of pension privatization that first began in Pinochet's Chile in 1981 has often been highly politicized and polemical. Economic and political conservatives portray the results of pension privatization as nothing short of miraculous for retirees and for Chile and argue that any rational country would follow Chile's example. Some economic and political progressives, on the other hand, describe the results in Chile as disastrous and a complete failure. What are the real lessons from pension privatization? Which side carries the argument?

In fact, the Chilean system of pension privatization has a mixed record, has undergone significant reforms in recent years, and is facing further sets of reforms, as evidenced in the campaign for the 2013 presidential elections where Socialist candidate and former (and now recently re-elected) president Michelle Bachelet seeks to significantly weaken Chile's pension privatization and create a state-run retirement fund (AFP). The changes to the system are already so extensive that the positions staked out by die-hard supporters and hard-core critics no longer make sense, with the two sides often arguing over a system that did not exist after the 2008 reforms.

Indeed, the continuation of the debate on Chile's original 1981 pension privatization without considering the extensive reforms reveals the key to understanding the puzzle of why the world looks to Latin America for pension policy lessons. This chapter argues that the unusual process of policy development and implementation in Chile, which used surrogates and pupils of Milton Friedman and other conservative economists and think tanks in the United States, resulted in the pension privatization that morphed into a real-world and high-profile demonstration or prototype to justify social security privatization in the United States.

In this chapter we will first describe the process of pension privatization in Chile and the use of the Chilean model as a blunt instrument for political ends. We will then describe the spread of the Chilean model throughout Latin America, the shortcomings of the model, and the reform of the reforms. It is argued that the lessons of Latin America cannot be based merely on the original privatization plans, but can only be accurately assessed by taking second-generation reforms into account. In the end, there are real lessons from Latin America for pension reform, but those lessons are different from the claims made by both cheerleaders and detractors.

9.1. PENSION REFORM IN CHILE AND SUPPORTERS ABROAD

Latin America has many firsts. Costa Rica was the first country to constitutionally proscribe the military in 1949. Argentina was the first country to have gender quotas by a political party in 1952 and the world's first woman president in 1976. And Chile was the first country to transform public PAYG pensions into privatized accounts in 1981.

José Piñera (b. 1948), the father of Chile's pension privatization, provides a detailed account of the reform process via his personal web page (Piñera 2010; see also Skousen 2008, ch.5). Piñera recounts how the University of Chicago began to provide scholarships to students from the Catholic University in Santiago, Chile, to study under the conservative economists at the University of Chicago, known as the Chicago Boys and led by Milton Friedman. These students would then carry the fervor and doctrine of the Chicago Boys to Chile and teach university students.

Piñera was one of the students who benefited from this educational experiment. He studied at the Catholic University in the late 1960s and earned a Ph.D. in economics at Harvard in 1975. Piñera returned to Chile in 1975 and worked at the Catholic University. This was just after the military coup, led by Augusto Pinochet, against the elected socialist President Salvador Allende on September 11, 1973.

Pinochet called in Piñera and other Chicago Boys, and together they implemented a radical new program of spending cuts, control of the money supply, expanded trade, and tax reform. Pinochet first placed Piñera in the cabinet in 1978 as Minister of Labor and Social Security and moved him to Minister of Mining in 1980. Piñera pushed through several far-reaching reforms, but the most important was the privatization of the public pension system. The Chilean pension-reform system has been heralded and replicated to some degree around the world, and Piñera is now the president of the International Center for Pension Reform and consults leaders around the world on privatizing pensions.

The original privatization was quite simple. Pensions would no longer be based in the traditional pay-as-you-go retirement system, but would instead be individual benefits based on individual contributions. Workers would own their own individual retirement accounts. Employees were required to invest 10 per cent of their wages and could choose to invest up to 20 per cent. Contributions would be tax deductible, gains would be untaxed, but withdrawals in retirement would be taxed. At retirement, workers could choose to set up an annuity with an approved insurance company, guaranteeing a fixed amount of retirement income for the rest of their lives. Employees could select from various funds run by several government-sanctioned companies for their retirement accounts. They could choose to invest in foreign stocks, as well as Chilean stocks, bonds, and government debt. They could change between the highly regulated AFPs (pension fund administrators).

The original idea for pension privatization came from the Chilean students at the University of Chicago, who observed the faculty participating in the professors' annuity plans, known as TIAA-CREF (Teachers Insurance and Annuities Association/College Retirement Funds). While the Chicago professors had a two-pillar retirement consisting of both a public pension system (social security) and a private retirement fund based on individual contributions (TIAA-CREF), the Chileans decided that the retirement program in Chile would rely entirely on the private pillar.

The Chilean experiment not only turned the practice of public pensions upside down, but also attempted to invert ideological practice. For example, the international observance of Labor Day is on May 1, inspired by mass worker protests that began on May 1, 1884, throughout the United States but centered in Chicago. The intellectual genesis of privatized pension plans also being in Chicago influenced the inauguration date of the Chilean program, in a clear attempt to counter traditional labor strategies and principles in the country:

> The privatized social security plan opened on May 1, 1981, which was Labor Day in Chile and most of the world. It was supposed to open May 4, but Piñera made a last-minute change to May 1. "When my colleagues asked why," he said, "I explained that May 1 had always been celebrated all over the world as a day of class confrontation, when workers fight employers as if their interests were completely divergent. But in a free-market economy, their interests are convergent." I told my colleagues, "Let's begin this system on May 1, so that in the future, Labor Day can be celebrated as a day when workers freed themselves from the state and moved to a privately managed capitalization system." (Skousen 2008, Ch. 5).

According to Skousen (2008), the benefits of the Chilean pension model have been nothing short of miraculous. Ninety-three per cent of the labor force is enrolled in 20 private pension funds. Annual real returns on investment have averaged an impressive 10 per cent over the past 3 decades. The pension funds have greatly expanded the capital markets in Chile and contributed to the country's high long-term economic growth rate of five per cent per annum. By 2008, Chile's private pension system held US$120 billion, or 80 per cent of GDP. By 2011, Chile's private pension system held 58.55 per cent of GDP (Federal Reserve Bank of St. Louis 2014). As Skousen says,

> In short, Chile provides a role model for successful privatization of the US Social Security system. According to Piñera, converting the pay-as-you-go system into a genuine savings program would dramatically increase capital formation and economic growth in the United States even though it would admittedly involve serious transition problems much greater than those experienced in tiny Chile. Some economists still oppose privatizing Social Security, but most are willing to experiment with a small percentage of the FICA tax to see what happens. For example, President George W. Bush proposed that two percentage points be assigned to personal investment accounts, but so far the bill has not been adopted.
>
> A wide variety of media have endorsed the Chilean model, including *Time* magazine and *BusinessWeek*. According to *BusinessWeek* (cover story, "Economic Growth: A Proposal," July 6, 1996) converting Social Security into a fully funded pension plan, complete with individual savings accounts, could boost national savings and increase U.S. plant and equipment by 25 percent by 2020,

and would dramatically increase the economic growth rate. The massive flow of funds into the equity markets would substantially reduce the cost of capital and encourage investment.

José Piñera thinks that the biggest boost to Social Security reform will come if China adopts private accounts. "Then the United States will have to act; otherwise, they will be left behind in rather dramatic fashion." (Skousen 2008, Ch. 5)

The Chicago School adherents and supporters in the United States were quick to applaud Piñera's pension reforms and to support his quest to spread privatized pensions and a reduced role of the state to the United States and around the world. Piñera was given a high-profile position in 1995 as the co-chair of the Project for Social Security Privatization, along with George Shultz, at the prominent libertarian think tank Cato Institute—one of many organizations supported by the billionaire industrialists and libertarian activists Koch brothers—to package and sell Social Security privatization to U.S. policymakers and the media. If tiny and Latin American Chile can embrace the free market for pensions, the argument goes, why can't the United States?

So how does José Piñera himself characterize the lessons and outcomes of the reforms?

A specter is haunting the world. It is the specter of bankrupt government-run social security systems. The pay-as-you-go system that reigned supreme through most of the 20th century has a fundamental flaw, one rooted in a false conception of how human beings behave: it destroys, at the individual level, the link between contributions and benefits—in other words, between effort and reward. Whenever that happens on a massive scale and for a long period of time, the final result is disaster.

Two exogenous factors aggravate the consequences of that flaw: the global demographic trend toward decreasing fertility rates and medical advances that are lengthening life. As a result, fewer workers have to support more and more retirees. Since increasing payroll taxes generates unemployment, sooner or later promised benefits have to be reduced, a telltale sign of a bankrupt system. Whether benefits are reduced through inflation, as in most developing countries, or through legislation, the result is the same: anguish about old age is created.

This comprehensive reform has changed dramatically Chile's economy and society. Six million workers (95 percent of the labor force) have a PRA and 1.5 million (almost 25 percent of labor force, and gradually increasing as higher wages allow their 7 percent of wages to buy the minimum health plan) have an ISAPRE plan.

The PRAs annual average rate of return for 26 years has been 10.3 percent, above inflation. Retirement benefits in the AFP system already are 50 to 100 percent higher—depending on whether they are old-age, disability, or survivors' retirement benefits—than they were in the pay-as-you-go system. According to William Lewis ("The Power of Productivity," 2004), total government expenditures in Chile as a percentage of GDP declined from 34.3 percent in 1984 to 21.9 percent in 1990, and of that 12.4 points decline, Social Security and Welfare changes accounted for half. By increasing savings and improving the functioning of both the capital and the labor markets, this reform was the single most important structural change that contributed to the doubling of the growth rate of the economy in the 1985–1997 period (from the historic 3 to 7.2%). (Piñera 2013)

Chile has been held up as a model for U.S. politicians for the past two decades, most recently in the public embrace of the Chilean model by Republican presidential primary candidates Herman Cain and Newt Gingrich in 2011–12. Cain, who briefly led the national polls for the Republican nomination, repeatedly pointed out that the Chilean model of 1981 would solve all of the country's social security problems. Cain pointed to Chile in two national debates and again in a Tea Party–sponsored Lincoln-Douglas–style debate with Newt Gingrich in November 2011 in Texas. "I am a strong proponent of an idea that President George W. Bush introduced, but it couldn't get any momentum," said Cain. "And that is the idea of personal retirement accounts—optional personal retirement accounts. Thirty countries have optional personal retirement accounts—the Chilean Model. I started studying the Chilean Model, and asked, why can't we do that? The answer is, we can. But the answer is, we have to fight the demagoguery whenever you try to fix the problem, and we have to fight all the people who don't want the system to change." Cain stated that Chile replaced its pay-as-you-go retirement system with personal accounts, starting 30 years ago. "And today they don't have the problems that we have trying to deal with Social Security," he said (Murphy 2011). The conservative *Investor's Business Daily* (2011) followed up Cain's support for the Chilean model on September 9, 2011:

> Herman Cain's victory in Florida's straw poll is notable, among other things, for his advocacy of "Chilean Model" Social Security reform in a state filled with retirees. It ought to be a wake-up call to all candidates. Aside from the analysis about Cain's victory being a protest vote against Texas Gov. Rick Perry, it's worth noticing that—in Florida, no less—both Cain and Perry, who finished first and second in the weekend's GOP straw poll, were the two most outspoken candidates about confronting the U.S. crisis in Social Security.
>
> It completely ends the notion that addressing the issue of unfunded pension liabilities—in Social Security, Medicaid and Medicare—is the third rail of politics. Voters migrated from Perry to Cain, but there were multiple Tea Party favorites to choose from. In moving to Cain, they went from a moderate to a strong stance on Social Security reform.
>
> Perry did call for a national dialogue on the matter. But Cain went much further, at least three times in debates calling for "The Chilean Model" to replace Social Security, bringing the idea to as many as 15 million viewers. Chile's system, enacted in 1981, took government out of the pension business altogether

and replaced it with a system of personal retirement accounts. It's one of the most successful fiscal reforms in history. It outperforms Social Security on returns, yielding about 9.23 percent compounded annual returns over 30 years under private management. That means Chilean retirees take home pension checks four times what they would have gotten if they had remained in their old Social Security system."

If all of the claims made by Piñera, Skousen, Cain, and the pension privatization supporters were correct, then Chilean pensioners would be living the good life and any reasonable person would want a similar system. Supporters claim that it provides universal high-return pensions in individual pension accounts to Chilean workers and that the workers have much higher pensions (four times higher, in fact) than they would in the pay-as-you-go system. In addition, the taxpayers and government coffers are freed of the burden of paying for retirement. Savings and investment rates soar, leading to a modern capital market and rapid economic growth. As we will see, however, these claims are highly misleading and ignore extraordinarily high commissions that undercut net gains, low effective participation rates, and large numbers of pensioners retiring into poverty.

9.2. THE CRITICS OF THE CHILEAN MODEL

Just as there are ardent supporters, there are also powerful critics of the Chilean model. For many of the critics, the Chilean system has been an absolute and unmitigated disaster, and no reasonable country should follow the example. José Cruz, the editor of *Nuestro Mundo*,[41] argues as follows:

The first generation of Chileans is retiring under the system put in place by Pinochet 25 years ago. The plan gets no funding from employers. All of it comes from the workers, who are required to "invest" 10 percent of their earnings in the plan, which is administered by one of 15 Pension Fund Administrators (two of which are owned by US corporations), investment firms that charge fees for "managing" the individual accounts.

Any financial company can set itself up as an AFP, as the companies are known by their Spanish acronym. While proponents of this system say that this promotes competition to get better returns, in reality all AFPs make more-or-less the same investments.

Because of poverty, unemployment, and the crapshoot of the stock market, together with the cut the AFPs take, Chileans are discovering that the promises made to them have not panned out. Retirees are also suffering because they haven't received cost-of-living raises.

---

41   The Spanish language section of *People's Weekly World*.

Today even the government itself and the AFPs have admitted that at least half of the Chilean people will never accumulate enough to be able to get the minimum pension equivalent to $100 (US) monthly. The Chilean Center for Alternative National Development (CENDA) has said that "two-thirds of the population will never qualify for a minimum pension." Manuel Riesco, CENDA's director, added that "the Chilean private pension system will provide pensions on its own only to the upper-income minority." (Cruz 2005)

Cruz further argues that the AFPs are the one sector in Chile that actually benefits from the system, and those AFPs are themselves populated by former Pinochet-era government officials. Cruz also notes that labor organizations in Chile are working to disband the system and to implement a pension system that guarantees a minimum retirement income of 70 per cent of employee wages. Cruz concludes: "If George W. Bush uses the 'good example' of Chile to revamp and privatize the Social Security System here in the US, it's a good bet that workers, women, African Americans, Latinos and other lower-income sectors of the population will be worse off" (Cruz 2005).

Popular U.S. website *The Daily Kos* ran a report in early 2006 titled "Private Accounts a Disaster for SS in Chile" (Acerimusdux 2006). And just as the supporters of private pensions used Herman Cain's debates to promote the Chilean model, the critics were quick to follow up the debates with their own interpretation. In the article "What Herman Cain Isn't Going To Tell You About Chile's Privatized Pensions," Susie Madrak reported the following exchange with her Republican chiropractor:

"I thought Herman Cain seemed pretty smart. He was talking about making Social Security like the Chilean model," he said. "What do you know about that?"

"Oh, jeebus," I said. "The *Chilean* model. The same one that right-wingers have been trying to shove down our throats for 30 years." (This was all mumbled, since I was face down on his table at the time.)

"First of all, it was a mess. It was imposed by Pinochet under his military dictatorship, and the generals revolted. They insisted they get to keep the old plan, and they did. Second, a lot of people didn't get anywhere near the money they actually needed to retire, but the administrators made a fortune." (Madrak 2011).

In *Mother Jones* magazine, Tim Murphy presented "Herman Cain's Chilean Model, Explained": "For the second consecutive Republican president debate, pizza mogul and talk radio host Herman Cain has suggested the 'Chilean Model' as a way to fix Social Security. Never mind that it's Medicare, not Social Security, whose runaway costs pose a long-term threat to the nation's fiscal health—what the heck is the Chilean

Model? And do we want it?" (Murphy 2011). The answer was a resounding no. The Chilean model, according to Murphy, produced poverty-stricken retirees and fabulously wealthy pension fund managers.

Activists and partisans thus remained extremely divided on the Chilean model. In recent years, however, several systematic analyses have taken place, both inside and outside Chile. It is clear that the benefits of the Chilean model are limited, that the system does not deliver what was promised to retirees, and that a national system based entirely on individual retirement accounts will not exist around the world, let alone in Chile.

In 2005 and 2006, 25 years into the Chilean experiment, the reliance on the individual account was seriously questioned on three separate fronts. The first challenge came from investigative journalism, the second from the political process in Chile and the bipartisan Marcel Commission, and the third from economic research at the World Bank. The combination of these three critiques strongly undermines the claims of Piñera and pension privatization supporters and confirms many of the claims by the opponents.

New York Times journalist Larry Rohter's reports on Chile's pension system in 2005 and 2006 played an important role in informing the world about the benefits and challenges in Chile. His January 27, 2005, article entitled "Chile's Retirees Find Shortfall in Private Plan" (Rohter 2005) revealed that only half of Chilean workers were actually captured in the private system, and that the government continued to direct billions of dollars to provide a minimal $140-per-month pension to the rest. Rohter notes that as a percentage of GDP, the government of Chile, in a privatized system, spends more on public pensions than does the United States. In addition, despite the rapid growth of the Chilean economy and stock market, the first waves of retirees under the private system were receiving far lower annuities than they had expected. Rohter uses the example of Dagoberto Saez, a 66-year-old laboratory technician who, though earning $950 a month and contributing to the system for 24 years, would receive only $315 per month in retirement. Had Mr. Saez stayed in the public system, he would have received 120 per cent more each month, or about $700. Indeed, most retirees who opted to stay in the public system were receiving monthly retirement annuities double those of retirees who switched to the private system.

Mr. Saez exemplifies the great mystery of the Chilean system. If the annual returns of the investment markets were higher than anyone predicted—the average 10-per-cent annual return on pension investments was double what was originally projected—why were workers retiring with much less than they expected? The answer, as detailed in 2005 in both the *New York Times* (Rohter 2005) and a World Bank report (Gill, Packard, and Yermo 2005), is the high commissions and other costs of the private pension companies, coupled with complicated quarterly statements that few could understand; one-quarter to one-third of all pension contributions went toward commissions and fees. Rohter acknowledges the benefits of the system, pointing out the creation of a modern capital market, cheaper credit for companies wanting to expand, and putting a brake on government deficit spending. He does, however, quote a government official who claimed, "What we have is a system that is good for Chile and bad for most Chileans."

The response from the political right in the United States, which used Chile as a model for social security reform—and who saw an opening for reform in George W. Bush's second term—was immediate. Brooke Oberwetter (2005), in the conservative *American Spectator*, lashed out at Rohter, calling him "all wet" and completely wrong. The International Center for Pension Reform and other supporters of the Chilean model joined the critique of Rohter, even referring to him as "Larry Potter for his legendary imagination." Nevertheless, Rohter followed up his 2005 story in a January 2006 *New York Times* article, "Chile's Candidates Agree to Agree on Pension Woes":

> The Chilean system of personalized accounts managed by private funds has inspired a score of other countries since the pioneer effort to create it here 25 years ago. It is endorsed by President Bush, who has called it a "great example" from which the United States can "take some lessons." Here at home, though, dissatisfaction with the system has emerged as one of the hot-button issues in the election. . . . (Rohter 2006)

It was not surprising that Michelle Bachelet, the front-running Socialist who ended up winning the presidency in 2006, described the public pension system as being "in crisis" and in need of major reforms in the areas of coverage and cost. What was surprising, and a most compelling argument in the Chilean electoral debate, was the position of billionaire conservative candidate Sebastián Piñera—the brother of privatization guru José Piñera—who stated that "Chile's social security system requires deep reforms in all sectors, because half of all Chileans have no pension coverage, and of those who do, 40 percent are going to find it hard to reach the minimal level. This has to be confronted now, and we agree with Michelle Bachelet and will, I hope, join forces behind this large undertaking" (Rohter 2006).

The original 1981 Chilean pension model was path-breaking, influencing some 30 countries to privatize pensions either partially or fully. The reforms produced some positive benefits for Chile but were not the overwhelming success that matched the rhetoric of their fans and supporters. Chileans from the right, center, and left agreed that the reform needed massive additional reforms. These reforms were introduced and passed, and they resulted in a very different system from the original. Interestingly, when Herman Cain or other supporters of privatization of social security in the United States refer to the Chilean model, they base their impressions on the original model and never mention the reforms; neither do the critics. "It is a big reform, not just patching a few things up," Bachelet advisor and former Minister of Economy Mr. Velasco said. While the rest of the world is still enamored of the original Chilean model, he noted, "we are moving to a Chile II model, and there is no blueprint to follow. We have to create from scratch" (Rohter 2006).

The third major examination of pensions in Latin America came from economists and started with Indermit Gill, Truman Packard, and Juan Yermo in their book, *Keeping the Promise of Social Security in Latin America*. The authors shatter the notion that the Chilean model was or even approached the status of panacea. They present pensions and retirement based on three pillars: government-guaranteed pensions that protect the population from falling into poverty in old age, mandated individual retirement accounts providing opportunities for self-managed pensions, and voluntary savings accounts. Among many other findings in this data-rich and detailed work, the authors conclude that the emphasis on the second pillar—mandated individual retirement accounts—was crowding out the other pillars, leading to too many individuals who were falling into poverty in old age. Privatized pensions revealed two major problems. First, the significant costs of commissions left many workers participating in the private pensions without sufficient retirement funds. Second, even with private pensions, the taxpayers would need to contribute heavily to retirement programs. The authors call for substantial new efforts in pillars one and three and for the abandonment of the reliance on the original Chilean model. Their work was crucial for a more dispassionate and nuanced assessment of pension reform.

9.3. THE SPREAD OF INDIVIDUAL ACCOUNTS IN LATIN AMERICA

Since the landmark work by Gill, Packard, and Yermo (2005), several academics have carefully tracked and analyzed the waves of pension privatization and reforms, including Sarah Brooks (2007); Barbara Kritzer, Stephen Kay, and Tapen Sinha (2011); Barbara Kritzer (2008); and Robert Holzmann (2012). This next section borrows heavily from both Kritzer's 2008 article on the 2008 reforms in Chile and the 2011 review by Kritzer, Kay, and Sinha.[42]

Since 1990, ten other Latin American countries have adopted some version of the Chilean model of privately managed individual accounts. These include Argentina (1994), Bolivia (1997), Colombia (1993), Costa Rica (1995), the Dominican Republic (2003), El Salvador (1998), Mexico (1997), Panama (2008), Peru (1993), and Uruguay (1996). There were significant differences in employer and employee contributions and the reliance on pay-as-you-go systems among the programs, as shown in Table 9.1.

Scholars have identified several problems with the first generation of private pension systems. The first is coverage. Coverage refers to the percentage of the population that is actively contributing to individual accounts. If coverage is low, then a large percentage of the population will not have adequate pensions upon retirement. Across the 11 Latin American countries with individual accounts, the proportion of contributors as a percentage of the labor force ranges from a low of 13.3 per cent in Peru to a high of 59.9 per cent in Chile in 2009, with a mean average of 29.6 per cent. This means that more than 70 per cent of the labor force across the region were not making regular contributions for their retirement.

There are many reasons for this low contribution rate. Latin America is home to a large number of informal workers, and there is a strong correlation across the region between the percentage of the labor force in the formal sector and the percentage of workers who contribute to an individual retirement account. There are

---

42   The authors are especially grateful for the work of, and their conversations with, Stephen Kay.

Table 9.1 Financing Individual Accounts in Latin America*

Country	Employee (%)	Employer (%)	Recognition of accrued rights under PAYG**
Bolivia	10	None	Yes
Chile	10	Voluntary	Yes
Colombia	3.85	11.625	Yes
Costa Rica	1	3.25	PAYG remains a first pillar
Dom. Rep	2.87	7.1	Yes
El Salv.	6.25	4.05	Yes
Mexico	1.125	5.15	At retirement, choice of PAYG or indiv. retirement
Panama	8.5 above $490	4 above $490	PAYG remains a first pillar
Peru	10	None	Yes
Uruguay	15 above $974	None	PAYG remains a first pillar

*Argentina nationalized the private individual retirement accounts in 2008.
**PAYG (Pay-As-You-Go) is the retirement system whereby current workers pay the retirement benefits of older retirees.

three potential solutions to this problem. The first would be to reduce the number of informal workers. This has been an objective in Latin America for decades and, while there has been some improvement in reducing informality in some countries, progress has been disappointing.[43] The second would be to provide a public pension for poor and informal workers, and to make participation in the individual account required only for formal, higher-income workers. Finally, the government and employers could increase the incentive to save by providing matching contributions to worker contributions. An additional group that was excluded from the pension reforms in Chile was the self-employed. Excluding the self-employed has a further impact on the low contribution rate.

A second major challenge of the first-generation privatization systems was the high level of administrative fees that greatly reduced the pensions of retirees. Pension funds in Latin America generally levy a charge, based on a percentage of workers' total income, on every contribution, leading to high fees and enormous profits in environments with limited competition and low levels of financial fluency on the part of the contributing population. For example, Mexican pension funds charge an average administrative fee of 1.87 per cent. This may seem like a small number, but remember that this is 1.87 per cent of the contributor's *total* income, not of the amount contributed. Since the mandatory contribution in Mexico is 8.5 per cent of income, the percentage of contributions that are collected as fees for a

---

43   The informal economy as a percentage of GDP ranges from 18.8 in Chile to 63.4 in Bolivia for 2006 (Schneider, Buehn, and Montenegro 2010).

worker making the minimum required contribution is 1.87 per cent of total income divided by 8.5 per cent of total income as mandated contribution, or 22 per cent! If a worker contributed 100 pesos to his pension, his net contribution would amount to only 78 pesos, as 22 pesos would go to administrative fees, and he would have to earn 28.23 per cent of compound interest just to get back to his initial contribution of 100 pesos.

In Argentina until 2002, the private-pension administrative fee was about 3 per cent and the minimum contribution was 10 per cent, resulting in a commission or administrative fee of about 30 per cent for each minimum contribution of 10 per cent. When Argentina faced an economic crisis in 2002, the government reduced the minimum contribution from 10 per cent to 5 per cent of total income. However, the administrative fees remained based on the total income, so the administrative fee doubled to a whopping 60 per cent! When an Argentine made a 100-peso contribution, only about 40 pesos made its way to the retirement account; the other 60 pesos went to fees and commissions. Argentines were incensed, but they received no mercy from the pension funds. It is no surprise that Argentines were relatively muted when the post-crisis government seized and nationalized the private pension system.

A complicated fee system and high fees endure in part due to widespread financial illiteracy, a universal problem. Research shows that only 18 per cent of citizens of the United States, for example, can successfully make simple interest calculations. In Chile, a survey revealed that

- fewer than 35 per cent of contributors knew the percentage of their taxable income that was directed to the pension system each month;
- only 15 per cent knew roughly how much money was in their retirement account;
- only 8 per cent knew how pensions were calculated;
- the poor and those with less education were less knowledgeable about the pension system. (Kritzer, Kay, and Sinha 2011)

In Peru, a large survey of heads of household by the Inter-American Development Bank (IADB) reveals that only 12.2 per cent of the population is aware of the monthly contribution rate, and 16.5 per cent know who paid the administrative fees. And in Mexico, surveys found that workers with higher levels of financial literacy were much more likely to select from funds with lower fees (Pagés et al. 2009).

Economic theory would predict that low competition among pension funds, mandated contributions from workers, and low financial literacy would combine for unusually high profits for the pension funds. Return on investment (ROI) is a measure of profitability in an industry. Without barriers to entry, if the ROI in one sector is unusually high, it will attract new investment that will lead to greater competition over time, and a normal return on investment will result.

Economic experts have been able to compare the ROI in the private pension funds with the ROI in the similar banking sector to test if the pension system earns unusually high profits. Unsurprisingly given the low competition, required contributions from workers, and low financial literacy, pension companies in Chile, Mexico, and Peru earn profits that are consistently far above those earned by banks. In Mexico, pension companies earned an average ROI of an extraordinary 36 per cent in 2000–2005, a rate that is six times higher than the ROI of the banks (Kritzer, Kay, and Sinha 2011). The pension-fund companies in Chile also have ROI much higher than the banks, suggesting that the limited number of funds is acting as an oligopoly and earning supra-normal profits. The high profits reduce the retirement benefits for the contributors, with lower-income workers suffering the most. A Mexican worker making the minimum monthly contribution pays about 22 per cent of all contributions in fees, while a worker contributing 20 per cent of his or her salary per month pays only about 9 per cent of contributions in fees. For low wage workers, studies calculate that a 1-per-cent reduction in the fixed contributory fee would result in a 9-per-cent increase in the worker's lifetime pension benefit!

An additional challenge of first-generation pension reform was gender inequality. Women's monthly pensions in Chile have been disappointing for two reasons. On the supply side, women are unemployed for longer periods than are men, and women's wages are lower than those of men. As a result, at retirement, women have a smaller balance in their fund than do men. There is also an important demand side or retirement feature that reduces the monthly pension of women. In Chile, monthly pension payments from the individual accounts are often based on an annuity, and companies must use gender-specific tables to calculate annuities. Since women live longer than men, the monthly payment to a woman would be lower than would the payment to a man with the same retirement balance. Overall, women's pensions have been 30 to 40 per cent lower than those of men.

9.4. THE 2008 REFORMS

Chile might have been the model for many countries to follow and for U.S. politicians to praise, but the Chileans themselves were unsatisfied with the first-generation pension reforms and instituted widespread changes with Law 20.255 in March 2008. These reforms are detailed in Kritzer (2008) and summarized below.

For many Chileans, pensions were simply inadequate. Law 20.255 adds a new dimension to the system, known as the System of Solidarity Pensions (SPS), to expand coverage and provide a minimum pension to the population. By 2012, an estimated 1.3 million people (in a country with a total population of 17 million) were receiving the basic solidarity pension. This pension is for all of those not eligible for any other pension, aged 65 or disabled, and a resident of Chile for a stipulated minimum amount of time. The previous pension for poor retirees restricted participation *de facto* to higher wage workers with full-time jobs in the formal economy. The pension in 2012 was about US$158 per month and went to over 1.1 million poor retirees. For those Chileans who had contributed sufficiently for a pension but whose pension was below US$494 per month in 2012, the solidarity pension also included a top-up amount of about US$33 per month.

To extend the degree of participation in the system, the self-employed are required to make contributions to individual retirement accounts, contributing a full 10 per cent of taxable earnings by 2015. As a further incentive for youth participation, the government subsidizes workers between the ages of 18 and 35 who earn less than about $462 per month and provides for an employer match of worker contributions to personal retirement accounts.

To improve gender equity, the new reforms provide a woman aged 65 or older with a bond equal to 18 months of contributions for each child born. The bond may be redeemed and added to the woman's individual retirement fund. Another measure provides additional retirement funds to women based on a reimbursement of the premiums women pay for disability and survivor insurance. In addition, retirement assets gained by a couple during their time of marriage are split evenly between the couple in the event of a divorce. And finally, wages for domestic workers must be no less than the minimum wage. This will increase the earnings of the largely female domestic worker labor force, theoretically resulting in higher pensions for these workers.

To reduce pension fund (AFP) fees and increase the competition among AFPs, the reforms made several important changes. The fixed monthly administrative fees that most AFPs used to charge account holders have been eliminated. In an effort to encourage lower contribution fees, the government now assigns all new labor-force entrants to the AFP with the lowest fees. An average 1-per-cent increase in the rate of return on pension funds can increase a pension by 20 per cent. In an effort to increase the often paltry size of retirement pensions from private accounts, the reforms aim to increase rates of return. There are three particular reforms in this area:

- to increase efficiencies, AFPs can contract out certain administrative pensions in an effort to reduce administrative fees;
- to increase competition and the number of AFPs, insurance companies are now allowed to set pension funds as subsidiaries;
- to increase the rate of returns, the law gradually increases the limits on foreign investments to 80 per cent of assets held in pensions. Previously, pension managers were largely limited to domestic investments.

Finally, in order to improve financial literacy in Chile, state and private donations finance a fund to develop financial education programs. In addition, a new accreditation system for pension advisors was established to provide expert and independent financial advice to workers and retirees. These advisors can charge up to about $2,400, a cap that is in place to limit the possibility of advisors taking advantage of the financially illiterate.

Even with these considerable reforms, many Chileans are still dissatisfied with the pension program. Michelle Bachelet, who oversaw the 2008 pension reforms as president, ran again in 2013 on a platform that included the creation of state-managed pension funds and even more reforms. She was re-elected president with a larger majority than in her first term.

CONCLUSIONS

Since Chile first reformed the PAYG to an individual account in 1981, 10 Latin American countries and 20 other countries have introduced some form of individual retirement account, including countries as diverse as Australia, India, Malawi, and Sweden. Few of them, however, tried the near universal individual account option that was implemented in Chile. Like Chile, countries such as Colombia, Mexico, Peru, and Ecuador are discovering the limitations of private retirement systems and are passing reforms inspired by the 2008 reforms in Chile.

The shortcomings of the Chilean system led the country to make extensive reforms, most notably in accepting that many Chileans will need public PAYG pensions and subsidies to retire with even a semblance of dignity, and in establishing an enhanced pillar of solidarity pensions and subsidies to low-income individual account holders. These changes are not cheap. The official Chilean estimate (by the official Marcel Commission, which evaluated challenges and proposed reforms) of the cost of the new solidarity pillar is estimated at 2.5 per cent of GDP, and the cost of the changes to subsidies and top-ups to the contributory pillar is estimated at 2.9 per cent of GDP. The military, while governing Chile in a dictatorship when pensions were privatized for most Chileans in 1981 always maintained a PAYG system for retiring soldiers, has a pension that costs the state approximately 1.5 per cent of GDP. The combined public cost of pensions in Chile, originally predicted to decline significantly after the 1981 transition, is now predicted to remain at about 6 per cent of GDP. In contrast, the social security system in the United States costs less than five per cent of GDP.

The Chilean lessons are numerous. Private accounts have many potential benefits. Workers have greater confidence in permanent ownership of retirement balances. Over time and with more transparent reporting, populations can gain greater financial literacy. Individuals in countries with historically low rates of savings can develop a much higher propensity to save. Large pools of savings enhance capital markets and domestic investment, both of which have been traditionally problematic in Latin America. However, the predictions of the most enthusiastic supporters of the Chilean model—that everyone would retire with great personal pensions, that public pensions would largely or totally disappear, and that the cost to taxpayers would be negligent—turned out to be both hollow and illusory. Extensive public pensions and significant taxpayer costs are not going to disappear with efforts to privatize pensions. Individual accounts can limit the liability of the PAYG system, but if the objective of pensions is to provide a robust and meaningful retirement, public pensions, subsidies, and significant taxpayer funds will remain a large part of the total retirement system.

LESSONS LEARNED

- There are no panaceas or quick fixes to provide dignified pensions to the millions of new retirees each year around the globe. The claims of the supporters of the Chilean pension system have been exaggerated.

- When considering returns in private pension plans, the costs or commissions must be accounted for and can seriously reduce retirement benefits.
- Financial literacy is crucial for a population to make informed decisions on national pension policy and personal savings decisions.
- All national pension plans, from the public system in the United States (Social Security) to the private system in Chile, require significant contributions from the taxpayer.

DISCUSSION QUESTIONS

- Why has the Chilean model spread outside of Latin America?
- Do reforms to the Chilean system make the system more or less credible?
- Do you find certain arguments for or against the Chilean model more or less convincing?
- Who benefits from the Chilean pension system?
- How could the Chilean model be adapted to suit the needs of larger countries?

ADDITIONAL READINGS

Madrid, Raul. L. 2005. "Ideas, Economic Pressures, and Pension Privatization." *Latin American Politics and Society* 46 (2): 23–50.
Piñera, José. 2000. "A Chilean Model for Russia." *Foreign Affairs* 79 (5): 62–73.

WEBSITES

Brookings Institute—National Retirement Savings system in Australia, Chile, New Zealand and the UK: Lessons for the United States. http://www.brookings.edu/research/papers/2010/01/07-retirement-savings-john.
Cato Institute—Chile's Social Security Lesson for the U.S. http://www.cato.org/publications/commentary/chiles-social-security-lesson-us.
Cato Institute—Economist Estelle James Examines Chile's Pension System. http://www.cato.org/publications/commentary/economist-estelle-james-examines-chiles-pension-system-1.
The International Labour Office (ILO) Social Security Reports. http://ilo.org/global/research/global-reports/world-social-security-report/lang--en/index.htm.
Stephen Kay, "State Capacity and Pensions." http://www.frbatlanta.org/filelegacydocs/StateCapacityandPensionsKay.pdf.
National Center for Policy Analysis—Pensions Reform in Chile: Closing the Gap, Not Scrapping the System. http://www.ncpa.org/pub/ba583.
New York Times—Chile rethinks its privatized pension system. http://www.nytimes.com/2006/01/10/world/americas/10iht-chile.html?_r=3&.

OECD—Chilean Pension System Working Paper. http://www.oecd.org/els/public-pensions/2429310.pdf.

Social Security in Other Countries. http://www.ssa.gov/international/links.html.

Social Security Programs throughout the World. http://www.ssa.gov/policy/docs/progdesc/ssptw/.

SSA—The Next Generation of Individual Accounts in Latin America. http://www.ssa.gov/policy/docs/ssb/v71n1/v71n1p35.html.

World Bank Pension Page for Latin America and the Caribbean. http://web.worldbank.org/WBSITE/EXTERNAL/TOPICS/EXTSOCIALPROTECTION/EXTPENSIONS/0,,contentMDK:22175646~menuPK:6111629~pagePK:210058~piPK:210062~theSitePK:396253,00.html.

CHAPTER TEN

GLOBAL LESSONS FROM THE BEAUTIFUL GAME

INTRODUCTION

In the book *Salsa, sabor y control, Sociología de la música tropical*, author Ángel Quintero Rivera (1998) presents the "contribution of the Caribbean to the happiness of the world" through its music. The same thing could be stated of South American football. Argentina, Brazil, and Uruguay embraced soccer[44] as part of the wave of globalization, port and rail construction, and immigration that swept the Southern Cone in the final decades of the nineteenth century. The creoles adapted and innovated the sport, with skilled passing and less dribbling, and by the 1920s Uruguay was the global power, subsequently joined by Argentina and Brazil as global leaders. These three countries have won 9 of 19 World Cups, 2 each by Argentina and Uruguay and 5 by Brazil.[45] To this stunning record we should add that Argentina and Brazil have also contested three World Cup finals: 11 of the 19 World Cup finals have featured one of these three South American countries. How is it that Uruguay, with a population of just over three million, was and is now again a global soccer power? What could larger countries with growing soccer fandom, such as the United States, India, or China, learn from South America?

---

44 While we prefer the word football to soccer, we use soccer in this chapter because of the quotations and language comparing football and soccer in the United States.

45 Uruguay was also Olympic champion on two occasions, 1924 and 1928, when the Olympics were regarded as the only world championship. In actuality, therefore, this tiny country, one-third the territorial size of Spain, with one-sixteenth the population of Spain, was the world champion on four occasions.

Indeed, what political lessons can we glean from Southern Cone soccer? There are few scholarly works that explore the sporting, political, and social lessons of this hegemonic sport, in part because social scientists traditionally have not systematically studied the phenomenon. Progressive intellectuals have largely decried the effect of soccer as the opiate of the masses and the principal source of alienation from politics and a distraction from the problems of corruption, inequality, poverty, and authoritarianism. For the rest of academia, soccer was a pastime, the domain of journalists and not serious academics. This dynamic is currently undergoing a radical change, as sociologists and political scientists are beginning to systematically examine the role of sport in general, and soccer in particular, in power dynamics, identity politics, civil society, corruption, organized violence, electoral politics, gender relations, and country branding.[46]

This chapter examines two principal lessons from soccer in Latin America. The first is the limits of sport as the opiate of the masses. Since Roman times, critics have observed that political elites with large masses of poor and deprived citizens could ensure security and eliminate political violence and unrest through "bread and circuses." One must merely keep the people fed and distracted by passionate entertainment in order to maintain privilege and power. In fact, 2013 was a watershed year in Argentina and Brazil for both the transparent attempts by political elites to use soccer as a distraction from political crises and the reaction from the population to these attempts.

The second lesson takes the example of Uruguay as the greatest per-capita soccer power in the history of the game, exploring precisely how the waves of Uruguayan soccer success occurred and providing a roadmap for other potential soccer powers to follow. Can Canada, China, India, Russia, or the United States, with a combined population of some three billion, learn enough from a country of some three million to someday challenge for a World Cup championship?

10.1. THE LIMITS OF CIRCUSES AND OPIATES

Journalists and academics have been charging politicians with using soccer as a political distraction for decades. Steve Bloomfield (2010) reveals the naked attempt by national rulers on the African continent to use the "beautiful game" for political ends. Franklin Foer (2004) vividly describes the use of soccer to boost ethno-nationalism and ethnic cleansing in Serbia. And in *Football and Fascism: The National Game under Mussolini*, Simon Martin (2004) argues persuasively that the Italian fascists used soccer stadia, Italy's success in the 1934 and 1938 World Cups, and the love of the game by the masses to create Italian national identity, shape public opinion, and reinforce conformity. The military junta in Brazil meddled in the team's composition to shape public opinion in 1970. Juan Domingo Perón was active in stadium construction and keeping the Argentines out of international competition in an effort to maintain his

---

46   See, for example, several works by Pablo Alabarces (2003; 2008) in Argentina and Ronaldo Helal (1997) in Brazil.

own public support. Most famously, the Argentine military junta in 1978 held a World Cup championship during some of the most violent days of the Dirty War and orchestrated an Argentine victory in search of political support and legitimacy. When Argentina won what was their first World Cup in 1978, both torturers and those that they tortured (and would perhaps later disappear) put aside their violent differences and celebrated arm in arm.

In the build-up to the 2010 World Cup in South Africa, Terry Eagleton (2010) voiced his complaint:

> If every rightwing think-tank came up with a scheme to distract the populace from political injustice and compensate them for lives of hard labour, the solution in each case would be the same: football. No finer way of resolving the problems of capitalism has been dreamed up, bar socialism. And in the tussle between them, football is several light years ahead. . . . Football offers its followers beauty, drama, conflict, liturgy, carnival and the odd spot of tragedy. . . . Like some austere religious faith, the game determines what you wear, whom you associate with, what anthems you sing, and what shrine of transcendent truth you worship at. Along with television, it is the supreme solution to that age-old dilemma of our political masters: what should we do with them when they're not working?. . . . Football these days is the opium of the people, not to speak of their crack cocaine. (n.p.)

The global importance of the beautiful game and its importance for local and national identity make soccer more likely than any other sport to be an opiate. While some 160 million people watch the U.S. Super Bowl, some 800 million watch a regular-season game between Barcelona and Real Madrid, and some 32 billion cumulative viewers watched the 2008 World Cup in Germany.

If soccer were an opiate around the rest of the world, then it would be crack in the Southern Cone. Soccer is, for these countries, what Markovits and Rensmann (2010) refer to as the hegemonic sports culture that fills most of the sports space and is a subject of a large percentage of daily conversations. In Brazil—in addition to a 38-game national first division *Brasilerão* or national championship, the South American Cup, the Liberators Cup all for club teams, and the international games for the multiple national teams—there are the state and regional championships. Brazilians are bombarded with more televised soccer games than any other people.[47] Brazil also boasts the most World Cup titles and is, by any measure, a soccer-crazy country.

No city, however, can compare to Buenos Aires for soccer passion. As documented by Gaffney (2009) the combination of neighborhood identity and politics produced a city with 69 professional soccer stadiums, more than any other city on the planet. In Argentina, first Diego Maradona and now Lionel Messi are referred to as lesser gods. Rabid fans of Maradona started the Maradona Church, with its own commandments,

---

47 In Brazil the weeknight soccer games are televised at 10 pm, so that Brazilians can watch the other opiate of the people, the television soap operas or *telenovelas*.

Figure 10.1: Diego Maradona at First National Team Game.

chants, and Christmas (Maradona's birthday of October 30, 1960). The church also uses the neo-tetragrammaton D10S to refer to the soccer star, fusing the Spanish word for god (*dios*) with Maradona's kit number (10). The commandments include: 2) Love football over all things; 3) Defend the colors of Argentina; and 9) Let Diego be your second name and that of your children. And the "Our Diego" chant states,

> Our Diego, who is on the pitches,
> Hallowed by thy left hand, bring us your magic. Make your goals
>   remembered on earth as in heaven,
> Give us some magic every day, forgive the English, as we have forgiven the
>   Neapolitan Mafia,
> Don't let yourself get caught offside and free us from Havelange and Pelé.[48]

48　Maradona scored the "hand of God" goal against the English in the 1986 World Cup that was won by Argentina. Fans accuse the Neapolitan mafia of conspiring against Maradona. João de Havelange (b. 1916) was the Brazilian president of FIFA, and Pelé (b. 1940) is the long-time Maradona rival from Brazil.

These two cases, Argentina and Brazil, are what political scientist Harry Eckstein (1975) refers to as the "most likely cases" for exhibiting the power of bread and circuses through soccer. Consequently, if we can establish the limits of soccer as an opiate of the masses in these most likely cases, then the claims of the strong relationship are exaggerated and undermined.

The summer of 2013 provides unique test cases of the limits of sports as a distraction from politics in both Argentina and Brazil. The case of Argentina is framed by a decision by the Argentine state to nationalize the televising of the professional soccer leagues. Until 2009, Argentine First Division games were televised as cable or pay-per-view by a private company, *Torneos y Competencias* (TyC), a company controlled by enemies of the ruling Kirchner governments. In July 2009, the Argentine government of Cristina Kirchner voided the contract and decreed that all games would be shown live on free public television. Watching soccer, the government said, should not be an activity only for those who can pay; soccer is a human right in Argentina, and it should be accessible and free to every citizen. The new television program would be known as "Soccer for Everyone" (*Futbol para Todos*), and the First Division championship would now be known as the *Torneo Nestor Kirchner*, named for Cristina Kirchner's late husband and former president of the republic. The televising of the second and third divisions of Argentine soccer has also been nationalized in the *Futbol para Todos* program. The games are shown sequentially from Friday to Monday, so that no two first-division games are shown at the same time. An Argentine has the right to watch every first division game for free!

The nationalization of soccer has been highly controversial. Opponents argue that taxpayers are underwriting not only popular entertainment and undermining market forces, but also providing a space for government propaganda. Nearly all of the advertisement in "Soccer for Everyone" is from and for the government. Supporters claim that the private broadcasters were abusing the soccer teams and the population with high prices to viewers and low payments to the league, that all citizens have the right to see soccer, and that the subsidy of the government is less than US$1 per viewer, who are largely working class, while the taxpayers subsidize the elitist Colón opera house in Buenos Aires with more than US$200 per spectator, who are largely elites.

The objective of the Kirchner government to use soccer as the opiate of the masses was never fully transparent until June 2013, when the government attempted to directly use soccer to undermine criticism of the government. Why did that happen and who won?

In April 2012, celebrated journalist Jorge Lanata started a satirical yellow-journalism weekly television show named "Journalism for Everyone," a clear play on words against "Soccer for Everyone." Week after week, the popular and talented Lanata would combine satire, stand-up comedy, and scandal-probing investigative journalism in an attempt to undermine the Kirchner presidency and expose corruption and misdeeds by Cristina Kirchner, the late Nestor Kirchner, and anyone associated with the government. Lanata's show is a mixture of similar shows in the U.S. hosted by Stephen Colbert and Glenn Beck. "Journalism for Everyone" became more and more popular with each new scandal, and the charges, often with limited evidence beyond the testimony of a single guest or two, would be supported with carefully timed reports in the major newspapers (*Clarín* and *La Nación*) that are unflinchingly critical of the government. The scandals included that the Kirchners had a huge vault of money hidden under one of their houses, that the vice-president was corrupt, and that governors associated with the Kirchners are feudal lords that abuse their own citizens.

By the southern hemisphere's autumn of 2013, the Kirchner government had reached its limit with the program and options were discussed to reduce the popularity, ratings, and influence of Lanata. Soccer was selected as the tool to reduce Lanata's viewers. There are plenty of popular soccer teams in Argentina, but the two largest teams with the biggest national fan bases are Boca Juniors and River Plate. Consequently, these two teams pull the highest ratings on "Soccer for Everyone." These two teams were integral to the government's plan.

The Argentine government informed the Argentine Football Association that it was to schedule the prime game for May 26, 2013 (Boca Juniors vs. Newells Old Boys) to begin at 7:30 pm, precisely the starting time for Lanata's "Journalism for Everyone." A new competition, much greater and more interesting than a mere soccer game, was now on. Who would win between Cristina Kirchner and Lanata? How could Lanata compete with the biggest soccer club in Argentina, the legendary Boca Juniors? Could soccer be the opiate to distract the population from Lanata's effective and entertaining yellow journalism?

This became a major question in café conversations and in the press in the days leading up to the Sunday-evening showdown. Lanata, ever a brilliant showman, executed a perfect game plan. The stage for his show was decked out as a soccer pitch, the announcers were the former soccer announcers for TyC, and Lanata and his crew all dressed as soccer players. And what was the final score of this showdown? All of Argentina was waiting for ratings to be released on Monday, May 27. The final score in the ratings war was "Journalism for Everyone" 24.7 vs. "Soccer for Everyone" 17. But Cristina Kirchner is a fighter and does not easily throw in the towel, so she tried again the following week by scheduling River Plate vs. Argentinos Juniors opposite Lanata. Lanata won again, 21 to 18.5.

The Kirchner government continues to use "Soccer for Everyone" to maximize government support. In September 2013, a long-awaited first part of a long interview with Cristina Kirchner was broadcast on public television, with a ratings share of a mere 1.9. The government changed the soccer schedule for the following Sunday and scheduled the second part of the Cristina interview in between the Boca Juniors and the River Plate games, which improved the ratings but also increased the critiques. This case in Argentina demonstrates the continuing attempts and limitations of politicians harnessing soccer as an opiate of the masses. While Argentines are passionate and crazy for soccer, they are also sophisticated political thinkers and do not like being manipulated with the beautiful game.

The limitations of soccer as a distraction were also tested in Brazil in 2013. Brazil is hosting the greatest and most popular sporting event on the planet—the World Cup—in 12 cities in June and July 2014. Brazil previously hosted the World Cup in 1950, losing a final in front of 200,000 fans at the Maracaná stadium. While the country has won a record five World Cups, that defeat is still a burden to carry. As a test-run of a World Cup, a smaller but important competition known as the Confederations Cup is held the year before in the host country. Eight national teams representing the different federations from around the world compete for the title and test the stadiums, infrastructure, and organization. Brazil has never won a Confederations Cup, and everyone knew that this would be a major event, held from June 15 to June 30, 2013.

Knowing that Brazilians would be focused on the Confederations Cup, government officials delayed the implementation of two unpopular policy issues until mid-June: increases in public transportation fares and a constitutional amendment known as the PEC 37. How successful was this plan of using soccer as a distraction? We explore this question below.

One of the major challenges for Brazilians is transportation. Subways are expensive and insufficient, public buses are crowded and expensive, and all surface transportation, including the huge numbers of first cars owned by the burgeoning middle class, often spends more time in traffic jams than moving. Several local governments announced bus and subway fare increases for early 2013. The national government of Dilma Rousseff, already facing criticism for the rising cost of living in Brazil, pressured those governments to delay fare increases until mid-June, during the Confederations Cup.

A second polemical issue that was also delayed until the Confederations Cup was the voting on the PEC 37. The PEC 37 is a constitutional amendment that would take away the Brazilian Public Ministry's authority to investigate corruption and other crimes committed by public officials, including elected officials. The Public Ministry is often referred to as the fourth branch of Brazilian government; it comprises independent public prosecutors who work at both the federal and state levels to investigate wrongdoing. The Public Ministry has brought charges against numerous officials, most notably the participants in the *Mensalão*[49] vote-buying scandal in 2005 that eventually led to convictions in 2012. The PEC 37 would not only eliminate the role of the Public Ministry in ongoing and future investigations of corruption, but would also provide impunity to those previously charged and convicted due to Public Ministry actions. The amendment would make corruption, already widespread in Brazil, that much easier and increase impunity by absolving the guilty from the *Mensalão*. It sailed though the committee process and was scheduled for what looked like a pro forma vote in the Congress in mid-June 2013.

Against this backdrop of the fare increases in transportation across Brazil, the impending vote of the PEC 37, and the glorious play of the title-winning Brazilian team in the Confederations Cup, the most unexpected thing happened. Brazilians initiated mass protests with millions of participants that exploded across the country. Ironically, the Confederations Cup, the upcoming World Cup, and the construction of the new soccer stadiums not only did not act as an opiate of the masses, but instead were kindling and gasoline for the political protests. The World Cup and the stadiums are examples of cost overruns, corruption, and diverting resources from transportation and health to unnecessary games and overpriced stadiums that would either end up as white elephants

---

49　*Mensalão*, or "big monthly," was a scandal in which the Lula government paid national legislators large monthly payments to vote with the government.

Figure 10.2: Protestor in São Paulo, June 7, 2013.
Credit: Maria Objetiva. Licensed under the Creative Commons Attribution-Share alike license (CC-BY-SA).

or privatized after being paid for by the taxpayer. Indeed, the stadiums are truly scandalous. For example, the World Cup stadium in Cuiabá will seat 43,000 when the average attendance for a soccer game in that city is 200. The Mané Garrincha stadium in Brasilia was originally expected to cost US$330 million but ended up costing US$750 million. The stadium seats 70,000, while local professional soccer crowds average 1000. There is also a stadium in Manaus, a city that does not have high-level professional soccer. These excesses and abuses to the taxpayer go on and on and are documented by many, including Gaffney at "Hunting White Elephants" (Gaffney 2014).

Protestors booed the president of FIFA and the president of the country at the opening Confederations Cup game. Brazilians attempted to delay the playing of the games by blocking access to the stadiums. In direct protest of the PEC 37, protestors attempted to seize the national legislative palace in Brasilia. Large-scale protests

continued from mid-June throughout the rest of the year. These protests had immediate effects in Brazil. Brazilians rarely protest in large numbers; in fact, the last such
event was in 1989. Government officials, business leaders, international soccer officials
at the World Cup, and those for the Olympics—Rio de Janeiro hosts the Olympics in
2016 and part of the 2013 protests were against the Olympic Games expenditures—are
worried that the brand of these mega-events in particular, and Brazil more generally,
will be extensively tarnished.

The two actions that were delayed until the expected Confederations Cup distraction were suddenly and unexpectedly impossible to pass. The Brazilian Congress,
expected to rubber-stamp the PEC 37 before the protests, voted 430 against and only
9 for. Transportation fare increases were rolled back throughout the country. It is too
soon to know the long-term transformations that will result from the mass protest
movement. We can, however, conclude that the opiate effect of soccer was not obtained,
and in fact the attempt of the government to use soccer as a distraction turned out to
backfire and inflame the protest movement.

10.2. U.S. EXCEPTIONALISM IN SOCCER

Soccer is not only the undisputed global game, but is also becoming the hegemonic sport
in many new nations, creating a population that eats, sleeps, drinks, and argues about it
even if they do not play it (Markovits and Rensmann 2010, 13). Soccer is the principal
game in almost every country with more than 100 million inhabitants, while only 1 of
the 15 most populous countries, Brazil, has ever won a world championship.

The disappointment of the United States is particularly informative. The United
States, a global sports power across a huge range of sports, finished third at the World
Championship and first World Cup in 1930 in Uruguay, beat mighty England in the
1950 World Cup in Brazil, advanced to the second round in the 1994 World Cup
played at home, and reached the quarter finals in 2002. Nevertheless, the United States
has never been considered a real threat to win a World Cup. While only a hegemonic
sport in a limited number of soccer cities such as Portland, soccer plays a fascinating
role in American politics. Some important conservative political voices associate
soccer with anti-Americanism and socialism. The antipathy that many Republicans
hold for soccer is part of a larger perspective in which American football is capitalist
and democratic while soccer is—as stated by former professional quarterback and
Republican vice-presidential candidate Jack Kemp—"European and Socialist." Soccer
is collectivist, foreign, uncomfortable, and a sport "that was not invented in the home
of the free" (Hertzberg 2010). Even though more U.S. citizens watch the national
team playing in the World Cup than watch the baseball World Series or golf's The
Masters, the sport is identified as something at battle with American exceptionalism.[50]
As conservative media star Glenn Beck exclaims, "I hate it so much, probably because
the rest of the world likes it so much" (qtd. in Hertzberg 2010).

---

50   Markovits (2001) has an entire book that elaborates the theories and history of the ideology
of U.S. exceptionalism and why that limits the appetite for soccer.

G. Gordon Liddy, another right-wing media host and head of the White House Plumbers who ended the Nixon presidency through their bungled Watergate burglaries, identifies soccer as a Latin American lesson that the U.S. should avoid, in a caricature worthy of the political cartoons of the nineteenth century:

> [Soccer] comes from Latin America, and first we have to get into this term, the Hispanics. That would indicate Spanish language, and yes, these people in Latin America speak Spanish. That is because conquistadores who came over from Spain—you know, tall Caucasians, not very many of them—conquered the Indians, and the Indians adopted the language of their conquerors. But what we call Hispanics now really are South American Indians. And this game, I think, originated with the South American Indians, and instead of a ball they used to use the head, the decapitated head, of an enemy warrior. (quoted in Hertzberg 2010)

Liddy's conservative radio guest added that "the whole Hispanic issue" explained why the left is pushing soccer in schools around the country. Sports are, now more than ever, part of the identity of a politically divided country.

In spite of these stereotypes, young people in the United States play organized soccer more than any other sport, and five million adults play the sport regularly (almost two million more adults play soccer regularly in the U.S. than the entire population of Uruguay). Yet it is still difficult to imagine that the country could win a World Cup any time soon, in part because the U.S. has yet to produce a single elite player, i.e., someone who is in the top five in his position. And the fanaticism for soccer is also exploding in China, with 1.3 billion inhabitants, yet their men's national team is FIFA ranked at number 99, behind New Caledonia, which has a population of 250,000. Why is it that in the global game that everyone wants to win, only a tiny number of countries can compete at the world level? What can we learn from the successful cases?

It is particularly useful, and absolutely fitting, to finish this book with the lessons from tiny Uruguay, that extreme case of soccer, with world-class players on top teams throughout Europe, four-time world champions (at the Olympics and in World Cups combined), winner of the most recent South American championship (2011), second place on the FIFA rankings in 2012, and the fourth-place team in the South African World Cup in 2010. How can we explain this accumulation of extraordinary successes? What are the lessons to be learned?

10.3. THE ORIGINS AND THE FIRST WAVE OF URUGUAYAN SOCCER GLORY

As they did to Argentina and Brazil, the British brought soccer to Uruguay in the second half of the nineteenth century.[51] The British business managers first imported cricket

---

51 Based on Franklin Morales (1969a, 1969b). We recognize and are grateful for the research of Juan Cristiano and his MA thesis in the Sociology Department at the University of the Republic, directed by Felipe Arocena, which was crucial for our writing the following sections on the Uruguayan case.

with the Victoria Cricket Club in 1842, but the sport did not catch on with the local population. A second cricket club, the Montevideo Cricket Club, formed in 1861, and it was here that soccer was first played in the country. The English High School began in 1874 and was the first Uruguayan institution with a soccer coach. The year 1878 witnessed the first of many games played between British residents of Uruguay and British sailors passing though the Montevideo port.

The Montevideo Rowing Club formed in 1874, and it differed in important ways from the Montevideo Cricket Club, which embodied a clear British identity and required members to speak English. The Montevideo Rowing Club and the National Rowing Club of 1888 both had a more Uruguayan and nationalist flavor. This new nationalist sports movement led Enrique Lichtenberger to organize the first Uruguayan club (named Football Association) dedicated to playing soccer, and the club prohibited foreign players. The club later changed its name to Albion, in honor of the pioneering English club of the same name, and adopted uniforms in the Uruguayan national colors of sky-blue and white. The nationalist trend in Uruguayan soccer reached its most durable and successful expression with the founding of Nacional Football Club on May 14, 1899. Nacional, the first creole club in Latin America, became one of the most acclaimed clubs in the world. Its founding was the result of a process that began with Montevideo Rowing opposing Montevideo Cricket, though officially Nacional is the fusion of two clubs: Montevideo Football Club and a breakaway group from Albion.

The other founding moment in Uruguay occurred in 1891 when managers of the English railroad company in Uruguay founded a sports club in Villa Peñarol, the Central Uruguay Railway Cricket Club. The club would eventually adopt the name Peñarol, reach the heights of global soccer, and represent a large contingent of creole fans cheering for the team colors of yellow and black.[52]

The sky-blue colors of the Uruguayan national team played its first game on August 15, 1910, at the Belvedere Stadium in Montevideo, beating Argentina 3–1. Héctor Rivadavia Gómez, president of the Uruguayan Football Association, pushed the idea of a continent-wide competition with the creation of the South American Football Association in 1916. A four-team tournament in 1916 was the preamble to the inaugural Copa América in 1917. The first South American Championship in 1916 featured host Argentina, as well as Brazil, Chile, and Uruguay. Uruguay won the title, and the leading scorer was Uruguay's striker Isabelino Gradín. Two Afro-Uruguayans were featured, Gradín and Juan Delgado, most likely resulting in the first national team in history to feature players of African descent. The Chilean delegation was sufficiently shocked to demand the annulation of the tournament because Uruguay was playing with "two Africans." Gradín gained such international fame that the Peruvian poet Juan Parra del Riego (1894–1925) dedicated the poem "Polyrhythmic Dynamic" to the player. The poem begins as follows:

---

52 Peñarol Football Club won five Liberators Cups: 1960, 1961, 1966, 1982, and 1986; three Intercontinental Cups: 1961, 1966, and 1982; and was Uruguayan champion 46 times. Nacional Football Club won three Liberators Cups and three Intercontinental Cups in 1971, 1980, and 1988; and was Uruguayan champion 44 times.

Palpitating and jubilant
like the shout that suddenly launches the aviator
all clear and nervous,
I sing to you, oh marvelous player!
That today you placed in my chest a trembling drum.
Agile,
refined,
fleet,
electric,
sudden,
delicate,
devastating,
I watched you play in the Olympic afternoon . . .

Figure 10.3: Isabelino Gradín, Uruguayan Soccer Star.
Credit: Photo provided by the Football Museum, Montevideo.

The South American Football Federation tasked Uruguay with hosting the first Copa América in 1917, the first official tournament of this nascent continental organization. The first Copa América was won by the Uruguayans, the same champions as in the four-team tournament from the previous year in Argentina. In fact, since the creation of the South American Football Federation, tiny Uruguay has won 15 continental titles,[53] nearly twice as many titles as Brazil's 8, making it the national team with the most South American titles and the current Copa América champion.

Uruguayan soccer reached new heights in 1924 in the soccer championship at the Paris Olympics. Twenty-two teams battled for the championship, and Uruguay played Switzerland in the gold-medal match, coasting to the championship with a 3–0 victory over the Swiss in front of 41,000 spectators. Even more impressive is the fact that the world's best team represented only half of the Uruguayan teams. In 1922, a schism divided Uruguayan soccer into two bands of clubs, managers, directors, and fans. Paradoxically, while one Uruguayan national team was winning the Paris Olympics, the other dissident Uruguayan team was playing the Newton Cup against a dissident Argentine team; the Olympic team was representing the Uruguayan Football Association and was harshly criticized by the dissident Uruguayan Football Federation, which believed that Uruguay would play poorly at the Olympics and embarrass the nation. In fact, the Uruguayan team caused such a sensation that the team won the Olympic Cup, a distinction that recognized the best champion of any Olympic event. Another Afro-Uruguayan player, José Leandro Andrade, became one of the first global international stars, earning the nickname "the black marvel."

Uruguayan national president José Serrato intervened in the beautiful game and unified the opposing factions in 1925, in part to prepare to defend Uruguay's title in the upcoming Amsterdam Olympics of 1928. The soccer of the River Plate dominated global soccer at the time, with Argentina and Uruguay regularly surpassing other teams and facing each other in the finals. After trouncing the opposition, Argentina and Uruguay played the gold medal match. The anticipation was so high that 250,000 people requested tickets. The teams tied the match, leading to a second sold-out final match, won by the Uruguayans 2–1.

In February 1929, directors of Nacional Football Club presented a project to the club's board in response to a request by the International Football Association Federation (FIFA) for Uruguay to organize the first World Cup. The other members of the South American Federation unanimously supported the Uruguayans. Finally, the FIFA congress in Barcelona unanimously selected Uruguay as host.

The principal task facing Uruguay was to build the infrastructure necessary to host such an international mega-event, as the country did not have a single suitable stadium. The new stadium would have a capacity of 80,000 spectators and would be named the Centenario, as homage to the hundred-year anniversary of the Uruguayan constitution of July 18, 1830. The construction was delayed and did not begin

---

53   In 1916, 1917, 1920, 1923, 1924, 1926, 1935, 1942, 1956, 1959, 1967, 1983, 1987, 1995, and 2011.

until February 1930. To meet the deadlines, workers worked three shifts, through the night under enormous lights. The stadium was completed on July 18, 1930, when Uruguay defeated Argentina 4–2 in the title game (Moreno 1970).[54]

The mythical Maracaná stadium in the Brazilian city of Rio de Janeiro, however, was the site in 1950 of the most glorious moment in Uruguayan soccer. Facing a home crowd estimated at 210,000, Uruguay defeated Brazil 2–1 and was crowned World Cup champion for the second time in a game that—because of idiosyncrasies of that World Cup—Brazil only needed to tie to secure the title. The visitors, captained by Obdulio Jacinto Varela, silenced the giant crowd that watched their celebration slip away even with everything on their side: the home grounds, the massive cheering crowd, and a 1–0 lead. To hold Brazil scoreless over the rest of the match, and to score two goals to secure the title, required the mythical *garra charrua*[55] or fighting spirit that characterized the Uruguayan people and national team. Uruguay's stunning victory left a deafening silence in its wake, along with reports of suicides by Brazilian fans. Uruguay had secured its fourth world title, unmatched in global soccer. Was it possible for this tiny country to continue its global dominance? It was possible but very unlikely.

10.4. STAGNATION AND DECADENCE

The same country that was the global power in the first half of the twentieth century stagnated on the soccer pitch, just as its economy and exceptionalism in economic development went into a long decline. The Switzerland of Latin America or the Athens of the River Plate, as Uruguay was often called, not only began a deep sleep in terms of international soccer, but also grew systematically poorer and fragmented. The socioeconomic decline reached its nadir with the military dictatorship of 1973.

By contrast, humiliated by the defeat at the Maracaná, Brazil reacted like a wounded tiger and invested energy and resources into soccer in order to become one of the greatest forces in the sport on the planet. With superstars such as Garrincha and Pelé, Brazil won its first world championship in 1958, again in 1962 without the services of an injured Pelé, and again in 1970 with a once-again sublime Pelé. The Europeans also improved significantly, with advantages in physical preparation, systemization of training processes for the players, and tactical discipline. In addition, the Europeans pioneered the importance of all aspects of elite performance, in advanced infrastructure for professional performance including the stadium and the turf, modern training grounds, gyms, and more. The most prominent example was the innovative playing style of the Dutch national team of 1974, identified as the "Orange Machine,"

---

54   A video of the inauguration, the stadium, and highlights from that first World Cup final are available at http://www.youtube.com/watch?v=1RqlyrXZ4KM.

55   *Garra charrua* is named for the Charrua Indians who inhabited the Uruguayan territory before the arrival of the Europeans. *Garra* is the Spanish word for talon or claw. Combined, *garra charrua* can be defined as brave tenacity or group survival instinct to never submit. It is a defining characteristic of Uruguay and of the national team.

with a soccer style of multifunctional players displaying a dominant tactical organization and devastating physical preparation.

The Dutch defeated Uruguay in the 1974 World Cup in a 2–0 match where the absolute Orange dominance from beginning to end exposed the sclerosis of Uruguay's reliance on *garra charrua*. The long sleep continued. In 1986, Denmark confirmed Uruguay's soccer obsolescence with the greatest humiliation of its history, in the form of a 6–1 destruction in which the Uruguayans were impotent while the Danes were explosive and owned the ball. In this period the Uruguayans developed a negative image as a rough and brutal team that employed excessive fouls to intimidate their opponents, as they could not win with their skill and game.

For their part, the Africans and the Asians slowly elevated the level of their game to reach the elite level of international play. With rare exceptions, a team should never underestimate the potential of any FIFA rival. The other South American teams, traditionally easily beaten by Argentina, Brazil, and Uruguay, began to approach their level and on occasion surpassed them. Bolivia eliminated Uruguay from the 1994 USA World Cup, and Colombia punished the Argentines with a historic 5–0 defeat in the Monumental Stadium of Buenos Aires in 1993, which forced the Argentines to compete in a play-off spot with Australia to reach the World Cup. Paraguay, Chile, and Ecuador have also arrived as serious threats in the qualifying matches in recent

Figure 10.4: Manuel Francisco dos Santos (Garrincha) Leading Brazil to the 1962 World Cup Title.

decades and have made an impact in some World Cups, occasionally leaving Uruguay on the outside looking in.

The triumphs of the first half of the twentieth century were sustained fundamentally by the technical quality of Uruguayan players and their *garra charrua*—courage to face adversity. Soccer of that era did not have the physical preparation, discipline, and speed of today's game. A bit of craftiness and exceptional technical skills self-taught to the Uruguayans on the *campitos* (empty lots with two rocks as goal posts) or on the streets were sufficient to beat the Europeans. The tactics in the games flowed not from a coach, but from the orders given by the most veteran players on the pitch. These senior players often also acted as sports psychologists, motivating their teammates to defeat the frustration that comes from losing a game or from a bad decision by the referee. José Nasazzi (Uruguayan captain of the Olympic winning team in 1924 and 1928 and of the first World Cup in 1930) and Obdulio Varela (Uruguayan captain for the 1950 and 1954 World Cups) were both impeccable leaders of their respective teams, and their wisdom in managing the tactical and psychological aspects were decisive in the success of those groups of players. The beautiful game, however, subsequently evolved from the spontaneous to the programmed and systematic, and the Uruguayan soccer institutions that socialized the players were unable to successfully adapt to these new trends.

The Uruguayan first-division soccer league is one of the least attractive markets for soccer players, due to the comparatively low salaries. This results in younger and younger players emigrating to Europe. Those players with possibilities to become stars are recruited at a very young age by sports agents who later place them in leagues with higher salaries. Not only are there salary asymmetries with respect to the richest global leagues (England, Italy, Germany, Russia, and Spain), but other Latin American countries with larger television markets, such as Argentina, Brazil, Chile, Colombia, and Mexico, are also more appealing and have higher salaries than the Uruguayan league. The smaller Uruguayan population results in a television market for soccer that is very small compared with other countries in the region. In addition, the market for merchandising (kits and other items with the team logos) remains small in comparison with other Latin American countries, let alone England and Spain. The revenues from members' monthly dues are also constrained by the small population. The insufficient resources to sign elite players at the South American level and to keep top Uruguayan players have meant that for the past 30 years no Uruguayan club has won the Liberators Cup (the top club competition for South America), or any other club cup organized by the South American Confederation. During these three decades Uruguayan clubs have reached only two semifinals (Danubio in 1989 and Nacional in 2009) and one final of the Liberators Cup (Peñarol in 2011). One telling indicator of the decline of Uruguayan clubs is the ranking of different leagues by the International Federation of History and Statistics (IFFHS). In 2012 the Uruguayan league was ranked 25th, and for South America only Bolivia, Peru, and Venezuela ranked lower.

10.5. RETURNING TO THE PEAK AFTER IMPORTANT TRANSFORMATIONS

In spite of the weakness of the Uruguayan league, the country continued to produce world-class players lured around the globe by higher salaries. A transformation of the national team was required to turn it once again into a global power. In March 2006, Óscar Washington Tabárez—a schoolteacher in his youth, thus called "el Maestro" ("the Teacher")—took the coaching reins of the national team for the second time. Tabárez was coach at the 1990 World Cup but was subsequently sacked. He had a successful career as a club coach in Argentina, Italy, and Spain. He coached giants Boca Juniors and Vélez Sarsfield in Argentina, Cagliari and Milan in Italy, and Oviedo in Spain.

Tabárez's 2006 return included a project entitled "Institutionalization of the processes of national teams and the formation of their players," which had the following objectives: 1) establish clear policies and processes that would provide stability and continuation of the national team, 2) raise the sporting performance and approach the level of soccer of international elite national teams, 3) positively influence the holistic preparation of players on the national team, 4) coordinate the objectives and activities of the national teams at all age groups to reach long- and mid-range objectives, 5) program all activities of the national teams in advance to match local and international calendars, 6) make competition an indispensable part of the evaluation of teams and the training of players, going beyond official international competition, and 7) develop a profile of Uruguayan national team players that includes technical, ethical, and disciplinary dimensions.

The institutionalization of policies and processes of the national teams and the socialization of the soccer players by the coaching staff headed by Tabárez have been key to the renewed success of the Uruguayan national team in recent years.[56] One crucial change was the decision to maintain continuity by securing Tabárez and his staff for six years. This contrasts with the trend in Uruguay of changing coaches on average every 1.85 years since 1955.

The other long-term blemish was the scarce coordination of objectives, style, and activities of the different Uruguayan junior national teams that feed into the senior team. This lack of coherence and continuity had seriously damaged the socialization of players on the national team. The players lacked a process to assimilate a Uruguayan style in all age categories. In addition, the players were never socialized from an early age into a set of common values that would orient their behavior on and off the pitch and contribute to a strong group identity. And the participation of the senior and junior players took place only at official international competitions. This was not enough to develop a well-functioning and unified team that could play well together. Since Tabárez took over, the under-15 and under-17 national teams train together twice a week and the under-20 team trains twice per week throughout the year, and for one solid month before any international competition. Now all activities of the junior national squads are overseen by coaches from the senior national team to ensure continuity.

As to the plan of increased international competition, Uruguay needed to play the maximum number of international games possible, taking advantage of all the open

---

56 We follow the inspiring theoretical work of Berger and Luckmann (2001), which discusses the importance of processes of institutionalization and socialization for the development and evolution of any social group.

play dates set by FIFA, and those games should ideally take place in Europe. This was difficult at first, as the rivals and venues were not adequate, but now the options have improved considerably and Uruguay has excellent choices for picking the best games for building the team and earning money. Uruguay has played more than 30 international friendly matches under Tabárez, in addition to twelve in the Copa América, seven in the 2010 World Cup, and dozens in World Cup qualifying matches.

Tabárez has put together a staff that includes youth coaches, technical assistants, and even sports psychologists. During the qualifying matches for the World Cup in South Africa in 2010 there were some very difficult times, but the coaching staff knew how to stay detached from the pressures from the press and the demands of a coaching change from the fans. Uruguay eventually finished fifth in a South American group where only the top four teams automatically qualified for the World Cup, placing Uruguay in a play-off spot with the fourth-place team (Costa Rica) of CONCACAF (Central and North America and Caribbean). Uruguay won the play-off with Costa Rica for a World Cup spot, 1–0 in Costa Rica and a 1–1 tie in Montevideo.

Another important change was the creation in April 2002 of a high-performance sports center known as "Uruguay Celeste," which functions as the training grounds for the various youth and senior national teams. The grounds feature several soccer pitches in excellent condition, a two-story building with rooms for 40 players from the national team and 70 junior players, with two to three players per room. The facility also has a gym, weight room, and press area. The facility cost US$1.7 million, with FIFA providing US$1.1 million and the Uruguayan Football Association (AUF) and the company Tenfield (a media company that holds the rights for the national team and the Uruguayan club league) each providing US$300,000. While the facility was inaugurated four years before Tabárez took over, it was an important element in the latest round of success. For many years the national teams had problems training, as they had no facility of their own. Tabárez took over with the benefit of the proper infrastructure for an elite soccer team, and he took advantage of it. The advances in training and facilities changed the negative image of the national team, one that used gratuitous violence and aggressive play to intimidate rivals.

Another factor for Uruguay's new wave of success was the utilization of innovative sports software that analyzes statistics and play in games: for example, the flow of passes, shots, centers, ball recovery, and plays that ended with goals. Kizanaro Sport Technology[57] provides the service, and one of the software developers was a Uruguayan company. The software meticulously analyzes the performance of the team and each player, and also provides in advance a bank of data of future opponents that can be used to plan games. One of the services of Kizanaro Sport is the real-time delivery of data for use at half-time in games in order to make adjustments and understand what is working and what is not. Since Tabárez arrived, the company has been a constant assessor for the coaching staff, providing statistics to analyze both the players and the opponents.

---

57   See http://www.kizanaro.com.

With respect to the current characteristics of elite soccer, Tabárez notes:

there is less space and time now to make plays. This is fundamentally due to the great development of physical preparation, the improvement in technique and skills, and the tactical organization of the teams. A game of elite soccer must take place with velocity. There is very little space to pass a ball to your teammate. Rapid passes are a distinctive trait of contemporary soccer. This must be incorporated in the conceptualization and methodology of training, and also the infrastructure. . . . You cannot play elite soccer on a bad pitch. . . . Elite soccer of today is a close relative or blood brother of velocity. Not only the speed of the moves . . . but also the speed of the execution of plays, which is associated with technique, and the speed of decision of the correct play to resolve a specific situation that is also linked to technique. (López 2012, 276–77)

Tabárez continues that the only way to compete at the elite level is to methodically train a system across all age groups and start at a very young age, so that play and behavior is imitated over and over until it becomes automatic.

The preoccupation that Tabárez has with the integral preparation and formation of the Uruguayan national teams' players of all ages is clear in the following quotation from an interview with the Argentine sports daily *Olé*, from January 2012: "In the junior teams we role play. What is the fundamental task of a player today? Communicate, speak. Therefore we must help them, but how? By playing. The kids designate a teammate to be the interviewer and we improvise a press conference. We have been doing this for four years. The player-journalists ask questions and the protagonist answers. When we finish the players give grades: and we continue until we improve . . ." (Bassahun 2011). The Uruguayan holistic training regiment includes education, studies, and high-school diplomas. The current nucleus of players on the national team, including Luis Suárez, Edinson Cavani, Martín Cáceres, Abel Hernández, and others have all gone through the process.

Some of the leaders of the Uruguayan team that took fourth place at the South African World Cup praise the socialization and methods of Master Tabárez (López 2012). For global superstar and Liverpool striker Luis Suárez, "you feel that you matter far beyond soccer. And as a player he helps you correct errors, he makes you see things that take place on the pitch that you are not seeing, and he explains so well. It is impossible not to understand the Master" (López 2012, 206). Diego Forlán, a striker who won the Golden Ball as the best player at the 2010 World Cup, noted that the Master transformed him from a great player into a leader on the team. Team captain Diego Lugano observed that Tabárez stopped him from trying to do too much and that "the Master does not change with the result. . . . We lose in the qualifying matches for South Africa against Peru, we beat Ghana, or Argentina in Argentina for the Copa América, he is always the same. The same schedules, the same behaviour. We beat Argentina and think that we will stay up til 3am, and no way. At midnight he announces 'off to bed, we have training tomorrow'" (p. 289–90).

We must stress that all of this process of perfection and exactness at all levels of Uruguayan national soccer is insufficient without remembering the fundamental importance of soccer in Uruguayan society. The first gift that a child receives upon learning to walk is a soccer ball, and there are few young men who have not played hundreds of games and participated in some type of competition, be it in school, neighborhood, or organized club. It is impossible to visit the beach, walk by a park, or pass a town square and not find a group of people playing the beautiful game. The game is of central importance on the radio, television, and the printed press, and occupies a permanent space in conversation. For all of the significant reasons that Uruguayan soccer has returned to the global elite, we must emphasize that the most important element for understanding the essence and distinctiveness of Uruguayan soccer is the ubiquitous presence of the sport in the daily life of the population.

CONCLUSIONS

The Latin American contribution to world soccer could not be greater: the South Americans have played a major role in making soccer the most important sport on the planet. Uruguay, Argentina, and Brazil have combined for more World Cups than any triad of countries in Europe. Argentina and Brazil have produced the two most idolized historical figures in Maradona and Pelé, and the best active player today is Argentina's Lionel Messi. Uruguay and Brazil played the most emotional, dramatic, and heroic championship game of all time. Uruguay is the country that, by far, is the most successful per-capita soccer power; no other country comes close to matching it.

Despite the unrivaled popularity of soccer in Argentina and Brazil, the conventional wisdom that soccer is the opiate of the masses and that politicians can use the beautiful game to manipulate the population is not supported by the evidence of events in 2013. The attempt in Argentina to use the government monopoly on televising and scheduling soccer to strip the viewership of a government critic was not successful. The attempt in Brazil to pass unpopular legislation and increase transportation fares behind the distraction of the Confederations Cup backfired and produced massive protests against those actions and against the World Cup itself.

In spite of its rich history, outside of the South American competitions, Uruguay dropped out of the soccer elite after 1970. Uruguay rarely qualified for World Cups, and when it did, it was usually eliminated in the group phase. The national team that dominated global soccer in the first half of the twentieth century became a second-tier power.

Yet Uruguay is once again a global soccer force, thanks in large measure to a modernization process led by Óscar Washington Tabárez. Leadership, a cohesive strategic plan, world-class infrastructure, institutional changes, common training regimens and playing systems across all national teams of different age groups, cultural shifts in education and formation of players, locally developed technology for advanced diagnostics, and a capacity to accept and learn from past errors—all have contributed to Uruguay's success.

Of course, even all of this does not ensure results, but these changes were absolutely essential. If Ghana had not missed its final penalty kick against Uruguay in the quarter-finals of the 2010 World Cup, sending Uruguay to a semi-final match with the

Netherlands, perhaps we would view Uruguay differently. Without the momentum of a fourth-place finish in the World Cup, perhaps Uruguay would not have defeated Argentina to win the Copa América in 2011. Would Tabárez still be the national coach without these successes? Soccer is a game, a sport that often ends in unpredictable results, and this is itself part of the beautiful game's extraordinary seduction. The results can come or not, but as Tabárez reminds us, the payoff is in the journey.

We would like to end with some final thoughts on global soccer. There are very few countries, only eight, that have won national team world championships, and also very few countries that have won club world championships. This demonstrates the enormous difficulties of winning and leads to the question of what factors are most important for winning. What does a country need to do to be the best in world soccer? There are so many countries with large numbers of players and high levels of passion, yet do not succeed. Sometimes the best teams do not win, such as Hungary in 1954.

For the Uruguayan case there are some necessary factors to understand success, though they are not sufficient. The first is the huge influence of the British at the end of the nineteenth century and beginning of the twentieth;[58] second is a high level of relative economic development, as Uruguay was one of the richest countries at that time; third is the creation of a singular local style and playing identity, based on the *garra charrúa* with its mix of austerity, liveliness, physical and aggressive play, and an instinct to never give up, that probably flowed from the mixing of African and European immigrants at the time of the creation of national identity; fourth is the exceptional team leaders and role models for the other players; fifth is the conformation of a middle-class society, largely urban, formed by a welfare state with strong social policies, including policies of sport promotion as a tool for social integration; sixth is the absolute pre-eminence of soccer as the national sport and a culture that leaves all other sports in its shadow; and seventh is the fact that Uruguay achieved extraordinary early triumphs that opened the path and provided the experience to repeat performances. After the relative decline and stagnation of nearly 40 years from 1974 to 2010, the eighth condition and source of recent success comes from the creation of modern sports organization and the most advanced conditions possible for teaching, training, and studying soccer.

Are these eight dimensions jointly sufficient to explain the history of Uruguayan soccer? Probably not, and certainly one could point to others. How many of these eight conditions are present in other successful countries? How many countries have many of these conditions but are not global soccer successes? How many successful

---

58   One interesting topic to explore is why not a single British colony developed championship soccer. Argentina, Brazil, and Uruguay adopted the sport so early due to British influence, but they were not colonies. British colonies adopted rugby or cricket as principal sports, not soccer. It would also be important to ask why a communist or former communist country never won a championship, despite huge numbers of players and considerable national effort. Other countries reached the peak of global soccer under authoritarian regimes or dictatorships such as fascist Italy under Mussolini, Argentina under the military junta of 1978, and Brazil with the dictatorship in 1970. Countries outside of the Western hemisphere have also never won (accepting that Latin America can be referred to as "the other West" as stated by Brazilian José Guilherme Merquior).

countries have their own idiosyncrasies that help us understand their victories, such as the influence of the Afro-Brazilian population in shaping the playing style of power-house Brazil? Ultimately, is it possible to satisfactorily name the essential conditions for a country to win a World Cup? There are only eight championship countries in the history of the tournament, so that may be a tall order.

LESSONS LEARNED

- Citizens are sophisticated and not easily manipulated just because they are passionate for sports.
- Uruguay, with only 3.2 million people, is an unlikely case for global soccer success, yet it has succeeded at the highest levels in different eras. It is a model to follow for other countries seeking success.
- It is incredibly difficult for a country to win a World Cup, and half measures will likely never produce a winner.

DISCUSSION QUESTIONS

- What will have to change for the United States to win its first World Cup, and how likely are these changes to happen?
- As soccer is often seen as the opiate of the masses, war is often seen as "wag the dog," or a manipulation of popular opinion. In what ways are sports and war similar and different in being used as distractions or an opiate by political elites?
- Do you think Uruguay will be able to compete in the future if other much more populous countries make a serious long-term attempt to develop a World Cup winning program?
- Why do conservatives in the United States view soccer as a socialist activity and leftist sport?

ADDITIONAL READING

Barbero, Raúl E. 1995. *La Copa América*. Montevideo: El País.

Bayce, Julio. 1970. "1928: Amsterdam." *100 Años de Fútbol* 11. Montevideo: Editores Reunidos.

Bellos, Axel. 2003. *Futebol: The Brazilian Way of Life*. London: Bloomsbury Publishing.

Burns, Jimmy. 2003. *The Hand of God: The Life of Diego Maradona, Soccer's Fallen Star*. Guilford, CT: Lyons Press.

Galeano, Eduardo. 1998. *Soccer: In Sun and Shadow*. London: Verso.

Kuhn, Gabriel. 2011. *Soccer vs. the State: Tackling Football and Radical Politics*. Oakland, CA: PM Press.

Manini Ríos, Carlos. 1970. "1924: Colombes." *100 Años de Fútbol* 7. Montevideo: Editores Reunidos.

Markovits, Andrei, and Lars Rensmann. 2010. *Gaming the World: How Sports are Reshaping Global Politics and Culture*. Princeton, NJ: Princeton University Press.

Suburu, Nilo J. 1970. "1950: Maracaná." *100 Años de Fútbol* 18. Montevideo: Editores Reunidos.

Taylor, Chris. 1998. *The Beautiful Game: A Journey through Latin American Football*. London: Orion.

WEBSITES

CONMEBOL. www.conmebol.com.

FIFA. www.fifa.com.

Christopher Gaffney. http://www.geostadia.com/.

CONCLUSION

This book represents a long journey shared by a sociologist from Uruguay and a political scientist from the United States. We have witnessed and experienced decades of economic transformations, political consolidations, cultural and social shifts, and policy innovations. Some of these policy innovations have inspired social scientists and policy makers around the world, but most of the changes in Latin America have not received the attention that they deserve. In addition to the ten foci of this book, there are many other lessons from the region. As just one example, several Latin American countries, including Costa Rica and Ecuador, have attempted creative and innovative environmental policies.

Chapter 1 introduced the conventional wisdom toward the region, the stereotypes, the pejorative descriptions—undeveloped, barbaric, backward—that shape the perceptions that people have not only of Latin Americans, but also of the political, social, cultural, and economic examples that could originate there. These perceptions of a Latin America that is lazy, innocent, and homogeneous/identical from the Rio Grande to Tierra del Fuego has a long pedigree, going back centuries. Cartoon caricatures are one of the most illustrative ways of examining these stereotypes, and several caricatures were reproduced as examples.

The first topical section of the book examined lessons from Latin America in the political domains of elections and participation. The perception of the region is one of institutional stagnation and a follower of the tutelage of external powers, particularly the United States. These three chapters established that the region is an incubator of impressive and pioneering innovations in various areas of political policy.

Chapter 2 examined gender and representation at the national legislative level. Argentina was the first country in the world with voluntary gender quotas by a political party, leading to a large number of women elected to the national legislature in 1951 for the Peronist Party. In recent decades, several countries have decided that electing a larger number of women is healthy for representation and democracy and have continuously enacted institutional changes to increase the number of women in congress. All of the countries of the region exhibit negative political attitudes toward electing women, and gender balance in legislatures is unlikely without binding quotas. The variance in the region is dramatic, with Brazil, Chile, Guatemala, Panama, and Paraguay electing women to fewer than 15 per cent of the lower house seats. Argentina, Costa Rica, Cuba, Ecuador, and Nicaragua elect women to more than 30 per cent of lower house seats. Argentina, Costa Rica, and now Uruguay have binding quotas that will guarantee a large percentage of women legislators, while Nicaragua has achieved a large number of women legislators due to the voluntary quotas of the currently hegemonic Sandinista Party. If the Sandinista dominance in legislative elections declines, however, these gains will be ephemeral. Brazil and Chile have electoral rules that make it particularly difficult to elect large numbers of women. Either attitudes or electoral rules—or both—must change in order for greater progress to take place.

Chapter 3 examined democratic political participation, from voting to more engaged acts of political behavior. For decades, elections in the region were open to charges of misconduct because electoral officials were partisans aligned with the ruling party. We examined the institutional reforms in Costa Rica in 1949 and Mexico between 1996 and 2006 that improved institutions and provided greater confidence in electoral results. Democracy is about much more than voting, and Latin America contains fascinating examples of enhanced political participation. The Kuna of the San Blas Islands in Panama have developed a mixed theocratic-democratic participatory process at the village level that flows into an autonomous congress for the larger Kuna nation. And in Brazil's southern city of Porto Alegre, participatory budgeting empowers citizens, particularly those from poor neighborhoods, to actively participate in the process that determines the spending needs of the city.

The unthinkable option of having a country without a military was the subject of Chapter 4. Ideas from comparative politics and international relations combine with diplomacy and military sales to create the conventional wisdom that all countries need a military. In fact, Central American countries did not historically have institutionalized militaries, with such institutions emerging and consolidating only in the post-1950 period as part of treaties with the United States during the Cold War. Costa Rica demilitarized in 1949; had it waited a few years it would have been much more difficult. The United States militarized previously demilitarized Honduras in the early 1950s, and the military quickly became the most powerful force in the country. The political and economic gains since demilitarization have been impressive in Costa Rica, as has the political and economic stagnation in Honduras since militarization. Latin American countries rarely fight each other, and the internal focus of the military makes this a particularly damaging institution in the region. Panama's demilitarization did not result in any lack of national security, and coincides with exceptional economic performance. Demilitarization is not a pipe dream, particularly for small countries in politically stable regions. Military powers should cease to encourage developing countries from spending precious resources on military weaponry, something that diverts spending from more pressing issues and does not provide for greater security.

The second thematic section examined cultural rights, racism, discrimination, and multiculturalism. The racial and ethnic mix in Latin America is much more varied than that held by conventional wisdom. For example, only five countries in Latin America have large indigenous populations: Bolivia, Ecuador, Guatemala, Mexico, and Peru. Bolivia is majority indigenous, and the subject of Chapter 5. The Aymara, Quechua, and other dozens of ethnic groups have long faced discrimination and poverty in Bolivia. Political organization and most voters produced the election of an indigenous president in Bolivia and a multicultural political movement of the newly empowered indigenous against the traditional white elites of the eastern section of the country. As a result, national identity in Bolivia is undergoing profound changes, including recent constitutional reforms that formally establish the country as multi-ethnic and the first pluri-national state. The indigenous of Bolivia have gained important cultural and political rights and powers, but it remains to be seen if this will translate in economic gains.

Chapter 6 explored the fascinating trends and outcomes of racial identity in Brazil. Brazil is the agglomeration of indigenous peoples and those from Europe, Africa, and Asia. Until the twentieth century, Brazilian elites regarded miscegenation as a national scourge that was undermining economic, social, and political development. This conceptualization changed rather dramatically in the first half of the twentieth century, however, as the new Brazil benefited from combining different peoples and miscegenation assimilated the best qualities of the European, the indigenous, and the African. Brazil never passed Jim Crow laws, and in many cultural and physical realms it is a model of racial integration. Many Brazilians deny that there is any racism at all. In fact, Afro-Brazilians have been subjected to racism and discrimination since the abolition of slavery. In the most recent decade, community leaders and politicians have discarded the nuanced and gradated conceptualization of race and developed a dichotomous racial categorization to combat racism and establish affirmative action programs in higher education and other areas of the public sphere.

Recent decades brought a demographic revolution to the United States, the growth of the Latino population to some 50 million. This was the subject of Chapter 7. This wave of immigration is unique in American history, not only for the numbers but also because the Latino population has been able to maintain their principal cultural characteristics such as the Spanish language. The majority of the Latino population are legal citizens, and with each passing year comprises a higher profile as governors, senators, athletes, musicians, and scientists. The Latino immigration is challenging the assimilation model of the past and can only be analyzed with theories of multiculturalism. A multicultural United States will have important ramifications for economics, politics, and culture.

The final section considered issues of social policy, inequality, and football. Chapter 8 dealt with the role of the state in distributing the benefits of economic growth. Should the state be actively involved in reducing inequalities or should the market determine distribution? Latin America exhibits multiple examples of both models. Costa Rica was one of the first countries to have an activist redistributive state with a capitalist economy. Costa Rica has long maintained activist policies for the poorest citizens and is an example of growth-with-equity. In contrast, Brazil followed a specific policy of growth-without-equity for many decades, believing that growth would eventually lead to a decline in inequality. In reality, Brazil's inequality continued to grow until the country abandoned trickle-down economics in 1994. Brazil then employed activist policies and three pillars to raise the living standards of the poorest Brazilians: higher state spending on education, conditional cash transfers, and dramatic increases in the minimum wage. As a consequence, Brazil's once notorious income inequality has declined significantly and now approaches that of Costa Rica. The June 2013 protest movement in Brazil was in part a result of the large growth of the middle class and the additional demands that they have for public services and clean government.

Chapter 9 described the lessons from pension reforms. Chile was the first country to switch from a pay as you go (PAYG) public system to private individual accounts in 1981. Thirty countries, ten of which are in Latin America, have since introduced some form of individual accounts. The Chilean system has long been heralded as nothing short of miraculous and a model for all other countries. However, the system never delivered the expected retirement income, in large part because the commissions were so large and misunderstood. Pension privatization matches many economic and political interests around the world, and subsequently the Chilean model will continue to be used as propaganda by privatization supporters. Chile implemented significant changes in 2008 and is again debating big reforms. Private accounts do have benefits, but they are no panacea to provide dignified pensions. Even with private individual accounts, the state and taxpayers must contribute a lot of money for pensions.

Sports and football in particular have considerable effects on culture, economics, and politics. Chapter 10 provided important lessons from the "beautiful game." The first section of the chapter tested the hypothesis that football is the opiate of the masses and can be used by political officials as a distraction. Two of the most football-crazy countries and most likely cases for sports as an opiate are Argentina and Brazil. In May and June 2013, the government in both countries explicitly used football as a distraction from the political situation. But the citizenry proved far too intelligent and informed, and the attempt backfired in both cases. The second half of the chapter explored precisely how the tiny country of Uruguay managed to become a global football power in the first half of the twentieth century and again at the beginning of the twenty-first century. Many much larger countries with rich sports heritages—such as the United States, Russia, and China—dream of competing at the level of Uruguay. Can they replicate the Uruguayan model?

Is this the historical moment for Latin America? Has Latin America matured and weaned itself from following the debilitating advice of the United States, and will it now prosper with domestic models?[59] Will we witness in the next few decades a deepening and consolidation of the surprising recent achievements, and will additional structural challenges be addressed? Can Latin American countries more successfully leverage globalization, integrate better among themselves, and capitalize on the cultural differences among immigrants, the indigenous, Afro-Latinos, mestizos, and

---

59   This most recent version of dependency theory comes from Weitzman (2012).

whites? Will consolidated democratic electoral regimes, unheard of in the past, remain the dominant form of regime? Is there a greater-than-trivial possibility of a return to a pattern of institutional breakdown, military coups, and guerrilla movements? Will the region finally move past the reliance on commodity exports and increase value-added goods, thus limiting the boom-and-bust cycles of commodity dependence? Can Latin American countries reach an environmental equilibrium and sustainably exploit the greatest reserve of potable water in the world, the largest green space on the planet in the Amazon, and one of the world's most extensive productive agricultural areas in the Southern Cone? Will the mega-cities of the region—including Bogotá, Buenos Aires, Caracas, Guatemala City, Lima, Mexico City, Rio de Janeiro, Santiago, and São Paulo—be urban innovators that set the pace for quality-of-life issues or urban jungles characterized by violence and urban decay? There are many questions here that do not have simple or easy answers. Nevertheless, there are some clear trends that appear irreversible and combine to produce an historic moment for the region.

The first great change to note is the relationship between Brazil and the rest of the region. Historically a cultural wall separated Spanish Latin America from Brazil, due to cultural and language differences, imperial rivalries, power disputes, and the relative backwardness of Brazil in contrast to Argentina and Mexico. The rest of Latin America knew very little about Brazil, and Brazil knew almost nothing about the rest of Latin America. Brazil shares borders with Venezuela, Colombia, Peru, Argentina, Bolivia, Uruguay, Guyana, and Suriname—in other words, with every South American country except Ecuador and Chile. Of course it was impossible for the region to encounter integration in the first century after the early independence movements of 1810, as Brazil remained an empire with an emperor until the end of the nineteenth century.

The divide between Brazil and the rest of Latin America has receded in the twenty-first century for several reasons: the impressive Brazilian democratic, economic, social, and cultural gains; an explicit strategy of Brazilian elites to connect with the rest of the continent and especially with its geographical neighbors; the advances in technology and telecommunications and the reciprocal influences through literature, music, cinema, and television; and the implementation of a program of scholarships from the Brazilian state to Latin American educational elites to study at the post-graduate level for various years in the top universities in Brazil. This new scenario has resulted in the deepening of integration in South America and has produced the most integrated Latin America in history. This permits the insertion of the continent into the globalized world, a world characterized by regional blocs such as the European Union, NAFTA, and zones of influence in Asia. Today the UNASUR (Union of Southern Countries) is a goal within reach, while the old utopia of integration of all of Latin America is still unrealistic, as Mexico and Central America are too close to the United States (and too far from god and from Brazil).[60]

---

60 Former Mexican president Porfirio Díaz (1830–1915) is credited with the now infamous characterization of "Poor Mexico, so far from God and so close to the United States," even though there is no strong evidence that he actually made the remark.

A second historic shift is that political democracy appears more and more solid. This is the first time in history that all South American and Central American countries have been functioning political democracies, albeit at varying levels. The only other regions that can match this are Western Europe and North America. To maintain this extraordinary achievement, the countries of Latin America signed an accord that obligates every country in the region to pressure any case of institutional breakdown and to encourage the restoration of democracy. This pact operated in practice to beat back coups in Venezuela, Paraguay, and Ecuador and to avoid a greater crisis in Honduras. Learning the value of democracy is a new resource for Latin American countries whose populations suffered through brutal dictatorships that they do not want to revisit. In 2010, all the presidents of the UNASUR countries ratified a protocol that includes the freezing of economic exchange, the elimination of commercial flights, the closing of borders, the interruption of energy delivery, and the refusal to recognize illegitimate governments whenever electoral democracy is interrupted. The costs for any new dictatorship are now too high, as they will be automatically converted into international pariahs.

A third important trend is the new model of economic development that consolidated after the crisis of the neoliberal model sustained by the Washington Consensus. After the 2001 economic collapse in Argentina, a group of center-left governments emerged in the region that bet on a new model of economic development with equity. Up until 2001, Argentina was, after all, the most disciplined student of the Washington Consensus economic model and where income and wealth should first concentrate in the rich and would subsequently drip down to the rest of the society, with a completely privatized and deregulated market, and a minimalist state. The strong social policies of redistribution of wealth analyzed in Chapter 9 of this book led to almost all the countries experiencing strong economic growth that largely benefited the poorer sectors of society. Many of the Gini co-efficients in the region show improvements in income distribution, most notably Brazil. Those who continue to claim that neoliberalism and a reliance on market forces still characterize Latin America are mistaken.

The combination of the second and third trends—the affirmation of democracy and the collapse of the neoliberal development model—have stimulated an exuberant experimentation in public policy, with a high degree of innovation and heterogeneity in the domestic models of each country. It is precisely this explosion of creative and innovative public policies—in politics, economics, culture, and society—that inspired the research and writing of this book.

Political democracy, along with the expansion of rights to marginalized populations, sustained economic growth, redistribution of income, and stronger social and environmental policies have combined to produce a structural shift in Latin America and undergird the lessons that we analyzed in this book. It is possible that the future will bring new crises to the region, and indeed this is likely, as no region is immune to them. The challenges and threats are enormous, for numerous reasons: because violence grows with drug trafficking, with Central American gangs, and with the state's inability to provide high levels of security in the large urban areas; because the economies of the region still depend far too much on primary products; because opportunistic populism creeps up in some countries; because the indigenous and the Afro-Latinos remain at the bottom of the social ladder; because machismo and domestic violence remains endemic; and because inequality continues at scandalous levels. These and many other grave problems are violent storms on the horizon and are serious threats to the long-term stability and prosperity of the region.

In spite of the serious weaknesses, the new coordinates that guide the most successful Latin American countries in recent decades are clear. We can summarize these coordinates as follows: politics (non-negotiable democracy); economics (maintaining the macroeconomic order with redistributional social policy and greater value-added exports); the social sphere (reduction of poverty and greater inclusion); the cultural domain (recognition of rights for historically discriminated populations); ecological issues (maintaining the rights of future generations to a sustainable environment); and all along with a deepening of Latin American regional integration, but with much greater emphasis in South America and less on the north. In a clouded sky the Southern Cross can illuminate not only the path to the end of the world, but also innovative policy options in politics, culture, and development.

REFERENCES

Abers, Rebecca. 2007. "Porto Alegre and the Participatory Budget: Civic Education, Politics, and the Possibilities for Replication." In *Building Local and Global Democracy (2004–2006)*, 81–93. Harrowsmith, ON: Carold.

Acerimusdux. 2006. "Private Accounts a Disaster for SS in Chile." *Daily Kos.* January 10. http://www.dailykos.com/story/2006/01/10/177387/-Private-Accounts-a-Disaster-for-SS-in-Chile#.

Adelman, Irma, and Sherman Robinson. 1978. *Income Distribution Policy in Developing Countries: A Case Study of Korea.* Oxford: Oxford University Press.

Alabarces, Pablo. 2003. *Futbologias: Futbol, Identidad y Violencia en America Latina.* Buenos Aires: CLACSO.

Alabarces, Pablo. 2008. *Futbol y Patria.* Buenos Aires: Prometeo.

Alcántara Sáez, Manuel. 2008. *Politicians and Politics in Latin America.* Boulder, CO: Lynne Rienner.

Andreski, Stanislav. 1954. *Military Organization and Society.* Stanford, CA: Stanford University Press.

Arguedas, Alcides. 1909. "Pueblo enfermo." In *Fuentes de la cultura latinoamericana,* ed. Leopoldo Zea. México: F.c.e. Reprinted as *Pueblo enfermo.* La Paz: Gisbert & Cía, 1975.

Argueta, Mario. 1988. *Tiburcio Carías: Anatomía de una Época.* Tegucigalpa: Guaymuras.

Arías Calderón, Ricardo. 2000. "The Demilitarization of Public Security in Panama." *Small Wars & Insurgencies* 11 (1): 97–111. http://dx.doi.org/10.1080/09592310008423263.

Arocena, Felipe. 1996. *Muerte y resurrección de Facundo Quiroga. Historia cultural de lo que ha significado 'ser moderno' para los latinoamericanos.* Montevideo: Editorial TRILCE.

Arocena, Felipe. 2008. "Multiculturalism in Brazil, Bolivia and Peru." *Race & Class* 49 (4): 1–21. http://dx.doi.org/10.1177/0306396808089284.

Arocena, Felipe. 2012. *La Mayoría de las Personas son Otras Personas. Un Ensayo Sobre Multiculturalismo en Occidente.* Montevideo: Estuario Ediciones.

Arocena, Felipe, and Jessica Elfstrom. 2008. "Brasil. De la Democracia Racial al Estatuto de la Igualdad Racial." *Argumentos* 20 (55): 97–121.

Banerjee, Abhijit, and Esher Duflo. 2011. *Poor Economics: A Radical Rethinking of the Way to Fight Global Poverty.* New York: Public Affairs.

Bassahun, Federico. 2011. "Uruguay ya ganó, su proyecto a largo plazo funciona como un reloj." *Perfil.* July 23. http://www.perfil.com/ediciones/deportes/Uruguay-ya-gano-su-proyecto-a-largo-plazo-funciona-como-un-reloj-20117-593-0009.html.

Berg, Janine. 2009. "The Minimum Wage as a Response to the Crisis." *ILO Notes on the Crisis*. Brasilia: International Labour Office.

Berger, Peter L., and Luckmann, Thomas. 2001. *La construcción social de la realidad*. Buenos Aires: Amorrortu editores.

Bigio, Isaac. 2002. "Nacionalismo Aymara." http://www.angelfire.com/rnb/17m/Bolivia/nacionalismoaymara.html.

Black, Jan Knippers. 1986. *Sentinals of Empire: The United States and Latin American Militarism*. New York: Glenwood Press.

Bloomfield, Steve. 2010. *Africa United: Soccer, Passion, Politics, and the First World Cup in Africa*. New York: Harper Perennial.

Bolivian Foundation for Multiparty Democracy

Bowman, Kirk S. 1997. "Should the Kuznets Effect Be Relied on to Induce Equalizing Growth? Evidence from Post-1950 Development." *World Development* 25 (1): 127–43. http://dx.doi.org/10.1016/S0305-750X(96)00093-9.

Bowman, Kirk S. 2002. *Militarization, Democracy, and Development: The Perils of Praetorianism in Latin America*. University Park, PA: Pennsylvania State University Press.

Bowman, Kirk S. 2013. *Peddling Paradise: The Politics of Tourism in Latin America*. Boulder, CO: Lynne Rienner Publications.

Brooke, James. 1993. "A Hard Look at Brazil's Surfeits: Food, Hunger and Inequality." *New York Times*, June 6. E7.

Brooks, Sarah. 2007. "Globalization and Pension Reform in Latin America." *Latin American Politics and Society* 49 (4): 31–62.

Buchanan, Patrick. 2001. *The Death of the West: How Dying Populations and Immigrant Invasions Imperil Our Culture and Civilization*. New York: Thomas Dunne Books.

Buenker, John, and Lorman Ratner. 1992. *Multiculturalism in the United States: A Comparative Guide to Acculturation and Ethnicity*. New York: Greenwood Press.

Butler, Eamon. 2011. "Chile's Pension System, A Model for the World." *Christian Science Monitor*, April 26. http://www.csmonitor.com/Business/The-Adam-Smith-Institute-Blog/2011/0426/Chile-s-pensions-system-a-model-for-the-world.

Cardona Quirós, Edgar. 1992. *Mi Verdad*. San José, Costa Rica: García Hermanos.

Carrio, Elisa Maria. 2005. "Argentina: A New Look at the Challenges of Women's Participation in the Legislature." In *Women in Parliament: Beyond the Numbers*, ed. Julie Ballington and Azza Karam, 164–73. Stockholm: IDEA.

Castells, Manuel. 2000. *The Power of Identity*. Cambridge: Wiley-Blackwell.

Centeno, Miguel Angel. 2003. *Blood and Debt: War and the Nation-State in Latin America*. University Park, PA: Pennsylvania State University Press.

CEPAL (Comisión Económica para América Latina y el Caribe). 2005. *Los Pueblos Indígenas de Bolivia: Diagnóstico Sociodemográfico a Partir del Censo de 2001*. Santiago de Chile: Documentos de Proyectos.

Comité de Abogados por los Derechos Humanos. 1994. *Análisis del Informe del Departamento de Estado Reporte de Países Acerca de los Derechos Humanos para 1993*. New York: Comité de Abogados por los Derechos Humanos.

Correlates of War. 1996. http://www.correlatesofwar.org/datasets.htm.

Cruz, José. 2005. "Chile's Privatized Pensions Spell Worker Hardship." *People's World*, February 11. http://www.peoplesworld.org/chile-s-privatized-pensions-spell-worker-hardship/.

da Silva Martins, Sérgio, Carlos Alberto Medeiros, and Elisa Larkin Nascimento. 2004. "Paving Paradise: The Road from 'Racial Democracy' to Affirmative Action in Brazil." *Journal of Black Studies* 34 (6): 787–816. http://dx.doi.org/10.1177/0021934704264006.

Del Campo, Esther. 2005. "Women and Politics in Latin America: Perspectives and Limits of the Institutional Aspects of Women's Political Representation." *Social Forces* 83 (4): 1697–725. http://dx.doi.org/10.1353/sof.2005.0060.

Denes, Christian. 2003. "*Bolsa Escola*: Redefining Poverty and Development in Brazil." *International Education Journal* 4 (2): 137–47.

do Nascimento, Abdias. 1968. "The Myth of Racial Democracy." In *The Brazil Reader*, ed. Robert M. Levine and John J. Crocitti, 379–82. Durham, NC: Duke University Press.

Eagleton, Terry. 2010. "Football: A Dear Friend to Capitalism." *The Guardian*. June 15. http://www.theguardian.com/commentisfree/2010/jun/15/football-socialism-crack-cocaine-people.

Eckstein, Harry. 1975. "Case Study and Theory in Political Science." In *The Handbook of Political Science*, ed. F.I. Greenstein and N.W. Polsby, 79–138. Reading, MA: Addison-Wesley.

The Economist. 2004a. "Brazil's Indians: The Amazon's Indian Wars." January 15.

The Economist. 2004b. "Indigenous People in South America." February 19.

The Economist. 2006. "Bolivia: A Champion of Indigenous Rights and of State Control of the Economy." December 14.

The Economist. 2008. "Brazil, Happy Families: An Anti-poverty Scheme Invented in Latin America Is Winning Converts Worldwide." February 7.

The Economist. 2011. "Focus: Brazil." November 11.

Federal Reserve Bank of St. Louis. 2014. Data download from http://research.stlouisfed.org/fred2/series/DDDI13CLA156NWDB.

Foer, Franklin. 2004. *How Soccer Explains the World: An Unlikely Theory of Globalization*. New York: Harper Perennial.

Foss, Sarah. 2012. "Ahora Todos Somos Panameños: Kuna Identity and Panamanian Nationalism Under the Torrijos Regime, 1986–1981." MA Thesis, Vanderbilt University.

Frank, Waldo. 1972. *Our America*. New York: AMS Press.

Freyre, Gilberto. 1989. *Casa Grande e Senzala*. Río de Janeiro: Editora Récord.

Funes, Matías H. 1995. *Los Deliberantes: El Poder Militar en Honduras*. Tegucigalpa: Editorial Guyamuras.

Gaffney, Christopher. 2009. "Stadiums and Society in Twenty-First Century Buenos Aires." *Soccer and Society* 10 (2): 160–82.

Gaffney, Christopher. 2014. "Hunting White Elephants." http://www.geostadia.com/2014/02/the-cup-of-cups.html.

Gerken, Heather K. 2009. "Mexico's 2007 Election Reforms: A Comparative View." *Mexican Law Review* 1 (2): 163–72.

Gil, Indermit, Truman Packard, and Juan Yermo. 2005. *Keeping the Promise of Social Security in Latin America*. Palo Alto, CA: Stanford University Press.

González-Vega, Claudio, and Victor Hugo Céspedes. 1993. "Costa Rica." In *The Political Economy of Poverty, Equity, and Growth: Costa Rica and Uruguay*, ed. Simon Rottenberg, 15–27. Oxford: Oxford University Press.

Hale, Charles. 1994. "Between Che Guevara and the Pachamama: Mestizos, Indians, and Identity Politics in the Anti-Quincentenary Campaign." *Critique of Anthropology* 14 (1): 9–39. http://dx.doi.org/10.1177/0308275X9401400102.

Helal, Ronaldo. 1997. *Passes e Impasses: Futebol e Cultura da Massa no Brasil.* Petrópolis: Vozes.

Hertzberg, Hendrik. 2010. "The Name of the Game." *The New Yorker.* July 12. http://www. newyorker.com/talk/comment/2010/07/12/100712taco_talk_hertzberg.

Heston, Alan, Robert Summers, and Bettina Aten. 2012. Penn World Table Version 7.1, Center for International Comparisons of Production, Income and Prices at the University of Pennsylvania.

Hewlett, Sylvia Ann. 1982. "Poverty and Inequality in Brazil." In *Brazil and Mexico: Patterns in Late Development*, ed. Sylvia Ann Hewlett and Richard S. Weinert, 317–38. Philadelphia: ISHI.

Hidalgo, Daniel. 2013. "Making Every Vote Count: Electronic Voting in Brazil." *Boston Review*, January 1. http://www.bostonreview.net/world/making-every-vote-count.

Holzmann, Robert. 2012. "Global Pensions Systems and Their Reforms: Discussion Paper." Washington, DC: The World Bank.

Honey, Martha. 1994. *Hostile Acts: U.S. Policy in Costa Rica in the 1980s.* Gainesville, FL: University Press of Florida.

Howe, James. 1986. *The Kuna Gathering: Contemporary Village Politics in Panama.* Austin, TX: University of Texas Press.

Htun, Mala. 2005a. "Racial Quotas for a 'Racial Democracy.'" *NACLA Report on the Americas* 38: 20–25.

Htun, Mala. 2005b. "Women, Political Parties and Electoral Systems in Latin America." In *Women in Parliament: Beyond the Numbers*, ed. Julie Ballington and Azza Karam, 112–21. Stockholm: IDEA.

Huntington, Samuel. 1968. *Political Order in Changing Societies.* New Haven, CT: Yale University Press.

Huntington, Samuel. 2004. *Who Are We? The Challenges to America's National Identity.* New York: Simon & Schuster.

Ikenberry, John G. 2002. "Beyond Racism: Race and Inequality in Brazil, South Africa, and the United States." *Foreign Affairs* 81: 1999.

Investor's Business Daily. 2011. "Cain's 'Chilean Model'." Investors.com. http://news.investors. com/ibd-editorials/092911-586464-cains-chilean-model.htm.

Janowitz, Morris. 1964. *The Military in the Political Development of New Nations.* Chicago: University of Chicago Press.

Johnson, John J. 1993. *Latin America in Caricature.* Austin, TX: University of Texas Press.

Jones, Mark P. 2009. "Gender Quotas, Electoral Laws, and the Election of Women: Evidence from the Latin American Vanguard." *Comparative Political Studies* 42 (54): 56–81.

Kamel, Ali. 2006. *Nao Somos Racistas.* San Pablo: Editora Nova Fronteira.

Klein, Joe. 1994. "If Chile Can Do It . . . Couldn't (North) America Privatize Its Social-Security System?" *Time*, December 12: 12.

Kritzer, Barbara. 2008. "Chile's Next Generation Pension Reform." *Social Security Bulletin* 68 (2): 69–84.

Kritzer, Barbara, Stephen Kay, and Tapen Sinha. 2011. "Next Generation of Individual Account Pension Reforms in Latin America." *Social Security Bulletin* 71 (1): 35–76.

Kymlicka, Will. 2007. *Multicultural Odysseys: Navigating the New International Politics of Diversity.* New York: Oxford University Press. http://dx.doi.org/10.1080/17449050701659789.

La Jornada. 2003. "Entrevista a Felipe Quispe," Bolivia.

LaFeber, Walter. 1984. *Inevitable Revolutions: The United States in Central America*. New York: W.W. Norton.

Langoni, Carlos Geraldo. 1973. *Distribução de Renda e Desenvolvimento Econômico do Brasil*. Rio de Janeiro: Editora Expressão e Cultura.

Lara, Fernando Luiz. 2013. "Converging Income Inequality in Brazil and the United States: Some Uncomfortable Realities." *Inequalities*, February 23. http://inequalitiesblog.wordpress. com/2013/02/23/converging-income-inequality-in-brazil-and-the-united-states-some-uncomfortable-realities/.

Lehoucq, Fabrice Edouard. 1992. "The Origins of Democracy in Costa Rica in Comparative Perspective." Ph.D. dissertation, Duke University.

Lehoucq, Fabrice Edouard. 1996. "The Institutional Foundations of Democratic Cooperation in Costa Rica." *Journal of Latin American Studies* 28 (2): 329–55. http://dx.doi.org/10.1017/S0022216X00013031.

Lieuwin, Edwin. 1965. *United States Policy in Latin America*. New York: Praeger.

Lloyd, Marion. 2004a. "In Brazil, A New Debate over Color." *Chronicle of Higher Education* 50: 38–40.

Lloyd, Marion. 2004b. "In Brazil, A Different Approach to Affirmative Action." *Chronicle of Higher Education* 51: 49–52.

López, Horacio. 2012. *El Camino es la Recompensa*. Montevideo: Aguilar.

Madrak, Susie. 2011. "What Herman Cain Isn't Going to Tell You about Chile's Privatized Pensions." *Crooks and Liars*. September 10. http://crooksandliars.com/susie-madrak/what-herman-cain-isnt-going-tell-you-

Markovits, Andrei. 2001. *Offsides: Soccer and American Exceptionalism*. Princeton, NJ: Princeton University Press.

Markovits, Andrei, and Lars Rensmann. 2010. *Gaming the World: How Sports Are Reshaping Global Politics and Culture*. Princeton, NJ: Princeton University Press.

Martínez Moreno, Carlos. 1970. "El Mundial del 30." *100 Años de Fútbol* 13. Montevideo: Editores Reunidos.

Marroquín, Alejandro. 1972. *Balance del Indigenismo*. Mexico: Instituto Indigenista Interamericano. Ediciones Especiales No. 62.

Martin, Simon. 2004. *Football and Fascism: The National Game under Mussolini*. New York: Bloomsbury.

Mayorga, Rene Antonio. 2002. Monitor Electoral Latinoamericano. August 21, 2002.

McCann, James A., and Jorge I. Domínguez. 1998. "Mexicans React to Electoral Fraud and Political Corruption: An Assessment of Public Opinion and Voting Behavior." *Electoral Studies* 17 (4): 483–503. http://dx.doi.org/10.1016/S0261-3794(98)00026-2.

Medeiros, Carlos Alberto. 2004. *Na Lei e Na Raça: Legislação e Relações Raciais, Brasil—Estados Unidos*. Río de Janeiro: DP&A Editora.

Meza, Víctor. 1981. *Política y Sociedad en Honduras: Comentarios*. Tegucigalpa: Editorial Guaymuras.

Mignolo, Walter. 2006. "Evo Morales, Giro a la Izquierda o Giro Descolonial?" In *Democracias en Desconfianza: Ensayos de Sociedad Civil y Política en América Latina*, ed. Jose da Cruz, 93–116. Montevideo: Editorial Coscoroba.

Mittelman, James H. 1988. *Out from Underdevelopment*. New York: St. Martin's Press.

Morales, Franklin. 1969a. "Futbol: Mito y Realidad." *Nuestra Tierra* 22. Montevideo: Nuestra Tierra.

Morales, Franklin. 1969b. "Los Albores del Fútbol Uruguayo." *100 Años de Fútbol* 1. Montevideo: Editores Reunidos.

Morse, Richard. 1982. *El Espejo de Próspero*. Mexico: Siglo XXI Editores.

Muñoz Guillén, Mercedes. 1990. *La Abolición del Ejercito*: 1914–1949. San José, Costa Rica: Editorial Porvenís.

Murphy, Tim. 2011. "Herman Cain's Chilean Model, Explained." *Mother Jones*. September 12. http://www.motherjones.com/mojo/2011/09/herman-cain-chilean-model-explained.

Noblat, Ricardo. 2009. "Candidatos 'Guarda Chuva.'" *Globo*. 13 September. http://oglobo. globo.com/pais/noblat/posts/2009/09/13/candidatos-guarda-chuva-13-9-1989-217406.asp.

Oberwetter, Brooke. 2005. "Chile Out." *The American Spectator*. February 17. http://spectator. org/archives/2005/02/18/chile-out.

Obregón L., Rafael. 1951. *Conflictos Militares y Políticos en Costa Rica*. San José, Costa Rica: La Nación.

Pagés, Carmen, J.P. Atal, J. Cuesta, L. Madrigal, and H. Nopo. 2009. "Why Are So Few People Contributing to Social Security in Peru?" Washington, DC: World Bank. http://siteresources.worldbank.org/SOCIALPROTECTION/.Resources/280558-1138289492561/2158434-1228317850075/5637583-1228317993563/Pages_Soc_Sec_Peru.pdf.

Paixão, Marcelo. 2003. *IDH de Negros e Brancos no Brasil em 2001: E a Desigualdade Continua!* Brazil: Revista Eletrônica Comciência.

Pastor, Robert A. 1999. "The Role of Electoral Administration in Democratic Transitions: Implications for Policy and Research." *Democratization* 6 (4): 1–27. http://dx.doi. org/10.1080/13510349908403630.

Pateman, Carole. 1970. *Participation and Democratic Theory*. New York: Cambridge University Press.

Pike, Frederick. 1992. *The United States and Latin America: Myths and Stereotypes of Civilization and Nature*. Austin, TX: University of Texas Press.

Piñera, José. 2010. "Econopower: How a Generation of Economists is Transforming the World (by Mark Skousen)." http://www.josepinera.com/josepinera/jp_econopower.htm.

Piñera, José. 2013. "Empowering Workers in Chile." http://www.josepinera.com/articles/ articles_empoweringworkers.htm.

Postero, Nancy G. 2000. "Bolivia's *Indígena* Citizen: Multiculturalism in a Neoliberal Age." Paper presented to LASA Congress. Miami, March 16–18.

Proyecto Estado de la Nación. 1995. *Estado de La Nation: En Desarrollo Humano Sostenible*. San José, Costa Rica: Proyecto Estado de la Nación.

Psacharopoulos, George, S. Morley, A. Fiszbein, H. Lee, and W. Wood. 1993. *Poverty and Income Distribution in Latin America: The Story of the 1980s*. World Bank Unpublished Regional Studies Program Report No. 27, Washington, DC: The World Bank.

Quijano, Aníbal. 2000. "Colonialidad del Poder, Eurocentrismo y América Latina." In *La Colonialidad del Saber: Eurocentrismo y Ciencias Sociales. Perspectivas Latinoamericanas*, compiled by Edgardo Lander, 201–46. Buenos Aires: CLACSO.

Quintero Rivera, Angel. 1998. *Salsa, Sabor y Control: Sociología de la Música Tropical*. México: Siglo XXI editores.

Rapoza, Kenneth. 2012. "In Brazil: The Poor Get Richer Faster." *Forbes*, September 25. http://www.forbes.com/sites/kenrapoza/2012/09/25/in-brazil-the-poor-get-richer-faster/.

Rivera, Ray. 2007. "In Mexican Town, Maybe a Way to Reduce Poverty in New York." *New York Times*, April 25. http://www.nytimes.com/2007/04/25/nyregion/25antipoverty.html?pagewanted=all&_r=0.

Roberge, Nicole. 2006. "Brazil Experiences the Growing Pains of Affirmative Action." *Issues in Higher Education* 23:16.

Rohter, Larry. 2005. "Chile's Retirees Find Shortfall in Private Plan." *New York Times*, January 27.

Rohter, Larry. 2006. "Chile's Candidates Agree to Agree on Pension Woes." *New York Times*, January 10.

Ropp, Steve C. 1974. "The Honduran Army in the Sociopolitical Evolution of the Honduran State." *The Americas* 30 (4): 504–28. http://dx.doi.org/10.2307/980035.

Salazar, Jorge Mario. 1995. *Crisis Liberal y Estado Reformista: Análisis Político-Electoral (1914–1949)*. San José, Costa Rica: Editorial de la Universidad de Costa Rica.

Schneider, Friedrich, Andreas Buehn, and Claudio Montenegro. 2010. "Shadow Economies All Over the World: New Estimates for 162 Countries from 1999–2007." Working Papers WP 322, University of Chile, Department of Economics.

Seligson, Mitchell A. 1987. "Development, Democratization, and Decay: Central America at the Crossroads." In *Authoritarians and Democrats: Regime Transition in Latin America*, ed. James M. Malloy and Mitchell A. Seligson, 167–92. Pittsburgh: University of Pittsburgh Press.

Skidmore, Thomas E. 1992. "Fact and Myth: Discovering a Racial Problem in Brazil." Kellogg Institute Working Paper #173. South Bend, IN: Notre Dame University.

Skidmore, Thomas E. 2003. "Racial Mixture and Affirmative Action: The Cases of Brazil and the United States." *American Historical Review* 108 (5): 1391–96. http://dx.doi.org/10.1086/529972.

Skousen, Mark. 2008. *Econopower: How a New Generation of Economists is Transforming the World*. Hoboken, NJ: John Wiley & Sons.

Smith, Peter H. 1996. *Talons of the Eagle: Dynamics of U.S.-Latin American Relations*. New York: Oxford University Press.

Solimano, Andrés, and Claudia Allende. 2007. "Migraciones Internacionales, Remesas y el Desarrollo Economic: La Experiencia Latinoamericana." Santiago de Chile: CEPAL.

Stavenhagen, Rodolfo. 2002. "The Return of the Native." University of London Institute of Latin American Studies, Occasional Papers No 27.

Tavener, Ben. 2011. "Brazil Minimum Wage to Top R$800 by 2015." *The Rio Times*, Sept. 27: 1.

Taylor, Charles. 1993. *El Multiculturalismo y "La Política del Reconocimiento."* México: Fondo de Cultura Económica.

Taylor, Lance. 1980. *Models of Growth and Distribution for Brazil*. Washington, DC: World Bank Research Publications.

Thames, Frank, and Margaret Williams. 2013. *Contagious Representation: Women's Political Representation in Democracies around the World*. New York: New York University Press.

Tilly, Charles. 1990. *Coercion, Capital and European States, AD 990–1990*. Cambridge: Basil Blackwell.

Toni, Ana. 2004. "For Brazil, First Steps Towards Affirmative Action." *Ford Foundation Report* 35: 26–27.

UNDP. 2005. *Human Development Report: Cultural Liberty in Today's Diverse World*. New York: United Nations.

UNDP. 2013. *The 2013 Human Development Report. The Rise of the South: Human Progress in a Diverse World*. New York: United Nations.

Vasconcelos, José. 1948. *Raza Cósmica. Misión de la Raza Iberoamericana*. Buenos Aires: Espasa-Calpe.

Veja. 2006. "Não o Remédio, Mas a Doença." October 25.

Velásquez Cerrato, Armando. 1954. *Las Fuerzas Armadas en una Democracia*. Tegucigalpa: Talleres Tipográficos Nacionales.

Veloso, Caetano. 2006. *El País*, October 15.

Wall Street Journal. 1996. "A Racial 'Democracy' Begins Painful Debate on Affirmative Action." August 6.

Wängnerud, Lena. 2009. "Women in Parliaments: Descriptive and Substantive Representation." *Annual Review of Political Science* 12 (1): 51–69. http://dx.doi.org/10.1146/annurev.polisci.11.053106.123839.

Wasik, John. 2012. "Voter Fraud: A Massive Anti-Democratic Deception." *Forbes*, November 6. http://www.forbes.com/sites/johnwasik/2012/11/06/voter-fraud-a-massive-anti-democratic-deception/.

Wicks, Ann, and Reylene Lang-Dion. 2007. "Equal Voice: Electing More Women in Canada." *Canadian Parliamentary Review* 30 (1): 36–39.

Weede, Erich. 1986. "Rent-Seeking, Military Participation, and Economic Performance in LDCs." *Journal of Conflict Resolution* 30 (2): 291–314.

Winddance, France. 1998. *Racism in a Racial Democracy: The Maintenance of White Supremacy in Brazil*. New Brunswick, NJ: Rutgers University Press.

World Bank. 2005. "Brazil's *Bolsa Família* Program Celebrates Progress in Lifting Families out of Poverty." http://go.worldbank.org/5NAMSEOR60.

Ybarra-Frausto, Tomás. 1992. "The Chicano Movement in a Multicultural/Multinational Society." In *On Edge: The Crisis of Contemporary Latin American Culture*, ed. G. Yúdice, J. Franco, and J. Flores, 207–17. Minneapolis: University of Minnesota Press.

Yrigoyen, Raquel. 2002. "Peru: Pluralist Constitution, Monist Judiciary—A Post-Reform Assessment." In *Multiculturalism in Latin America: Indigenous Rights, Diversity and Democracy*, ed. Rachel Sieder, 157–83. New York: Palgrave Macmillian.

INDEX